Dimensions of Older Adult Ministry

A Handbook

Richard L. Morgan, contributing editor
Martha Gilliss, general editor

WITHERSPOON
PRESS

Louisville, Kentucky

Book interior and cover design by Michelle Vissing

First edition

Published by Witherspoon Press
Louisville, Kentucky

Web site address: www.pcusa.org/witherspoonpress

PRINTED IN THE UNITED STATES OF AMERICA

06 07 08 09 10 11 12 13 14 15—10 9 8 7 6 5 4 3 2 1

Library of Congress Cataloging-in-Publication Data

Dimensions of older adult ministry: a handbook / Richard L. Morgan, contributing editor ; Martha Gilliss, general editor.— 1st ed.
    p. cm.
  Includes bibliographical references.
  ISBN 1-57153-059-2 (pbk. ; alk. paper)
1. Church work with older people—Presbyterian Church (U.S.A.) 2. Aging—Religious aspects—Presbyterian Church (U.S.A.) 3. Older Christians—Religious life. I. Morgan, Richard Lyon, 1929- II. Gilliss, Martha S.
  BV4435.D46 2006
  259'.3—dc22
                            2005035561

Dedication

This book is dedicated to older adults everywhere with thanks for your wisdom in leading the church, your guidance of youth into the faith, your willingness to give time, talents, and money to meet the needs of those around you, your faithfulness to the church, and your serving as a model for living. May God continue to bless you.

Contents

Contributing Authors

Sally L. Campbell

Coordinator of pastoral education at St. Luke's Hospital, Bethlehem, Pennsylvania. A licensed marriage and family therapist as well as an ACPE (Association for Clinical Pastoral Education) associate supervisor.

Donovan Drake

Pastor of Trinity Avenue Presbyterian Church, Durham, North Carolina, on the campus of Duke University. A graduate of Princeton Theological Seminary, he holds a doctorate from McCormick Theological Seminary.

Miriam Dunson

Retired associate for older adult ministries, Presbyterian Church (U.S.A.). Holder of an M.A. from the Presbyterian School of Christian Education and a doctor of ministry from Columbia Theological Seminary; missionary in Korea for 18 years; author of *A Very Present Help: Psalm Studies for Older Adults* and *Facing Forward in Older Adult Ministry;* member of the Delegate Council of the National Interfaith Coalition on Aging.

Steven P. Eason

Senior pastor of Myers Park Presbyterian Church, Charlotte, North Carolina; former pastor of Mount Pleasant Presbyterian Church, Mount Pleasant, South Carolina. A graduate of Duke Divinity School, Durham, North Carolina, he holds a doctorate from Columbia Theological Seminary.

Peg Wittig Lewis

Developer of an innovative program for older adults at La Jolla Presbyterian Church, La Jolla, California. Holder of a B.S. in nursing, an M.A. in theology from Fuller Theological Seminary, and a professional certificate in Gerontological Counseling.

Harry R. Moody

Senior associate, International Longevity Center–USA and director of academic affairs for the American Association of Retired Persons (AARP), Washington, D.C. Author of *The Five Stages of the Soul* and a leading researcher in the field of aging for the past two decades.

Richard L. Morgan

Leader of workshops across the country on "Aging as a Spiritual Journey." Former editor of *AGEnda*, Presbyterian Church (U.S.A.) quarterly newsletter on aging, and author of eleven books on aging and spirituality, including *Fire in the Soul* and *Remembering Your Story*; his latest book is *Meditations for the Grieving* (Herald Press, 2005).

Dwyn M. Mounger

Interim minister of Memorial Presbyterian Church, St. Augustine, Florida; former pastor of Presbyterian churches in North Carolina, South Carolina, Georgia, and Tennessee. Author of numerous journal article and sermons.

Andrea Reiter

A nationally certified counselor, resident pastoral counselor in training at Care and Counseling, Inc., St. Louis, Missouri. Holder of certification in gerontology, spiritual direction and formation training, National Board of Certified Counselors, and an M.A. in counseling and guidance, University of Missouri, Kansas City, Missouri.

Isabel W. Rogers

Professor of applied Christianity for thirty years, Presbyterian School of Christian Education; in retirement a much sought-after speaker across the country. Holder of an M.A. in English literature, Florida State College for Women; an M.A. in political science, University of Virginia at Charlottesville, Virginia; and a Ph.D. in Christian ethics, Duke University, Durham, North Carolina.

Steven Sapp

Dean of the Department of Religion, University of Miami, Miami, Florida. Author of *Fullness of Years* and *Coping with Alzheimer's* and a leader of seminars on aging across the nation.

Henry C. Simmons

Director of the Center on Aging, Union Theological Seminary—Presbyterian School of Christian Education, Richmond, Virginia. Co-author of *Thriving After 55* and *Soulful Aging;* former president of the Religious Education Association and member of the board of directors of the National Council on Aging and of the National Interfaith Coalition on Aging.

Samuel M. Stone

Executive director of Glenaire in Cary, North Carolina, since this continuing care retirement community (CCRC), managed by The Presbyterian Homes, Inc., opened in 1993. A licensed nursing home administrator and an ordained minister in the Presbyterian Church (U.S.A.).

T. Ronald Vaughan

Pastor of New Salem Presbyterian Church, Stony Point, North Carolina. An ordained minister in the United Church of Christ who spent many years bivocationally in health care and ministry, a published prize-winning poet, author of numerous articles for professional journals, and a licensed nursing home administrator.

Foreword

Miriam Dunson

The issues in the field of older adult ministries are so broad, so massive, so diverse, and so very important that it is difficult to address all of them in one book, or in a series of books. We sought to address many of the most requested issues in a ten-book series, *Older Adult Issues Series*, published by Westminster John Knox Press (Geneva Press) in 1999. This series has met many needs and has been used widely in congregations. However, requests continue to pour into the Office of Older Adult Ministries, asking for resources on even more issues. This book is a result of those requests.

The purpose of this book is to engage persons in congregations in discussing these important issues as they are appropriate for their own situations. It is designed to be an information resource as well as a practical guide for those persons who have need in these particular areas of study.

The topics for the various chapters were chosen because they were the most requested. The authors were chosen because they seemed to be the most appropriate and most knowledgeable on those particular issues. Therefore we present this book, recognizing that "one size does not fit all." Some of the chapters will speak to some congregations and other chapters will meet other needs in other places. Our hope is that the issues are important enough and presented in such a way that the various chapters can be used in congregational study groups for discussion and can be used to build programs and plan events that will touch particular needs of the participants. Each chapter includes discussion questions that can be helpful to leaders.

Richard L. Morgan has done most of the selecting of authors. He has organized the chapters and has read and edited most of the manuscripts. He has corresponded with and guided the writers and has led the way for this book to become a significant tool for congregations to use in their older adult programs and events. Deepest gratitude is due to Richard Morgan for his hard work and for his expertise in writing and editing, in choosing good writers, and in organizing the manuscripts.

We hope you will find this book to be a very effective tool in meeting the needs and utilizing the skills of older adults in your congregations.

Preface

There is little doubt that there is a need for help in ministering to older adults in the church. The twenty-first century has seen only the beginning of an "age wave," a demographic revolution with increasing numbers of persons living longer and better than anyone could have imagined.

Recent years have witnessed the publication of numerous writings about aging and religion. Regrettably, many of these writings have been directed to professionals in the field and not to congregations.

In the latter months of 2001, Miriam Dunson and I envisioned a readable, user-friendly book that would be valuable to congregations in their ministry with older adults. This book is the result of that dream.

I would be amiss not to express deep appreciation to all the writers who volunteered their gifts to make this book possible. They were chosen because of their special work and interest in ministry with older persons. Without the dedication of their time and talents this book could not have been written. Appreciation is also due to Greg Cohen, associate for older adult ministries for the Presbyterian Church (U.S.A.), for helping to revive the publication of this book, and to Martha S. Gilliss, associate for curriculum development for adults, Presbyterian Church (U.S.A.), for serving as its general editor. From the very beginning this has been a cooperative effort by many people.

We face incredible challenges in older adult ministry in the mainline churches and synagogues in America. The percentage of older persons in our global society is growing and expected to nearly double between 1990 and 2030. Soon churches and synagogues will have to respond to the imminent retirement of the large boomer generation, as seventy-eight million more people will retire. The writers hope that this anthology will help minister to this population, realizing it is an awesome task. But we must begin!

Look ahead. You are not expected
to complete the task. Neither are
you permitted to lay it down.
—*The Talmud*

I trust that this book will inform, inspire, and empower each reader to be proactive about ministry to and with God's people.

—*Richard L. Morgan, Contributing Editor*

In God's Time: Aging as People of God

Donovan Drake

Genesis 1—A Time for Creating

In the beginning, before God was busy creating the heavens and the earth, the sun, the moon, the hippopotamus, the beetle, the sponge, and the human race, God created time. The result of this earliest of creative acts is that in all the glory and wonder "Eden saw play." Eden also knew that its days were numbered. "There was evening and there was morning, the first day." Gone! "There was evening and there was morning, the second day." Gone! The third day . . . gone! This numbering hardly seems a concern of the rock, the tree, and my old cat lying belly up on the living room floor. It does, however, concern me and those of us who remember the garden, notice the gray, feel the newest ache and wonder, "Where has all the time gone?"

While we manage perhaps too well the domination and subjugation of most of creation, it is the creation of time that succeeds in having power and dominion over us. As much as we try to hide the gray, fix the face, or remedy the aches, time has the power to keep counting off our days. Time has the power to call into question the meaning of our existence.

How do we understand this powerful creative force? How as people of God can we understand the process of aging? This chapter will examine through story and reflection how our culture and theological tradition make sense of the aging process.

Going for Broke—Aging as Surviving

A grieving heart with the power of attorney sat in the office of a stockbroker. It was nearing Christmas. Helen's eldest son, Andrew, was seeing through on his mother's last wish.

Not long ago Helen had been priding herself on her ability to drive herself to the hairdressers, to the supermarket, and to church for both Sunday worship and Wednesday night meetings.

Now she was in a hospital room some three miles away in the intensive care unit as the result of two months of a slow spiral downward. It was unlike her to give up. Earlier she had had heart surgery and lung surgery, and both times she surprised the doctors by her tenacious ability to recover and live an independent life.

Since a stroke in September Helen had had to rely on her family for a timely washcloth, a readjustment of pillows, a cup of ice water. Covers on. Covers off. Mixed with Helen's sense of helplessness was her sense of guilt for taking so much of her family's time.

"Momma! Shh!"

While Helen could not do things for herself, she could *think*, and what she thought about was a wish—a wish to assuage the guilt. Gifts were to be purchased for Christmas: for grandchildren, great-grandchildren, the church, and other loves of her life. The wish required Andrew, who had her power of attorney, to sell some stock. "You'll see to it! Right?"

"Yes, Momma."

Andrew loved his mother and hated the dilemma of not wanting to see his mother suffer and not wanting to have her die.

By November Helen had contracted pneumonia and by December was on life support. Helen had a living will, but the difficulty for the family was that they had seen their mother come back from debilitating surgeries many times. Mom was a fighter. Maybe if the doctors could clear up the pneumonia she could get off the machine and regain her strength.

Remembering his mother's wish, Andrew broke away from the hospital. It was a crazy wish to think that a big Christmas would somehow make up for the loss of a mother. Andrew, however, made his way to the broker's office partly to make good on a promise and partly as a diversion from decisions that he would have to make the next day.

The broker called him into his office with the words "How is your mother doing?"

"Ummm. Not well, she's on a machine right now, but we haven't given up hope," came the reply.

The broker and Andrew reviewed stocks to be sold, and as Andrew was ready to leave, the broker offered him some monetary advice: "I want to remind you—if you can keep your mother alive until January first, the new tax laws will kick in and there will be a huge tax advantage for the estate."

Stunned silence followed Andrew out of the office and back to the hospital.

The next day, with Andrew's permission, a nurse disconnected the machines and then invited Helen's family into the room. "The LORD is my shepherd, I shall not want . . ." These words came from Andrew's lips, and gradually the words grew louder as daughter-in-law and grandson picked up the cadence. "Surely goodness and mercy shall follow me all the days of my life; and I shall dwell in the house of the LORD for ever" (Psalm 23:1, 6 RSV).

Reflection

Our growing old is, in one sense, a testimony to our survival skills. Every day that we add to our life bears testimony to our ability to survive disease, environment, and our genetic flaws. We are now a nation of people who spend billions of dollars a year and a great deal of our time on trying to live as long as possible. Our days testify to the task at hand as they are filled with brisk walks, bottled water, and cholesterol-lowering oatmeal. Protection is purchased in airbags, sunscreen, air filters, and smoke detectors. We want to survive! Surely this is the wisdom of the proverb to "not forget my teaching, . . . for length of days and years of life and abundant welfare they will give you" (Proverbs 3:1–2).

While aging is a testimony to our survival skills, aging comes with a curse that over time loses what it so skillfully acquired. Lost one by one are the driver's license, the ability to dress oneself, the ability to get up stairs.

In the preceding story Helen lived independently for most of her adult life. A stroke made her totally dependent. The meaning of life had boiled down to surviving—surviving not as a means to enjoy life but now the only alternative to death. Rather than have a life devoid of meaning, Helen tried to use her time in any way that would give meaning. Helen's "wish" might be construed as an opportunity to still mean something to others in her world.

The broker's view of life was one void of feeling. Life has nothing to do with love, friendship, faith, or memory. Life whittled down to a monetary moment. "Can she survive until January first?" While crass, the motivation, it seems, is again to give life purpose. If a machine is keeping her alive, why not have a purpose for that way of existence?

Even though Helen had a living will, Andrew and his family wrestledwith guilt, feeling that in agreeing to disconnect the machine they were in some way defying their mother's fighting spirit.

Ultimately for Andrew and the rest of the family the meaning of life was not found in terms of aging as mere survival, but in terms of a God who finds a way into the sterile environment of an intensive care unit and offers to each day and age both love and comfort.

Blessed Assurance—Aging as Blessing

All the houses on South Park Drive are designed to capture attention. Long driveways are bordered by perfect grass that leads to white pillars, bricks, and bay windows—but they are no match for Beverly's home. Built before prestige rolled in, Beverly's home is a cottage. Painted quietly pink behind an agonizingly twisted dogwood tree, it is enough to hold attention, and so is Beverly.

Imagine a stout woman, cane in hand, climbing a sidewalked hill. She is dressed in a tweed sports coat and a stocking cap that mirrors the colors from a roll of Lifesavers and covers her cropped gray hair. Aqua sweatpants are tucked into a pair of black leather high-tops.

She is passed on both sides by crisp walking suits with headbands and Raybans. They walk for health, for conversation, and to wave at passing motorists. She walks because if she does not move, the traffic piles up: She will worry. She will worry about worrying. What will happen tomorrow? How will she get up in the morning? Then, for a moment, she worries about whether or not she will get up in the morning. If she is not concentrating, will her heart make another beat?

On a bad day Beverly is anxious, so she moves and her life moves, she writes poetry, she paints watercolor portraits of members of the A.M.E. Zion church, and she takes long drives in her truck.

She travels down country roads, stops haphazardly, walking onto the porches of strangers and asking directions, telling stories, and accepting their invitations to dinner.

I had an invitation to visit Beverly.

"Come in! Come in!" she greeted me, and I entered her living room. It was a room splashed by paintings in bright colors, all created by her hand, except for the large portrait of John, her deceased husband.

"John, we have a visitor," she said to the painting. Her next words were, "Do you think I'm odd?"

"Are you talking to your husband or me?" I inquired. (I know Beverly well enough to know that she enjoys being noticed for her eccentricities.)

She laughed and we sat down. "Oh, Donovan! It's young John. I'm just worried," she said. "My son John, who's a psychologist in Charlotte, was recently diagnosed with lymphoma. Do you know, I called him yesterday, and he said to me, 'Mother, I need for all of your friends to quit praying for me and to start praying for my cancer. I'm getting so sweet I can't stand myself!' He sounds just like his father, oh dear." She said this with a slight laugh and then added, "I don't know what I would do without him. It's hard, you know. We must pray for a miracle."

As a pastor I pray for miracles. I pray for miracles to stop a disease from coursing through the veins of good people. This disease, I have seen, drags its prey for months or a tortuous year until finally it makes a mistake. It kills and in so doing takes its own life. I pray for miracles. I know nothing more to do.

Three months later John died. I sat with Beverly, not knowing what to say. I simply sat. I did not know God on that day. What I did know was that cancer had taken too many fine people—people who were gentle and kind and loved. I know that God is too selective in his miracles, and there are days when I feel weak and it threatens my faith.

The Sunday morning after John's death came. I got up in the pulpit and preached a sermon that will not be remembered. The truth that morning sat on the back row, for there was a woman who had watched her husband die, and who had prayed countless prayers and wept over her son. In spite of it all, there was a woman who sang a song on a Sunday morning and came to worship God.

Faith is as strong as it is fragile, and I am amazed.

Reflection

Scattered about our Scripture is the thought that old age is a blessing of God, a reward for righteous living. An example of this is found in the Ten Commandments. "Honor your father and your mother, so that your days may be long in the land that the LORD your God is giving you" (Exodus 20:12). Proverbial wisdom tells us: "The fear of the LORD is the beginning of wisdom, and the knowledge of the Holy One is insight. For by me your days will be multiplied, and years will be added to your life" (Proverbs 9:10–11).

While it is easy to attribute all good things to God, one needs only the eyes of Job to look around and see that "the tents of robbers are at peace, and those who provoke God are secure" (Job 12:6). Observation says there are plenty of tyrants who live long lives and far too many of the innocent who have lives that are cut tragically short. The death of Jesus is the most compelling of examples.

The Bible is then at odds with itself—but then so are we. As one gerontologist, Robert Kastenbaum, put it, "While reaching a good old age has been a common hope, being old has rarely been anyone's ambition."[1]

For Beverly aging is a blessing. Aging brings forth the surprise of mixed paint on a pallet, a new road, and the laughter of grandchildren. But for Beverly with the blessings of age also come new fears, new worries, and painful losses. She endures the pain and celebrates the joys. The dark colors and the light colors are often at odds with one another and yet, says the painter, "working together to say something beautiful."

> We know that all things work together for good for those who love God, who are called according to his purpose. . . . For I am convinced that neither death, nor life, nor angels, nor rulers, nor things present, nor things to come, nor powers, nor height, nor depth, nor anything else in all creation, will be able to separate us from the love of God in Christ Jesus our Lord (Romans 8:28, 38).

Saintly Ambition—Aging toward Victory over Death

Sadie Webb lived on the last road in western North Carolina, and then some. Her mailbox introduced me to her gravel drive, which lingered through the smell of tall pines, a display of black-eyed Susans, and the front porch to a smile. "Oh, come in! Sit down! Would you like some tea?"

"Yes, thank you," I said.

Glasses rattled in the kitchen while I surveyed the pictures that crowded her walls. I already knew some things about Sadie. I had been cautioned by a few in our congregation to wear orange on my visit. Apparently Sadie was a deadeye with a rifle. She was ninety years old and capable of picking off a gray squirrel on a rainy day from one hundred yards. It was not that Sadie despised squirrels. It was that the garden needed a fighting chance.

The garden was her joy. Photographs testified to it. Old black-and-whites washed into color snapshots were along a wall and even on the television console. The garden is shown growing in the background and Sadie, Robert, and their two daughters growing up in the foreground.

"Janet lives in Hickory and Carol lives in Alabama," she said, handing me a large glass of iced tea. "I hope you like it sweet."

I do not, but my mother had instilled in me to respond in silence and a nod. "Here's my husband, Robert. He passed away five years ago on October 12. He had gone out to the shed, and you know it wasn't like him not to come in for lunch. So I went out to the shed, and he was on the ground, and I knew.

"He flew an airplane, and when we were courting he buzzed my home. The next day when he came to the door, my father told him if he did it again, he'd shoot him down. It never happened again."

I laughed. I had been her pastor for ten minutes, but Sadie was comfortable. She was in control of the conversation.

"Janet is the oldest. She married a real estate agent in Hickory. They don't have any children. Carol doesn't have any children, either. I don't understand these girls. Carol is remarried and her new husband flies a plane, too. I guess she's a lot like her mother after all. That girl wants me to fly down with her husband to Alabama in his little Cessna for a few weeks. I don't know . . . " Sadie paused.

She moved over to her recliner. "Where are my manners? Have a seat." She slowly lowered herself into the chair, but then gave up on the last five inches. "Ever since my treatments I haven't been able to get around very well. I have cancer, you know." She waited for me to respond.

I had been told by the women of the church, who were the most reliable source for information, that Sadie had cancer of the liver and had been taking chemotherapy for the last year. The chemo had made Sadie's hair fall out, and on a good day she wore a white wig;

on a bad day she just tied on a bandana. I caught her on a good day.

"I heard that you had cancer. I was wondering . . . " She cut me off. "Preacher," she said, "what do you suppose heaven is like?" A question, I have come to find, that a pastor will have to field about twenty-seven times a year. This was my first time out. I had just graduated from seminary. I had my Christology down pat, but what was heaven like? I had no answer. I offered silence.

In that silence rose the face of my second-grade Sunday school teacher. I remember clearly his description of the hereafter—a city with streets of gold and pearly gates. In the second grade the only city I was familiar with was Sioux City, Iowa, a town that was filled with meatpacking plants and grain elevators. So for a good part of my life heaven was Sioux City, but cleaner. It was not the answer I thought Sadie was looking for. I also knew the silence had gone on long enough. After all, I was ordained. I said, "I think heaven will be a place that is better than your most favorite thought, and it will last forever."

As it turned out Sadie wanted Sioux City. "Do you suppose we'll live in houses?" she said. "The Bible says we'll live in houses. Do you think people will be able to recognize other people?"

I thought less and replied, "Yes."

"I'm not sure I'd want to see a good many of them." She sipped her tea. "I don't know, I don't think I'll be going," she said.

It was then I remembered a seminary professor saying, "When you get old enough to see death over your shoulder, heaven becomes something you doubt or something you believe in with all your heart, and even then you have your doubts."

My heart reached out to this dear lady. My words ran to reassure. "Sadie," I said, "my goodness, you love God. I know you do! God certainly loves you. You're one of the saints in the church! Everyone I know has told me about how you were always the last one out of the church on Sunday morning because you'd make sure the place was clean before you left. You brought up your daughters in the church. Of course you're going to heaven!"

"Heaven?" Sadie exclaimed. "I know I'm going to heaven! I was talking about Alabama!"

I visited Sadie every week or two until she died in the fall of that year. A gardener is good at timing things. I will remember that when

I visited her, at first I was greeted at her door. Then, in her last days, I was greeted near her bed—but always with a smile and an hour's worth of conversation. She would talk, and I would listen. Before I would leave I would always remind her that she was going to heaven. We would laugh and share a wink. Sadie I will remember because she smiled, because she loved a garden, and because heaven, for her, is a lot easier to get into than a Cessna.

Reflection

"Now the gardener is the one who has seen everything ruined so many times that (even as his pain increases with each loss) he comprehends—truly knows—that where there was a garden once, it can be again, or where there never was [one], there yet can be a garden." 2

Our aging journey toward death is a conversation in which we can all relate and contribute, but most of us choose to fill our traveling years with conversation about the scenery rather than the final destination. Ultimately it is disease, tragedy, and old age that are the triggers that cause us to speak of what it means to die.

From a scientific view death is merely the end of life. The heart and mind stop functioning. Decay. We leave on this earth a residue.

While science provides the facts, our faith provides a mystery. "What no eye has seen, nor ear heard, nor the human heart conceived, what God has prepared for those who love him" (1 Corinthians 2:9).

A mystery in which instead of leaving a residue, body and soul are resurrected and celebrated. How is this possible? In this world we can only wonder!

Sadie wondered, "What do you suppose heaven is like?"

Our fear is that heaven will be less pleasing than the memories that decorate the walls: the photographs of a tanned husband standing beside his plane, daughters dressed in Easter's best that day when the garden was more dazzling than expected. Our fear is that there is a certain worn comfort that life has given that heaven cannot replicate.

Our Scriptures are well aware of our fears, and instead of offering details into the afterworld they offer comfort. Jesus imparts these words to his disciples:

In my Father's house there are many dwelling places. If it were not so, would I have told you that I go to prepare a place for you? And if I go and prepare a place for you, I will come again and will take you to myself, so that where I am, there you may be also (John 14:2–3).

Our future is like our past and our present. Time after time, in this age and the next, God is with us. It is what Sadie took comfort in, and so can we.

Genesis 1—A New Creation

In the beginning Eden knew that its days were numbered. We do, too, and we can choose to accept the fact of our aging with fear, changing hair color, face-lifts, and trembling, or we can choose to embrace this wonder of creation that allows us to love God, glorify God, enjoy God, at any age and in any age. Time will tell, and so can we!

Questions for Discussion

1. In what ways were you created to survive? What does it mean to live a long life? Would you want to live to be 100?
2. List twenty things you have that help you live in your day-to-day life. If those things were narrowed down to ten, what things would you keep and what would you give up? What if you had to narrow them down to three?
3. List ten ways that aging has been a blessing. List ten ways it has been a curse.
4. Can you think of ways in which the good and the bad in your life have worked together for good?
5. What are your feelings about death?
6. Does old age prepare someone for dying? Why or why not?
7. What are some words that describe heaven for you?
8. In Sadie's story in what ways might redemption be considered a positive blessing?

Notes

1. Robert Kastenbaum, "Exist and Existence," *Aging, Death and the Completion of Being*, ed. David D. Van Tassel (Philadelphia: University of Pennsylvania Press, 1979), p. 77.
2. Henry Mitchell, *The Essential Earthman: Henry Mitchell on Gardening* (Bloomington, IN: Indiana University Press, 2003), p. 3.

Jung's View of the Later Years

Richard L. Morgan

A human being would certainly not grow to be seventy or eighty years old if this longevity had no meaning for the species. The afternoon of human life must also have a significance of its own and cannot be merely an appendage to life's morning.[1]

Although Carl G. Jung died in 1961, years before the age boom descended on our world, his views on aging speak with incredible meaning for our time. If Freud was the psychologist of sexuality, Jung was the psychologist of spirituality. More than any other psychologist of his day, Jung saw that the focus of life changed at midlife from the outer to the inner world. Aging was a time for soul-making.

Jung believed that even as the sun reached its zenith at high noon and then began to descend into darkness, so humankind reached a major crisis at midlife. No longer would meaning be found outside in the world, through career success, productivity, and family, but within oneself, in the life of the soul. In the outside world women develop feminine traits and men master the art of being strong and masculine. One-sidedness is necessary to achieve mastery of the outside world.

At midlife former goals lose their meaning, children leave home, and a void seems to exist in one's life. It is then that a person needs to focus on his or her inner self to learn about unrealized potentials.

If Jung were living in this technological age, midlife would probably begin at age fifty-five, but his insights remain valid. We are living through the greatest miracle in the history of humankind—the doubling of life expectancy since the start of the Industrial Revolution. At that time life expectancy was about thirty-five years. In 1900 it reached forty-seven years. Now the average male life span is seventy-three, and the average female span of years is seventy-nine. This blessing of extended years means we must prepare for the possibility of another life—as different from the traditional roles and responsibilities of earlier years as winter is from spring. In an age when some still dread or deny aging, Jung shows that aging is a time of growth, not decline. His views were mirrored in his own life; the last decade of his life before death was filled with personal and spiritual growth.

Jung's views about the changes that come with midlife are especially relevant for the boomer generation. They point to a meaningful way to spend one's last years that go beyond the usual preoccupation with travel, recreation, and games. Jung claims that aging is a time of growth and transformation, that "the afternoon" of life cannot follow the same programs as life's morning. He mirrors the words of Jesus, "For what will it profit them if they gain the whole world but forfeit their life?" (Matthew 16:26).

So, Jung argued, aging has its own challenges and meaning. He wrote: "A human being would certainly not grow to be seventy or eighty years old if this longevity had no meaning. The afternoon of life must also have a significance of its own and cannot be merely a pitiful appendage to life's morning."[2]

Jung used Chinese vocabulary to explain life's two major stages: Life's morning is a *yang* time. The sun has its ascent, and so do the ego's powers as the young man or young woman sets out to conquer the world. Life's evening time is a *yin* time. The sun is descending in life's afternoon, but that also means the *yin* is growing. "Yin is in!"

Stages of Life

Jung believed life had four major stages: childhood, youth, middle age, and old age. He wrote:

> The one hundred and eighty degrees of the arc of life are divided into four parts: the first quarter, lying in the east, is

childhood, that state in which we are a problem for others, but not yet conscious of any problems of our own. Conscious problems fill out the second and third quarters. . . . While the last, in extreme old age, we descend again into the condition where, unworried by our state of consciousness, we again become something of a problem for others.[3]

Anne Brennan and Janice Brewi call Jung's stage of old age *the mature years*. Jung's descriptive essay on the four stages of life is found in *Modern Man in Search of a Soul*. Surely today he would have called it *The Modern Men and Women in Search of a Soul*. Jung describes life's major crisis as appearing at midlife. He uses the analogy of the sun to describe what he means. As the sun rises during life's earlier stages, we are more inclined to see the world as something to be mastered. We must achieve, make our way in the world, discover and explore our talents, and make our mark. We are ambitious, active, eager to control and to accomplish. While we are doing that we have an outward focus, and for that reason we turn our backs on some essential resources of the soul. Among these resources are such things as emotional life, creative potentials, and spiritual possibilities. So our development during the first stage of life seems to be somewhat one-sided, more *yang* than *yin*.

Later on in life we may well turn back toward some of the spiritual resources we have neglected and seek transcendence. But at high noon (midlife) the sun begins its inevitable descent in the west. So now we focus on our inner selves and want to claim an inner life that our outward activity has held in check. Jung warns, however, of an "ambush" at midlife if we are not prepared for the change. He says:

Instead of looking forward, one looks backward . . . one begins to take stock, to see how his [or her] life has developed up to this point. The real motivations are seen and the real discoveries are made. . . . But these insights do not come to him [or her] easily; they are gained only through the severest shocks.[4]

It is also during our middle years that life is often disturbed by such events as the death of parents, the necessity of adapting to increasing age, and major losses.

First Half of Life	Second of Half of Life
ego	self, new center of wholeness
conscious personality	unconscious personality
outer events	inner event
outer world	inner world
persona, role-playing	coming to terms with *shadow*
achievement	wholeness
dependence on other's opinion	transparency
doing	being

The second half of life brings major changes. Our friends begin to die. Death begins to hang over us like the sword of Damocles.

We find ourselves often out-of-sorts with a youth-oriented culture. In their book *The Passion for Life* Brennan and Brewi propose that we do one of three things. We can regress. We go into a second childhood, abandoning responsibilities and denying our aging. If we do not regress, we can decide not to change. We refer to the "good old days" and cling to the past as the butterfly clings to the cocoon. We say, "It's too late to change." People may live to be eighty, but some die at fifty. Many people get stuck at midlife. They decline and, like Lot's wife, turn into pillars of salt. People who are one-sided are critical, judgmental, endlessly complaining.

The third response is to see this new stage of life as a spiritual journey, an adventure, and an invitation to become whole, find our true self, and discern the image of God in us. The blinders are off. Jung calls this the process of individuation.

Achieving Wholeness

Jung saw the later stage of life as a new rooting in the Self, finding wholeness and God in us. This growth of the soul prepares us for the great transition of death.

In his autobiography, *Memories, Dreams, Reflections*, Jung ascribes his theory of the structure of the psyche to a nocturnal vision. In his dream Jung is standing in the upper room of a strange house. He feels the urge to go downstairs, and when he does he finds that everything there is old and musty. He explores the whole house and discovers a stone stairway that winds down to a lower level. Descending, he finds himself in a beautifully vaulted room, extremely ancient. For Jung, the dream represents the hidden parts of our own psyche, hidden from us by the veil of our consciousness.

It is in the later stages of life that we can get in touch with these other parts of our personalities.

During life's earlier stages, when career success and achievement dominate our lives, we have to don a mask (what Jung called the *persona*) to relate to the world and satisfy social demands. In the opera *Phantom of the Opera* there is a classic scene at a masquerade party.

> Masquerade!
> Paper faces on parade. . . .
> Hide your face,
> so the world will never see you.
> Masquerade!
> Every face a different shade. . . .
> Masquerade!
> Look around—
> there's another mask behind you!

The *persona* includes such forms of social behavior as personal appearance, posture, dress, facial expression. While a person must learn to adjust to society, there is always the danger that the *persona*, the face or role, can dominate one's personality and prevent selfhood.

One of the tasks of later life is to drop the *persona* and become oneself. In fact, the closing years of life are like the end of a masquerade party, where the masks are dropped. May Sarton said it well: "At seventy I am more myself than I've ever been."[5]

Aging also demands that we acknowledge the *shadow* within us. The more we wear masks in life, the more we repress or disregard the *shadow* in us. The *shadow* is the opposite of the image we project on society. How do we recognize the *shadow*?

At times we may acknowledge the unpleasant parts of our personality, but we excuse, cover up, or refuse to admit to them. At other times they are projected onto others. The very qualities we dislike in another person may well be those aspects of our own personalities we don't want to admit. When another person angers or irritates us, it may well be that they are expressing outwardly our own faults or weaknesses that we try to conceal.

> I do not like thee, Dr. Fell,
> The reason why I cannot tell.
> But this alone I know full well,
> I do not like thee, Dr. Fell.

The reason we do not like Dr. Fell is that he is us. Or, as the comic strip character Pogo said, "We have met the enemy and he is us." Another aspect of Jung's theories is related to the Chinese philosophy that the earth is composed of two opposites, the *yin* and the *yang*. The *yang* is the active, warm, bright masculine force, and the *yin* is the fertile, cold, mysterious, and feminine force. The yin-yang symbol shows that both forces are necessary; at the expansion of one is the narrowing of the other. Jung called these forces *animus* (masculine) and *anima* (feminine). He believed that when one of the opposites reaches its greatest strength, the other will begin to assert itself. "When *Yang* has reached its greatest strength, the dark power of *Yin* is born within its depths, for night begins at midday when *Yang* breaks up and begins to change into *Yin*."[6]

Jung's concept of the *animus* and *anima* has real meaning for older persons. He believed in the unity of the opposites. In our older years, changes can occur. Women can begin to manifest *animus* characteristics, activating their masculine component, while men manifest *anima* characteristics, activating their feminine component. Therefore to develop wholeness in later life means that both opposites are part of the personality.

However, in the first half of life these poles are unequal. Men are more *yang* and women more *yin*. However, in life's second part repressed parts of the soul demand their due. Aggressive businessmen need to relax, downshift, find time for the soul. *Yang* energy changes over to *yin*.

There is anima awakening for the male. All the feminine tendencies in a man's psyche that are ignored or repressed in the first half of life emerge in midlife. Conversely, during midlife the woman discovers that her *yang* side is emerging. All masculine tendencies in a woman's psyche that are repressed or ignored in the first half of life will come out at midlife. Each sex adds some of the traits that distinguished the opposite in early adulthood, women becoming independent and assertive and men more expressive and emotionally responsive. The goal of later life is individuation or the realization of our true potential as persons.

Telling Our Story to Find Meaning

Telling our story and preserving our memories as a legacy for future generations is another task of individuation in the later years. Jung believed that older persons have the need to review, reflect upon, and sum up their lives. Telling one's story prior to death helps one discern the meaning of one's life.[7]

An integral part of this life review is recognizing the meaningful occurrences in one's life. Jung had a lifelong interest in coincidences and coined the word *synchronicity*, which he defined as "meaningful occurrences." When there are two simultaneous meaningful occurrences that have no causal connection, we have a synchronistic event, a coincidence.

Jung had many synchronistic experiences, the most famous being the case of the golden beetle. As a client described a beetle, that very insect flew into the room, a "birth" symbol to Jung. Many older people who revisit their stories can discern meaningful occurrences in their lives. Lynn Huber claims that these coincidences are "a miracle in which God wishes to remain anonymous."[8]

Facing and Accepting the Reality of Death

Jung challenged people to confront the reality of death. In *Memories, Dreams, Reflections* he wrote: "A man should be able to say he has done his best to form a conception of life after death, or to create some image of it—even if he must confess his failure. Not to have done so is a vital loss. For the question that is posed to him is the age-old heritage of humanity . . . which seeks to add itself to our own individual life in order to make it whole.[9]

The question asked by Job, "If mortals die, will they live again?" (Job 14:14) becomes real at midlife. Thoughts of death change from the abstract to the concrete, from something that happens to others, to something that will happen to us. It is, as Gene Cohen writes, "the first time with depth of consciousness, that we confront our mortality. We look to the horizon and see the sunset rather than the sunrise. If the uncertainty of life leaves us daunted, the certainty of death fills us with sudden dread."[10]

Jung believed that understanding death and immortality helps to displace the center of the personality from the ego to the deeper Self. In 1944 at the age of sixty-nine Jung was hospitalized by a heart attack. While on the operating table he felt himself lifted up from the surgical room miles into outer space. It seemed to him as though he was detached from his body, his consciousness no longer confined to his physical self. Gazing into space, he saw glorious sights. The earth was bathed in beautiful blue light. Looking south, he saw an enormous block of brown granite floating in space. The granite had been hewn out to form a candle-lit temple, where an ancient sage greeted Jung and told him that now he would discover the meaning of his life. As Jung approached the temple, he felt all his past existence drop away from him like a snake's discarded skin. Only the essence of him was left, his true being.[11]

Jung was about to enter a room within the temple where he sensed that he would meet all the people in his life with whom he had formed lasting connections. Suddenly, however, he was summoned to return home. He was told his life was not finished and that he must return to the body immediately. Jung obeyed, but he was deeply dismayed that he must come back to the material world. As the weeks flew by, Jung found himself caught between the repeating joy of the breakthrough moments and the dread of the return to his ordinary life with its limitations.

Jung knew that he had more work to do, but his heart attack was a wake-up call and marked a transition to old age. He resigned his professorship in Zurich and spent increasing amounts of time at the retreat he had built at Bollingen. The last fifteen years of Jung's life, from the age of seventy to eighty-five, were some of his most prolific years in terms of his ideas and writing.

On June 6, 1961, the last evening of Jung's life, his son Franz was with him, and also Ruth Bailey. As Ruth left the room Jung asked Franz to quickly help him out of bed before she came back. He wanted to look at the sunset. The summer sun set like a ball of red flame beneath the Alps. Jung returned to his bed for the last time and died. The sun had finally descended on his life. It was said that a violent thunderstorm broke out in Kusnacht two hours after his death. Just about the time of his death lightning struck his favorite tree in the garden.

Jung always called death "the great adventure," and he believed that what came after death was "unspeakably glorious." He would concur with Paul's words that "what no eye has seen, nor ear heard, nor the human heart conceived, what God has prepared for those who love him" (1 Corinthians 2:9). It is significant that on the right and left side of Jung's grave in Kusnacht are these words from 1 Corinthians 15:47:

Primus homo de terra terrenus.
Secondus homo de caelo caelesti.
(The first man is of the earth, and is earthy.
The second man is of heaven and is heavenly.)

Little doubt that Jung believed that transformation and individuation did not end with this life!

Deepened Religious Faith

It was Carl Jung who introduced to psychoanalysis crucial questions about religion and the soul that Freud mishandled or ignored. In his book *Future of an Illusion* Freud characterized religion as a massive neurosis. He believed that God was nothing but a "father replacement," which neurotic people needed as a crutch. Jung differed radically. The only son of a Swiss Reformed Evangelical minister, Jung had eight uncles in the clergy as well as his maternal grandfather, Samuel Preiswerk.

Jung saw our spiritual history going through three phases: (1) The phase seen in the Book of Job, where God's presence in human beings is unconscious; (2) the phase in the Gospels, where God's presence is conscious in the One (Jesus), and finally, (3) the phase where consciousness of God is present in the many. Jung wrote, "The Indwelling of the Holy Ghost, the Divine Person, in [humanity] brings about a Christification of many."[12] Jung would concur with Paul's hope expressed to the Galatians, that "Christ [be] formed in you" (Galatians 4:19). Although Jung spoke of individuation and Jesus of love, Paul and Jung were thinking of the fullness of living to which we all are called. For Christians, to be like Christ is to love.

In an essay entitled "Psychology and Religion" Jung made clear his religious views: "No matter what the world thinks about religious experience, the one who has it possesses a real treasure, a thing that has become for him a source of life, meaning, and beauty, and that has given a new splendor to the world and to mankind. He has faith and peace."[13]

Jung's faith was well reflected in a stone carving over the door of his home in Kusnacht, words Erasmus had written in Latin:

Vocatus sed non vocatus,
deus aderit.
("Called or not called, God will be there.")

For Jung, God was always there, known or not known, present in the collective unconscious, calling him to live and be his true self. For Jung, unlike Freud, God was no illusion. God was "one of the soul's deepest and closest intimacies."[14]

What is the significance of Jung for the later years? He reminds us that late life is a time for growing our souls and developing our spirituality. In an interview for the BBC Jung, at eighty-one, said he treated many old people. He observed that the unconscious side of aging adults ignores the fact that they are threatened with death. "We are not sure that it is a complete end," he said, "because life behaves as if it is going on. So, I tell old people to live on, as if they had centuries, and then they will live properly."[15]

In his later years Carl Jung modeled this belief as he lived out a full life to the very end.

Gerotranscendence: Jung's Views Revisited

In recent years Swedish gerontologist Lars Tornstam of the University of Uppala has developed a theory of aging he calls gerotranscendence. Like Jung's individuation theory, the new theory of Tornstam (1989, 1994) states that gerotranscendence is a natural progression toward maturation and wisdom.[16] Tornstam bases his theory of transcendence on studies of fifty Swedish men and women between the ages of fifty-two and ninety-seven. He discovered that these individuals experienced a series of changes. They redefined the Self and relationships to others, and they had a new understanding of existential questions.

Tornstam believes that old age is not merely the continuation of midlife patterns and values, but rather a development of something qualitatively different, as Jung described it in 1931. Tornstam also revisits the 1960 Cummings theory of aging, which states that older persons want to disengage and withdraw. In their rush to abandon this theory, gerontologists introduced the activity (transcendence) theory.

The theory of transcendence was born of the feeling that something was lost when the old theory of disengagement was abandoned. Tornstam records that when Joan Erikson, a co-worker of Erik Erikson, turned ninety-one she became aware that the words "wisdom" and "integrity" fell short of expressing her experience in her later years. She was so bold as to revise her colleague's eighth stage to include a ninth and a tenth stage, addressing "gerotranscendence."[17] Among the marks of gerotranscendent persons are the following:

View of Time and Space
- sense of greater connection with previous generations
- decrease in borders between past and present

Self-Understanding
- awareness of one's good and bad qualities
- need for solitude

Decrease in Self-Centeredness
- heightened sensitivity to the needs and feelings of others
- increase in altruism and concern for society
- reduced self-centeredness in ambitions and goals

Transcendent Wisdom
- greater tolerance of human limitations
- practical wisdom

Meaning of Relationships
- fewer acquaintances, more close friends
- less feeling of competitiveness
- more selectivity in choice of friends and social activities
- diminished boundaries between self and others

Mystery Dimension of Life
- sense of the numinous dimension of the world
- awareness that there is more to life than rational knowledge
- boundary between self and universe transcended

View of Life and Death
- no fear of death
- view of life as continuing until death

Attitude toward Material Assets
- little concern with material assets
- real happiness found beyond material resources
- material assets seen as means to help family, serve others

Life Satisfaction
- acceptance of present life situation
- acceptance of past without regret
- pleasure in small aspects of daily life
- acceptance of present age[18]

One can clearly see that Tornstam's discovery mirrors Jung's view of the later years as a time for growth toward wholeness. The decreased interest in material things coupled with a deeper need for solitude, a feeling of cosmic communion with the spirit of the universe, and movement away from the ego to a new Self all sound like Jung. Although a relatively new theory, transcendence warrants more study in the years ahead.

Summary

Jung believed that the second half of life was a spiritual journey to achieve wholeness. These were the tasks he considered crucial:

1. Letting go of the dominance of the ego to grow the Self
2. Integrating all the opposites of our personality to become who were meant to be
3. Facing the reality of age and death
4. Reflecting on our story to find the meaning of our lives
5. Closer communion with God

Jung's view of later age as a spiritual journey is a challenge and a call to adults and the Christian church. Wallace B. Cleft has written that Jung believed that the future of Christianity lies in the realization of the Christ within each person, which is another way of stating the presence of the Holy Spirit in humanity.19 Jung could echo the words of Paul that his greatest hope was that "Christ is formed in you" (Galatians 4:19).

Glossary of Jung's Terms

The Ego—consciousness (includes internal and external awareness, dominant in the first half of life).

The Personal Unconscious—First layer of the unconscious, which contains all feelings repressed during one's lifetime; includes *shadow* and most of *animus/anima*.

The Collective Unconscious—The personal unconscious is limited to a person's experience; collective unconscious is inherited and shared by all humankind. It is made up of energy forces called archetypes. We can only learn about them through dreams, fantasies, and myths.

The Persona—The ego's mask or personality one projects on society. It is necessary to survive in the world. A balanced person will have *persona*, but also other aspects of the psyche.

The Shadow—Adverse traits or feeling we cannot admit in ourselves and often project on others we do not like because they reflect the *shadow* in us.

The Animus/Anima—Anima is the feminine side in man, "the woman within." When the *anima* is repressed, men are one-sidedly aggressive, independent and domineering. *Animus* is the male side of woman, "the man within." When women repress their *animus*, they are passive, withdrawn, and submissive.

The Self (Selbst)—Most important archetype, the person who fulfills their potential and unites all opposites in their personality and become a whole person (self-actualized person). Ultimate goal of life.

For Further Reading

Primary Sources

Jung, Carl G., *Modern Man in Search of a Soul.* New York: Harcourt, Brace and World, 1933.

Jung, Carl G., *The Portable Jung.* New York: Penguin Books, 1976.

Jung, Carl G., *Psychological Reflections: A New Anthology of His Writings, 1905–1961,* ed. Jolande Jacobi. Princeton, NJ: Princeton University Press, 1970.

Jung, Carl G., *The Undiscovered Self.* New York: New American Library, 1957.

Books Related to Jung's View of the Later Years

Brennan, Anne and Janice Brewi, *Mid-Life Spirituality and Jungian Archetypes.* York Beach, ME: Nicolas' Hayes, 1999.

Brennan, Anne and Janice Brewi, *Passion for Life: Lifelong Psychological and Spiritual Growth.* New York: Continuum, 2001.

Crowley, Vivanne, *Jung: A Journey of Transformation.* Wheaton, IL: Quest Books, 1999.

Crowley, Vivanne, *Principles of Jung's Spirituality.* London: Thorson, 1998.

Hall, Calvin S. and Vernon J. Nordby, *A Primer of Jung's Psychology.* New York: Penguin, 1973.

Jacobi, Jolande, *The Psychology of C. G. Jung.* New Haven, CT: Yale University Press, 1973.

Singer, June, *Boundaries of the Soul.* New York: Doubleday, 1972.

Stein, Murray, *In Midlife: A Jungian Perspective.* New York: Springer Publishers, 1973.

Wallace, Cliff B., *Jung and Christianity.* New York: Crossroads, 1994.

Questions for Discussion

1. Reflect on your earlier life and career. What were your greatest achievements or the highlights of your life?
2. If you are now at midlife (fifty-five to seventy-five), how do you see your life now?

3. Jung called the *persona* the roles we play in life. What roles did you play in society?
4. Think of all your negative qualities that you do not admit to others. Then think about the characteristics you dislike in other people. Do you see any connection? When you find that you dislike someone at a church meeting, could that be your "shadow self"?
5. Jung believed in synchronicities, meaningful occurrences you neither planned nor controlled. Can you recall such moments in your life? What about in your church life? Would you say they were coincidences or God moments, when God was present in mysterious ways?
6. If you are "retired," what insights from Jung's view of later life appeal to you?
7. Does Jung's view that men become more prone to affiliated relations and women more assertive make sense to you? Cite examples.
8. If the latter half of life is more focused on developing the inner self (soul work), how can the church help older adults do that?
9. Do you know people who are described by Lars Tornstam's concept of gerotranscendence? Is that the kind of older person you would like to become? Explain.
10. Do Jung's views of later life make any sense in a society that still evaluates people by their productivity and achievement at any age?

Notes

1. Carl G. Jung, Gerald Adler, R. F. C. Hull, *The Structure and Dynamics of the Psyche*, vol. 8 in *Collected Works of C. G. Jung*, 2nd ed. (Cambridge, MA: Bollingen Publishing Company, 1970), p. 17.
2. Ibid.
3. Carl G. Jung, *Modern Man in Search of a Soul* (New York: Hartcourt, Brace and World, 1933), p. 112.
4. Carl G. Jung, *Psychological Reflections: A New Anthology of His Writings*, 1915–1961, ed. Yolande Jacobi (Princeton, NJ: Princeton University Press, 1970), pp. 132–136.
5. May Sarton, *At Seventy* (New York: W. W. Norton, 1993), p. 14.
6. Carl G. Jung, *The Collected Works of C. G. Jung*, vol. 13, *Alchemical Studies* (London: Routledge & Kegan Paul, 1967), p. 13.
7. Richard L. Morgan, *Remembering Your Story: Creating Your Own Spiritual Autobiography*, 2nd ed. (Nashville: Upper Room Books, 2002).
8. Lynn Huber, *Revelations on the Road* (Boulder, CO: WovenWord Press, 2003), p. xii.

9. Carl G. Jung, *Memories, Dreams, Reflections* (New York: Continuum, 2001), p. 121.
10. Gene Cohen, *The Creative Age* (New York: HarperCollins, 2002), pp. 82–83.
11. Vivianne Crowley, *Jung: A Journey of Transformation* (Wheaton, IL: Quest Books, 1999), pp. 132–133.
12. Carl G. Jung, *Answer to Job* (New York: Meridian Publishers, 1960), p. 2020.
13. Carl G. Jung, *Symbols of Transformation*, vol. V in *Collected Works of C. G. Jung*, 2nd ed. (Cambridge, MA: Bollingen Publishing Company, 1967), p. 105.
14. Carl G. Jung, *Civilization in Transition*, vol. X in *Collected Works of C. G. Jung* (Cambridge, MA: Bollingen Publishing Company, 1970), p. 279.
15. Anne Brennan and Janice Brewi, *Passion for Life* (New York: Continuum, 2001), pp. 50–51.
16. Lars Tornstam, "Gerotranscendence—A Theory about Maturity into Old Age," *Journal of Aging and Identity*, January 1996, pp. 37–50.
17. Ibid., p. 48. (Joan Erickson's conversation with Tornstam.)
18. Feresh Ah Madi, "Reflections on Spiritual Maturity and Gerotranscendence: Dialogue with Two Sufis," *Journal of Religious Gerontology* 11 (2), pp. 73–74.
19. Wallace B. Clift, *Jung and Christianity: The Challenge of Christianity* (New York: Crossroads, 1997), p. 157.

"Old Souls, New Shoes": Transitions and Stable Periods in the Last Third of Life

Henry C. Simmons

Pick up today's newspaper and turn to the obituaries. Look for people who died in their eighties or nineties and try to figure out from the text what they did between retirement and their deaths. Only in a few cases will you find any clues. These people may well have lived twenty-five or thirty years past retirement (and you may well, too), and yet it did not strike the writer of the obituary that it was important to say what they did for this last third of their adult lives.

At least in part, the problem is that we do not have any standard vocabulary to describe the events, changes, and transitions and stable periods that take place predictably in the last third of life. We hear phrases like "good years, bad years," "young old, old old," "go-go, slow-go, no-go." Or, within the life of a congregation, we may hear that a person is designated for pastoral care of the frail, or that there are programs for widows, or that there is a special service in Older Adult Month, or that there is a Seniors group. But nothing in all this gets at what transitions and stable periods can be expected if one lives a full life from the time one retires until one dies.

The story of those predictable transitions and stable periods (James C. Fisher and Henry Simmons, forthcoming) is the focus of this chapter. As you read this chapter, keep in mind that there are predictable transitions and stable periods (what we will likely share in common) and there are individual differences. The latter have to do most notably with four factors: gender (length of life, available financial resources, patterns of relationships, and interaction), context (familial, racial, and place on the urban-rural continuum), cohort (year of birth and the social attitudes one carries from that era), and socioeconomic status (personal and financial resources).

Finally, as you read this chapter note that we have moved our attention away from *chronology* toward a vocabulary that identifies the transition or stable period a person is living through. Common sense tells us that this shift is useful. If we say that a child is a "normal seven-year-old girl" we have a pretty good sense, within a range, of the child's physical, social, linguistic, emotional, and educational development. We get a picture that gives us a good starting point. But if we say that a person is a "normal seventy-three-year-old woman" we cannot get a picture that has any kind of clarity. She may be in a nursing home with a chronic disease or she may be off hiking the Appalachian Trail. But if we say that a person is in the process of retiring, or is coming out of the dark times surrounding a spouse's death, or is struggling with a loss of independence, or is dying, we do get a lot of clarity. We do not know the person's age, but that does not matter because we have a good starting point for connecting with the person and understanding his or her life. We are not arguing, of course, that chronology means nothing. Sixty is predictably different from 106. It is just that knowing where a person is in terms of life tasks and transitions gives us a better picture.

Retiring

"Retiring" is the transition that marks for many or even most the beginning of what we are calling later life or the last third of life. It is an active word and denotes a relatively short period of one's life of about a year's duration that has a *before*, a *during*, and an *after*. There is a *before*: the time of planning, meeting with the human resources staff, tidying up projects, and so on. Then there is the *during*: the actual retirement event itself, perhaps with a festive lunch, the proverbial gold watch, good-byes to colleagues, and promises to keep in touch. And there is the *after*: the weeks and months following, when one starts to build a new rhythm of life, finds new things to do and people to do them with, and ultimately discovers a new sense of self.

This is not a small or insignificant transition. It involves life decisions about who I am now that I am no longer defined by my job, what I will do that is worthwhile, and with whom I will do that. These are, in Erik Erikson's understanding of life, deep redefinitions of identity, generativity (supporting the development of the next generation), and intimacy. "Nothing can minimize the psychological adjustment of leaving the world of work for the retired life. Work provides not only a sense of worth and prestige, but valued friendships and opportunity for self-expression. The shock when that is gone cannot be measured."[1] The movement from work to redirection can be one of life's great challenges.

Opportunities for Spiritual Growth and the
Role of the Community of Faith

In the losses that inevitably accompany retiring, we engage in a struggle to redefine life's agenda in light of some new and compelling vision that may include a new and compelling vision of God.[2] Retiring—or other evidences that we are entering a new phase of life, such as a sudden awareness of the altered faces of those one has known since youth—can be a spiritual event of great magnitude. It can be a moment that sets us on a new course toward wholeness of self and relationship with God. But if there is potential for growth, there is also peril. Personal length of days is an absolutely nonrenewable resource. Retiring may open us to a world of opportunity, but the awareness that we do not know our length of days brings the reflective person up short. If retiring causes us to reimagine identity, generativity, and intimacy, it should also face us starkly with the realization that we are dependent on God in ways we have not hitherto experienced. It is by faith that we will cope and grow.

There is little formal religious education for retiring. Retiring may bring with it a sense of uselessness, often masked by great bursts of activity. Retiring does not mark the end of human growth. But the paucity of religious literature or religious education for this life transition is appalling. There is great need for counseling and educational programs for the retiring in congregations. Careful consideration of vocation is particularly crucial at this time of life, when a person has greater voice now than at any time in life about how his or her time and resources will be used.

Retiring needs to be celebrated liturgically.[3] Women and men in peer relationships need to support each other in arriving at understandings of retiring that raise up a sense of promise, of vocation, of responsibility, of giftedness. These are realities far removed from the glossy images of consumption or scarcity that are presented in popular culture. They need the leadership of communities of faith to support people to take seriously the possibilities and importance of this doorway into the last third of life.

Extended Middle Age

Although it often takes the best part of a year, people do get through the transition of retiring. They then embark on a time of life that we call extended middle age. Unlike the transition of retiring, this is a stable period of life—with its ups and downs, certainly, and with its challenges, promises, hopes, dreams, tasks, and losses, but a time of life that feels like it holds together. This period of life is of indeterminate length: six months, five years, fifteen years, twenty years. The indeterminacy is unnerving to many people. There are few or no clues about one's length of days in this period of life. There is a common wisdom that one ought not waste these precious days. "Do whatever you want to do while you can do it! The day will come when you can't travel, or volunteer, or whatever it is you can now do." "Do it while you can" is a sort of mantra that holds this time of life together.

In its simplest articulation, extended middle age is much like middle age, except that work has been replaced by another set of activities. People in this stable period see themselves as still in their middle years, but now with opportunities for leisure they did not previously have. They do not relate as peers with those further along the journey of life. They look back to middle age rather than ahead to the uncertainties that will eventually come. Yet people in extended middle age both are and are not the people they were in their middle-age work years. Indeed, to the extent that retiring was a deeply successful transition, they are engaged in a spiritual quest that makes this a new part of the human journey.

Opportunities for Spiritual Growth and the Role of the Community of Faith

The meaning of this part of the journey is not likely to emerge with clarity without conversation among thoughtful, supportive, and highly motivated peers.[4]

Those who have left behind the world of paid work have also left the tyranny of the paycheck. They are liberated to learn, to develop and to strengthen social relationships, and to read. They can adopt a lifestyle of their choice and choose to slow down. Without the social pressures that once pounded upon their lives, they are free to think for themselves and to challenge the prevailing ethos of fear and greed.[5]

It continues to startle this author that congregations and communities of faith have so little insight into the radical possibilities of extended middle age. Congregations ought to be privileged places for groups of elders to engage in a high level of self-reflection and growth in social awareness, free from "the lifelong pressures of orthodoxy and educational conditioning."[6] Not everyone will have the personal resources or aptitude for this kind of attention to the meaning of life and the social demands of the Word of God. But surely groups of such thoughtful, supportive, and highly motivated peers in extended middle age, gathered in faith in their congregations, should not be almost unheard-of exceptions.

Some might argue that communities of faith have no particular responsibilities to structure opportunities for such groups. Individual people have their own responsibilities and opportunities for insight and faithful service. As plausible as this might sound, it misses the complicity of communities of faith in devaluing aging. There are many pastors who have come to retirement with a great sense of failure and guilt because they failed to "grow young churches." This reflects an unspoken assumption in churches that church growth is only valid when there are increasing numbers of people under thirty-five years of age, not increasing numbers of people of any age. It also misses the reality that churches opt into a very socially specific view of the last third of life.

A study of denominational literature on grandparenting, for example, showed "a complete lack of attention to the demographic, economic, and social challenges facing the United States: widespread dissolution and reconstruction of families, eroding incomes, eroding job opportunities, a sharply divided class structure, growing threats to the stability of urban families and communities, a world in which cultural continuity is increasingly difficult to achieve."[7]

The sole focus of these books was on companion or leisure grandparenting. This suggests that communities of faith have opted into a very socially specific view of the last third of life, and one that is far from providing a supportive context for grappling with the vocation of the later years.

Uncertain Journey

Extended middle age ends in loss. With or without warning, one begins, unwillingly, an uncertain journey whose outcome cannot be predicted. A major loss interrupts one's life. The world is turned upside down. Typically losses are of this magnitude: death of a spouse, disabling illness of self or partner, a one-sided divorce, a dulling of cognitive ability, or a realization of the need for a more supportive environment.

During extended middle age people wonder uneasily about what this transition will look like in their own lives. There may be a sense of dread: "What will happen if she dies first?" There may even be some anticipatory grieving, as one imagines life alone. Yet when the reality hits there is an element of shock or surprise. "Just yesterday we seemed to be doing so well . . . "

Anthropologists use the term "liminal" when studying complex patterns of major life transitions. The young boy who goes through a ritualized yearlong process of initiation into manhood enters as a boy and emerges as a man. In that year he is "betwixt and between."[8]

The uncertain journey is very much a betwixt-and-between experience: in a year or less one goes from a sense of self that is clearly consistent with one's previous adult experience, to a sense of self that is forced to look forward to the real limits of a future that is not "business as usual." It is a liminal or threshold experience. And the threshold one crosses is not a threshold one would choose. But there is no choice. There is only the struggle to cope, to stay strong, to hold true to one's core values, and to grieve one's losses in a healthy way.

Opportunities for Spiritual Growth and the
Role of the Community of Faith

The wilderness of change that is the threatening landscape of the uncertain journey can reveal the shallowness of a socially sanctioned death that denies spirituality. A church community can be powerfully supportive if it is able to walk with individuals in the wilderness—but only if it recognizes the absolute mystery of loss and death. This is a puzzling and painful time. It can feel as if there is a black hole, a great emptiness, at the center of one's very being.[9]

Loss and death are not subject to logical explanation because "they are part of the awesome mystery of creation. When we attempt to alleviate [their] terror by the use of reason and analysis, we destroy the possibility of personal encounter with God because neither God nor God's creation can be reduced to a logical formula."[10]

The uncertain journey must be endured. Life will not return to what it was before. There may be light in the future, but the person who comes to that light will find that the former sense of identity, generativity, and intimacy all need to be renegotiated. From outside the uncertain journey we can only stand in awe at the resilience of the human spirit.

The New Me

As daunting as it may seem, there is nothing to do but to pick up one's losses and begin to build a new stable life structure that has its own sense, its own integrity, and ultimately its own joys and sorrows. There are new routines to set up, new or renewed relationships to be formed, new tasks and projects to be fulfilled, and above all a new sense of self, a new me, to be discovered or created. For example, if one's partner has had a debilitating stroke or injury—even something far less debilitating than Christopher Reeves' injury—life does not simply go on. Every facet of every day has to be invented anew.

A very clear example is the death of a deeply loved and loving spouse. The one left behind has a huge hole ripped out of the fabric of his or her life. Especially if this happens early on after retirement, at a time that is "not normal," there is great disruption and even a sense of suddenly being half the person one was. With dramatically diminished resources, again one has to accomplish the creative and responsible ordering and living out of one's life. Issues of identity, generativity, and intimacy have to be faced. Even where there is a clear sense of consistency and continuity with the goals and commitments of one's earlier life, these goals and commitments will be shaped differently from within and without. What was "normal" cannot be reclaimed and a new sense of "normal" must be constructed within new defining parameters. Widowhood (an outcome more likely than widower hood) is potentially quite different from other kinds of losses. When the loss that creates the uncertain journey is one's own health, or the loss is the incapacity of a spouse who will need constant care, there are limited resources left to turn outward to the church community or the larger community. Widows have, on the other hand, from the days of the apostles, had a place in the church that was honored, responsible, and often quite unique. For some, this is a time of a new sense of the spiritual. The shock of loss breaks open a lifelong belief in the importance of the physical, material world. As patterns shift, reconfigure, and develop, there is a palpable awareness of the Unknown, the Mystery, the Divine.[11]

It can be a privileged moment of grace—painful, costly, but ultimately rich in mercy.

Opportunities for Spiritual Growth and the
Role of the Community of Faith

The "new me" phase of life is a stable period that can last for years. Again chronology does not help much in our understanding of this stage. What does help is our attention to issues of identity, generativity, and intimacy. For months and years—in some cases twenty or more years—people will create new visions of themselves and live within these visions, intentionally, making and keeping promises, honoring themselves and others, and finding life-sustaining relationships. And if, as Jane Thibault writes, "the development of an intense, mutual, love relationship with God is the primary spiritual task of later life,"[12] a deepening love affair with God will become part of the abundance of life-sustaining relationships.

The church community has a role to play in opening up spaces for people in this stage of life to flourish and contribute. The church community must first realize, however, that it stands "under the oppression of cultural metaphors and images. This is critical if a group is to move from the experience of the *problems* of aging to a dawning sense of agency for the individuals and the group."[13]

It is not the place of people in the church to pity those who work out their lives in ways not of their choosing. The church community must move beyond cultural norms that require the widow or the chronically ill or partially disabled person to be cheerful, to smile all the time, to acquiesce in being invisible and docile, to participate in their own erasure.[14]

It is only when a community of faith grasps and lives the truth that God's promise and human vocation is for the whole of life that this time of life can be seen as a time of growth, freedom, and responsibility.

Reluctant Journey

The third transition of the last third of life is the reluctant journey from independence to dependence. The reluctant journey may take as long as a year as people teeter on the edge of not being able to make it on their own (physically, emotionally, mentally) without sustained help. The actual "tipping point" can often be marked with some precision: a fall, an accident, getting lost close to home, a stove-top fire, an admission of deep-seated fear of being alone. The previous stable period of revised lifestyle has come to a dreaded point: coping with the ins and outs of daily life is no longer possible without help. Some of the most ordinary tasks of life can no longer be accomplished on one's own: toileting, eating, bathing, getting from bed to chair—the activities of daily living that we mastered as very young children.

Home may become a strange place; one gets turned around going to the bathroom, or suddenly the basement stairs (down to the laundry) seem too steep. A once-familiar neighborhood may seem to be a maze. A trip to the library or dry cleaner's may end in driving block after block looking for familiar landmarks. The control of bowels and bladder so hard-won in childhood becomes unpredictable, and going out even to church (or perhaps especially to church) becomes unthinkable. No longer is walker or cane enough help to get from bed to chair and back again. Preparing meals and even the act of eating becomes arduous, and poor nutrition takes its toll. Taking a bath or shower is felt to be dangerous and lifelong habits of hygiene give way. Whatever the cause, however it plays out, persons in this stage of adulthood cannot get by on their own. They are going through a transition we can hardly imagine for ourselves—the reluctant journey.

Some have adult children, grandchildren, nieces or nephews, friends, spouses, or fictive kin to ease the terrors of this reluctant journey, although when the burden falls on a spouse or partner the cost may tip the balance for that person. Some few plan and execute the plan to move ahead of this transition to a life-care community or other place of assisted living.[15]

The more likely scenario, however, is that people hold on well past any reasonable hope of being able to manage on their own. Fierce independence can lead to a downward spiral of increased immobility, poor nutrition, out-of-date or poorly monitored medications, and so on. Friends or family who have been called in to help at the last minute are often appalled at the filth and squalor people endure rather than accept help or move to a care facility. A generation that prided itself on self-sufficiency runs the risk of depleting the very resources needed to initiate change.

But for those who do plan ahead and accept care, there are more options than were available even a decade ago. This is the good news. The bad news is the cost of care—frighteningly high for those who do not have long-term care insurance or personal wealth.

Opportunities for Spiritual Growth and the
Role of the Community of Faith

This transition tests faith—or shows, perhaps, that much of what we thought of as faith was simply a naive and unexamined confidence that things would "turn out okay." The later years, however, reveal the paradox at the heart of the gospel: "that in losing our lives we somehow find them, that loss can be gain, and weakness, strength; that death is the path of life."[16] A stark example of how difficult this paradox is to live is seen in the lives of those whose "reluctant journey" ends in a nursing home. Whatever the benefits of needed physical care, the human spirit is likely to be stifled by anger toward one's family and God, a sense of uselessness, and a highly personal and threatening feeling of loneliness. Anger toward family and God is almost inevitable. Anger toward the family comes from a profound sense of abandonment. And as the image of God is born and nurtured in family and supported by familial relationships, this sense of abandonment somehow makes the universe untrustworthy.[17]

And yet the new nursing home resident has to adapt—has to come to the point of being thankful for being in this facility. This is an arduous and lonely struggle. It involves a new relationship with the self and new ways of relating to others. It involves making new friends—quite unlike any friends the person ever knew before. And it involves learning how to relate to God all over again. These are tasks accomplished in the depths of one's heart and soul.

The community of faith may be too threatened to interact appropriately with people going through this transition. After all, any one of us could wind up in that same place someday. Yet if we see in those enduring this reluctant journey "only the destruction and loss of all we have known, then we will cling to our present experiences, stunting their growth by our sense that they hold no future promise."[18] The truth is that these people do have a future in the last stable period of life we call "while the light lasts." And they have a final journey to take, dying, without which the whole human project is not understandable.

While the Light Lasts

This stable period of indeterminate length has stark boundaries: the reluctant journey into dependence and dying itself. It is a period of life with a beginning, a middle (potentially long, and with much variation), and an end. One enters in dependency and frailty, one ends in dying. Between, there may be months or years—even many years—of a life that needs its own goals, promises, struggles and hardships, joys and friendships, freedoms and meaning.

"While the light lasts" has its own integrity, variations, and distinctiveness. It has integrity because it is a human life, lived in continuity with the whole of life. It has variations because the losses that shape this period may be physical, cognitive, emotional, or social. It has distinctiveness because it has moved beyond the normal processes of aging and is dominated by some biological or mental pathology. Giving and receiving care are core realities of this period and they are complex. Some environments of care—individual or institutional—are person-friendly, some are simply dreadful, and most fall in between.

Opportunities for Spiritual Growth and the Role of the Community of Faith

"While the light lasts" can only be understood in the context of a whole life, and it is most certainly best interpreted to us by people who are themselves in this stable period. There are two psychological mechanisms that people use to keep themselves "okay." The first is a process of selecting elective life goals that are realistic in relation to their present lives, and of compensating (by getting help, for example) in relation to what they cannot manage on their own. The second mechanism involves learning new ways of managing or accommodating. Instead of choosing a goal and going for it no matter what, they learn new ways—leaving more time for tasks, changing routines, letting someone help them with bathing or dressing.[19] The specifically spiritual dimension of these psychological strategies has to do with a decision that goes to a core belief, namely that one is okay, not because of what one does but because life, God's gift, is worthwhile and precious. Further, even in the face of diminishing time, people in this time of life can, paradoxically, take time. Rather than being frustrated by an awareness that they cannot do what they once did, they can witness to the sacramentality of the present moment by staying focused on the task at hand, whatever time it takes. Lastly, in accepting help where needed, they let go of that icon of adulthood, independence, and point toward the truth of adulthood, interdependence, and, where necessary, dependence with dignity. It is a wonderful basis for healthily reaffirming one's dependence on God. This is not the same as passivity in the face of physical and moral evil. "God is not simply present in human passivities, but where people choose to grow in the face of opposition. There is no time in one's declining years when the human growth process is at an end."[20]

The role of the community of faith is made complex because of a general unawareness of how much the church has to learn from the spiritual struggles of people in this period of life. As Ruth Howard Gray wrote, "If we are unafraid to draw close, we have much to learn and thus to preach. The lessons have a pointedness that gives new meaning to religious convictions that all life is holy and is part of God's gift. The [person] who has learned anew to thank God for this life can be a powerful teacher and witness."[21] The astonishing reality of this period of life for those of us who have come less far in the journey of life is this: It is not as dark or bleak or unnuanced as we might expect or dread; indeed, some people who are quite sick, frail, and dependent are nevertheless happy, committed, generous, satisfied—in a word, okay. This is a word of witness and good news that needs to be heard and believed by the community of faith.

Dying

Dying refers to the actual transition from life to the silence of death. Unlike all other transitions and stable periods of life, during which we have informants aplenty, no one can tell us about the experience of life's denouement. But the transition is long enough and complex enough that there is much to learn about dying. Dying is a process, a transition that ideally takes time.

As with the other transitions, it is not always clear when life's balance tips irrevocably toward change. Something happens. For reasons that may not be physically clear, a person is "unto death" and this final transition has begun. There is a series of developmental tasks that begins with a sense of completion with worldly affairs and ends with a surrender to the transcendent, to the unknown, to God.[22] If it has not already happened, the business of life—the focus of so much life energy until now—is handed over to others, and formal social and legal responsibilities are brought to a close. Only a clear sense of the approach of death could bring a person to accomplish this task—to give up what has been worked for so hard.

When all that is done, the person turns inward to try to come to a sense of meaning about life. This process is often one of storytelling, to oneself and to others. In this process failures, wrongs, and things left undone may take on power. But so too may a sense that much good has been done. In this interplay of light and shadow, the individual has to own the good and forgive the bad. This needs an experience of the love of others. People can only truly forgive themselves when they know forgiveness from others. The person must then bring to completion relationships with family and friends. This is the time to ask forgiveness, accept forgiveness, express love, acknowledge self-worth, and say good-bye.[23]

The final steps have to do with an acceptance that it is okay that one's individual life is coming to an end because there is a transcendent. In the surrender to the transcendent, to the unknown, the final task is completed: one lets go, actively. One wills to surrender. "Here," says Ira Byock, "little remains of the ego except the volition to surrender."[24]

Opportunities for Spiritual Growth and the
Role of the Community of Faith

The first task of the community of faith is to reclaim dying as "sacred dying."[25]

Mainstream American culture no longer thinks of death as "sacred dying," nor are people who are dying treated as if the were in the midst of an important, life-defining spiritual journey. Death is either medicalized so that medicine serves as the dominant framework for understanding dying and death, or death is simply secularized so that the good death is one that is only quick, uneventful, and painless.

The spiritual nature of sacred dying—as Byock has described his empirical findings about dying well—is transparent. Worldly goods have never been meant to be the be-all and end-all of life; there is much in each life to celebrate and to regret; there is an irreplaceable need for forgiveness and the expression of love; when all is said and done, it is only the Transcendent, the Mystery, God who can draw us, in love, into the surrender of the ego.

The lack of engagement of the community of faith as a community in sacred dying is equally transparent. Good individual pastoral care will never bring the whole community of faith to a conviction that death is ultimately too deep for tragedy. "Glory is incandescent and ascentional, and . . . 'the dying of the light' can be a dawning; requiem, a rainbow. . . . [We do not] rejoice in some starless night, but . . . suggest that one cannot see the stars save by night. . . . Done is our own nocturnal passage, illumined by the same Easter fire, and it is as dawn."[26]

Conclusion

These are the transitions and stable periods that give shape to the last third of life for those who do not die an untimely death. They point to a journey we will all take, and one about which we know relatively little individually or as communities of faith. Ruth Howard Grey writes in her eighty-fifth year: "In order to be better prepared for their own old age, I suggest to those coming along that they have more association with old people. Much can be learned from them." [27] If the church is going to be faithful to its commission to teach all nations, it will have to once again, and with renewed interest, engage with the new world of aging. This framework may help make sense of a long journey that is radically new. "Aging is a moral and spiritual frontier because its unknown, terrors, and mysteries cannot be successfully crossed without humility and self-knowledge, without love and compassion, without acceptance of physical decline and mortality and a sense of the sacred."[28]

Questions for Discussion

1. What does the author mean when he writes, "Retirement is both a possibility for growth and a peril"? What are these possibilities and perils?
2. How could your church provide programs that would be helpful to members who retire? What kind of recognition would be appropriate?
3. As a person enters "extended middle age," why does the mantra "Do it while you can" become so important?
4. A pastor states, "There is no reason to provide groups for people who are 'retired.' They just fit into the traditional structures of the church." Do you agree or disagree? Why or why not?
5. What are some signs that a person has departed "extended middle age" and moved into a time of "uncertain journey"?

6. How can a church help a person struggling to find the "new me" after experiencing major losses in later life?

7. What are some of the "tipping points" of entrance into the life transition of dependence on others?

8. How can adult children recognize some of these "tipping points" in their aging parents? What are their options in handling this situation?

9. What can pastors and congregations do to assist persons in the "while the light lasts" times, when they turn inward and want to find the meaning of their lives?

10. How does a church reclaim dying as "sacred dying"? How can people who are facing death be helped to recognize that "they are in the midst of an important, life-defining spiritual journey"?

Notes

1. Richard L. Morgan, *Beyond Retirement: Toward a Redirected Life* (Louisville: Geneva Press, 1999), p. 9.

2. David Johnson Maitland, *Looking Both Ways: A Theology for Midlife* (Atlanta: John Knox Press, 1985).

3. John H. Westerhoff and William Willimon, *Liturgy and Learning Through the Life Cycle* (New York: Seabury Press, 1980).

4. Maxwell Jones, *Growing Old: The Ultimate Freedom* (New York: Human Sciences Press, 1988).

5. Jones, *Growing Old*, p. 10.

6. Jones, *Growing Old*, p. 107.

7. Henry Simmons, "Grandparenting: A Bibliographic Review," *Journal of Religious Gerontology*, October 2003:78.

8. Bob Trubshaw, "The Metaphors and Rituals of Place and Time: an introduction to liminality," (1995), http://www.indigogroup.co.uk/foamycustard.

9. Kathleen Fischer, *Autumn Gospel: Women in the Second Half of Life* (New York: Paulist Press, 1995).

10. James Adams, *The Sting of Death: Leader's Guide for A Study Course on Death and Bereavement* (New York: Seabury, 1971), p. 57.

11. Raymond J. Stovich, *In Wisdom and Grace* (Kansas City: Sheed and Ward, 1988).

12. Jane Marie Thibault, *A Deepening Love Affair* (Nashville: Upper Room Books, 1993), p. 19.

13. Henry C. Simmons, "Spirituality and Community in the Last Stage of Life," *Dignity and Old Age*, ed. R. Disch et al. (Binghamton, NY: Haworth Press, 1998), p. 85.

14. *Worlds of Difference: Inequality in the Aging Experience*, ed. Eleanor Stoller and Rose Gibson (Thousand Oaks, CA: Pine Forge Press, 1994), p. 83.

15. Henry C. Simmons and E. Craige MacBean, *Thriving After 55: Your Guide to Fully Living the Rest of Your Life* (Richmond, VA: PrimePress, 2000).

16. Kathleen Fischer, Wider Grace: *Spirituality for the Later Years* (New York: Paulist Press, 1985), p. 5.

17. Henry C. Simmons, "'Teach Us To Pray': Pastoral Care of the New Nursing Home Resident," *The Journal of Pastoral Care*, 45/2 (Summer, 1991), pp.169–175.

18. Fischer, Wider *Grace*, p. 13.

19. Jochen Brandstädter and Bernard Baltes-Götz, "Personal Control over Development and Quality of Life Perspectives in Adulthood," *Successful Aging: Perspectives from the behavioral sciences*, ed. Paul Baltes and Margaret Baltes (Cambridge, UK: Cambridge, 1990).

20. James L. Empereur, *Prophetic Anointing; God's Call to the Sick, the Elderly, and the Dying* (Wilmington, DE: Michael Glazier, 1982), pp. 174–175.

21. Ruth Howard Gray, *Survival of the Spirit: My Detour Through a Retirement Home* (Atlanta: John Knox Press, 1985), p. 92.

22. http://www.dyingwell.com.

23. Ira Byock, Dying Well: *Peace and Possibilities at the End of Life* (New York: Riverhead Books, 1997).

24. http://www.dyingwell.org, click on Landmarks and Taskwork for the End-of-Life

25. Megory Anderson, *Sacred Dying: Creating Rituals for Embracing the End of Life* (Roseville, CA: Prima Publishing, 2001).

26. Christopher Nugent, *Mysticism, Death and Dying* (Albany, NY: State University of New York Press, 1994), pp. 101, 104.

27. Gray, *Survival of the Spirit*, p. 93.

28. Thomas Cole, personal communication.

Later-Life Learning

Peg Wittig Lewis

Ageism abounds! Statements like "You can't teach an old dog new tricks" or "She's having a senior moment" are repeated so often they are assumed to be true. These stereotypes have become firmly affixed to older persons in our culture and consequently persons in their later years are not considered to be serious learners. And the church is not immune to this thinking. Programming for older adults is often "dumbed down" because of the conviction that those who have reached a certain age are neither interested in nor capable of significant learning and growth.

Faulty beliefs such as these, however, have been soundly debunked by solid neurological research evidence. It is not only the exceptional older persons like John Glenn, Grandma Moses, and Art Linkletter, who often symbolize active, productive aging, who are able to learn and process information at a ripe age. Ordinary older adults can learn, process, and retain information well into old age. More important, the existential *experience* of later-life learning can be enriching and life-changing and instrumental in persons being brought toward wholeness in Christ.

In its ministry with older adults the church has an opportunity to create an entry into that rich experience. This may require a reconceptualization of our approach to older adult learning—an attitude change tantamount to a conversion experience. Programs designed for older adults often focus on their social needs, and thus trips, outings, and entertainment become the primary activities. These legitimate activities are important for their lives, but as Henri

Nouwen so poignantly observed in *Aging: The Fulfillment of Life:* "When we are primarily concerned with giving old people something to do, offering them entertainment and distractions, we might avoid the painful realization that most people do not want to be distracted, but heard, not entertained, but sustained."1 Instead, with teaching and learning that is transformational at its heart, older adult ministry can sustain persons, grow them toward maturity, and enable them to deal effectively with the contingencies of aging. Real, significant learning can take place—learning that fosters self-understanding, promotes growth, nurtures the spirit, and stimulates the intellect.

The Capacity to Learn in Later Life

Creating ministry of this kind first requires an understanding of the older adult learners themselves. What actually are their cognitive abilities? Are there deficiencies that need to be compensated? How do they learn?

When speaking of the cognitive abilities of the older person, three interconnected elements are to be considered: intelligence, learning, and memory. The first, intelligence, or one's capacity to learn, historically has been thought to diminish with aging. Until recent paradigm-shifting research results surfaced, it had been believed, for example, that we lose brain cells as we age. Not only has this been shown to be untrue, but in 1998 a group of American and Swedish scientists demonstrated that new brain cells are actually generated in adult humans.[2]

The brain does not have to go into decline in older age! It is true that some aspects of innate intelligence are affected in the aging process—our speed of processing information, some abstract thinking, and some spatial abilities. But the more than encouraging news is that the kind of intelligence that involves all of our life-acquired learning—our education, experiences, skills, and abilities—all that intelligence associated with the learning *accumulated* in a lifetime not only is intact, but can actually improve. Additionally, any diminishment in these areas is offset by gains in other areas. Researchers have contended some areas of intelligence, including the ability to make decisions based on experience, setting priorities and determining the appropriate action to take, and interpersonal skills do not actually even develop until middle age or later in life."[3] The strengths and potential of older learners have been grossly underestimated for years. While "use it or lose it" is not necessarily true, Ronald Manheimer reports that "intellectual functioning is maintained where life situations continued to be stimulating and challenging, where people had to use their skills and where they had access to educational activities."[4]

The second and third components of cognitive ability are learning and memory. These are two sides of the same coin and should be thought of together. We cannot retrieve information from the memory bank until it has been properly deposited.

Factors Affecting Learning

As teachers of older adults, it is helpful if we are conscious of some of the factors affecting learning in this age group. For example, as we age some acuity is lost because of sensory changes in hearing and seeing. We are slower, too, to perceive and process information. Also, information presented must have some personal significance or perceived relevance to the learner. Because older persons are more easily distracted and it is harder to focus and concentrate, attention to the environment is essential. Older persons may be less willing to use complicated learning strategies. It becomes necessary for them to "push through" their inclination to stay out of uncomfortable areas.

Memory Changes

Memory changes associated with aging are neither as common nor as severe as believed. The same lapses in memory associated with older persons are common in persons of any age but are rarely noted or thought to be significant. This is not to say there are not some things that can be done to better maintain the connections between the brain cells. The hairlike endings of the nerve cells, which can become thinner with disuse, can be strengthened and maintained by learning new things and by doing routine things in new ways.

As we age it takes a bit longer for information to pass from the "working memory" into "long-term memory." This means additional rehearsal and repetition of material becomes necessary. Great improvements in learning and memory can be achieved by practicing two simple things: improving *concentration* on what is being learned, and giving the material meaning and significance by *associating and connecting* it to previously stored information.

How we learn affects how we remember. We all have preferred styles of learning. We can begin to recognize the way we generally prefer to learn, capitalize on it, and then practice additional ways of acquiring information. This way there are some back-up methods to use when we get stuck. Memory stores do not become "overloaded" as we age, so we do not need to worry about putting too much in. Of course poor nutrition, depression, fatigue, inactivity, medications, anxiety, and physical illness affect memory and learning at any age.

Characteristics of Learning in Mid and Later Adulthood

Understanding of adult learning theory gives us a starting point from which to plan ministry programs that are effective, age appropriate, and transforming. Several salient principles characterize adult learning. Various adult education theorists have described these as: internal rather than external motivation, incorporation of prior life experiences, real-life task or problem orientation, and immediate application of material learned. Transformation of persons and the significance of learning in community further characterize adult learning.

Self-Motivation

As we mature we become increasingly self-directed; our motivations are from within rather than imposed from without. Increasingly the goals of learning are determined by the learner—they know what they want to learn and assume more responsibility for the learning. Rather than planning classes for them, we can involve older persons in their determination and design. We have to give up being "in charge" or directive in our approach. We have to trust the learners enough to relinquish our tendency to control and allow them to be self-directive in the process.

Building on Life Experiences

In later -life learning there needs to be an acknowledgement of the depth and breadth of the learner's own life experiences that are being brought to the situation. Learners themselves are a rich resource for the class experience. Much can be learned in dialogue and discussion. Peers lecturing peers is also very effective. Participants teach each other—and the teacher.

Task or Problem Orientation

Another characteristic of adult learning is that real-life tasks or problems generate the adult's learning needs. While some seek classes for intellectual stimulation, learning for its own sake is much less often the motivation for the older adult learner. Ministry programs planned and offered around need-based subjects are much more successful.

Immediacy of Application

Another principle that follows from this is that there is an immediacy of application of the learned material. Adults want to apply the new skills and knowledge to their immediate circumstances and problems. Their thinking is not usually "maybe this will come in handy to know someday."

Transformational Learning

Professional educational literature speaks often of the concept of "transformational" learning. Simply put, transformational learning is learning that produces change within the person. M. Carolyn Clark writes: "It shapes people; they are different afterward, in ways both they and others can recognize. It is intimately connected to our developmental process and contains the concepts of meaning and reflection, social praxis, and relationship with the teacher."[5]

Finally, adult learning takes place in the context of relationship. While adults are learning, they are benefited by relationships with others. As participants encounter others, learning that is indeed transformational can occur. Not only are new insights gained from the experiences of others, but also the community experience itself is life-shaping. In an environment of respect, collaboration, trust, openness, and authenticity, transformation can take place. The facilitator has the responsibility to provide an atmosphere that is caring, accepting, respecting, and helping.

Uniquely the Church

Opportunities for older adult learning are widely available in many settings. Universities, community programs, Elderhostel, hospitals, social service organizations all provide excellent, helpful programs. The church not only has the opportunity to create learning experiences undergirded with the key principles of adult learning, but because of its very nature it can actually enhance and make the experience even more meaningful. All of the ingredients are potentially present for life-changing, authentic, and transformational learning to take place. The church provides a gift to the world because it places all learning within a spiritual dimension whether or not the actual material being covered is "spiritual" in nature. At the heart of the *learning experience* there is a spiritual dimension.

Authentic Community

As we have seen, adult learning takes place in a context of relationship—a supportive, positive relationship between the learner and the group of fellow learners and between the participants and the teacher. The creation of *authentic community* is what the church is already about. This should be what we do best! God is in the business of creating community. We invite people into the relational process—in theological terms, the very relationship that exists in the Trinitarian persons of the Godhead—the giving and receiving of love. Mutual trust, respect, and acceptance are essential elements in the formation of community. Likewise are the affirmation of the uniqueness and contribution of each person. Community life is a shared life, delighting with each other and sharing sorrows. It is this organic, living, dynamic interconnectedness that fosters real learning.

Hope of the Gospel for Aging

In the church we have the opportunity to integrate the hope of the gospel as we plan learning opportunities. Societal views of aging seem to be either pessimistic or overly optimistic. Neither the view that aging is one problem after another, nor the view that promotes the successful "good life," denying the realities of older age, is particularly helpful. Instead the gospel provides a realistic hope, fully embracing the contingencies of aging, yet bringing God's redemptive purposes into every situation. Programs can address very real problems and issues and help people deal with them effectively. At the same time creative programs assist older persons to find meaning and to see in new ways how God works in the midst of the things they are experiencing.

The Teacher

As a ministry leader the person in the role of teacher is more a "mentor" than an "educator." The focus is on the learner and we simply guide older adults in discovering and learning, and we seek to create an environment in which they can be freed to do it. Humility is essential to learning and to teaching. In Deuteronomy

4:1 and 5:1 *teach* and *learn* are the same root word in Hebrew. We are present to the persons we minister with when we are aware of our own brokenness and are able to be authentic and transparent in our interactions. Humility takes courage and the emotional involvement of the teacher.

We teachers, of course, are not in this alone. Our task as teachers is to cooperate with what the Holy Spirit is doing in persons.

Purpose and Meaning

Adults look to the learning experience, not as a means to acquire facts, but as a way to gain a sense of purpose and meaning for their lives. Eric Erikson, in his well-known exploration of life stages and consequent tasks for each, has described *generativity* as one of the later stages of adult life. According to Erikson, mature individuals have as a major task supporting the development of the next generation. Most often this is demonstrated in volunteerism in a variety of activities and in an awareness of the need to leave a legacy for others. In the church we can help people understand their role in ministry with others. We can help people, even at an advanced age, explore their giftedness and help direct them into productive and meaningful service to others. We can help them discover where their lives intersect with the kingdom of God and equip them to be about what God is doing in the world.

Transformational Learning

Finally, if the secular world is aware of transformational learning, how much more are we able to effectively participate in God's transformation of persons into the image of Christ. What an opportunity the church has to do the "soul work" that is spoken of in "secular" literature! The church as "disciple maker" has as one of its primary tasks the influencing toward change in a person's ways of thinking, behaving, and being.

The spirit of older persons can be nurtured by helping them reflect on what is being learned and on how it is being integrated into their souls. Bible "facts" are now far less important than how God is speaking to them and changing them through God's Word. We can help people "listen for God's Word." We can be participants when those serendipitous "transforming moments" occur and help people see where God is present and what God is doing.

Models for Transformational Ministry in Later Life

It appears that older adult ministries adopt one of several models as they develop. One model is that of a community center in which a church designs programs for and encourages participation of the wider community. The programs may be held from several hours a day to a weekly basis. Often they are activity-focused and are similar to community senior centers. A second model is that of pastoral care that is focused primarily on the homebound or those in nursing homes. Visitation, transportation, and deacon-type care are the substance of the ministry. Yet another form, which could be termed a medical model, came into being with the advent of parish nursing. The focus here is on health education, connecting persons with resources, and follow-up care. Finally, the most common model has a socialization and fellowship orientation. Groups are brought together for day trips, travel, luncheons, speakers, and many other enjoyable activities.

Each of these forms—community, pastoral, medical, and social—meets important needs of older adults. However, perhaps as ministry leaders we could look at the older persons in the congregation more holistically than these models allow. The creation of ministry with transformative learning experiences at its core meets the needs of its constituents within the church. It can also extend in outreach to involve the burgeoning aging population in this country. With a holistic approach to ministry the church has the opportunity to lead the way.

The components of a *comprehensive* transformational learning program would include concentration in each of these areas: spiritual nurture, life enrichment, aging and transition, health and wellness, and equipping for service. All of these would be done in a context of intentional community- and relationship-building.

One church where the foundations for this type of ministry were laid, in defining its purpose, says it "seeks to provide an integrated ministry to persons in their middle to later years that values their gifts and experiences, nurtures body, mind and spirit toward wholeness in Christ and equips them to serve in the faith family and the world."[6] This is comprehensive and a solid basis for growth and expansion beyond the immediate church. It can reach out to a community having great need.

Spiritual Nurture

The goal of spiritual nurture is that older adults will be built up into a mature faith, a faith that is integrated into all other aspects of their lives and that enables them to cope with the contingencies of aging. Jane Thiebault, noted writer on the subject of spirituality and aging, reminds us that "the one thing we can take with us is our relationship with God." We need to be investing in that relationship throughout our lives.[7]

How does this relate to later-life learning? Jesus said in Matthew 11, "Take my yoke upon you, and *learn* from me" (italics added). Or as Eugene Peterson poetically translates these familiar verses in *The Message*,[8] "Walk with me and work with me—watch how I do it. Learn the unforced rhythms of grace. I won't lay anything heavy or ill-fitting on you. Keep company with me and you'll learn to live freely and lightly." We need to teach people how to learn from Jesus, no matter their age. We need to help them learn the "unforced rhythms of grace" in their lives for when the losses come, when the tough things most of us will experience with aging at some point come. Being a disciple does not end at retirement—in fact, some of the richest years of growing intimacy and maturity in Christ are ahead.

Older persons are, for the most part, open and ready to embrace serious spiritual nurture in a variety of forms. For some it is only in these later years that they have begun seriously to consider spiritual matters. A fascinating health study done at the Durham VA Medical Center and reported by Dr. Harold Koenig[9] revealed that 31 percent of the persons studied had experienced a significant change in their faith, one that could be termed a conversion experience, after the age of fifty. This is a ripe time in people's lives, primarily because we have begun to experience losses, leaving a vacuum that we yearn to have filled.

In a weekly session, "Growing Together in Faith," a group gathered faithfully to study, learn to listen to God, apply the Scriptures to their inner souls, and learn to walk with Jesus. In a retreat format while visiting a monastery they learned to be still with God, perhaps for the first time. The process of life review or spiritual autobiography is a notable means of nurturing faith. Learning about ourselves and our past and discovering where God has been with us and how God has brought us to where we are is a deep learning experience.

Life Enrichment

The content of classes that enrich the lives of older persons has almost limitless possibilities. Again, rather than selecting those for "learning's sake" alone, we can provide classes that are transformational. A wonderful example of later-life learning occurred in a church that had been given a special grant of ten computers intended for use by the children in their Sunday school classes. Seizing the opportunity that an empty computer lab offered during the week, older adult ministry leaders scheduled computer skills classes for seniors on weekdays. Hundreds of seniors entered the world of cyberspace, and e-mails began flying around the country connecting them with grandchildren and children. The joy on the faces of these folks when they came to the lab and saw on the screen, "You've got 3 messages!" was priceless.

Bob, a special inspiration to all because of his dedication to learning, at the age of ninety-two began taking the computer classes. His goal was to write his life story using the computer. So every week he would faithfully attend the class, and then stay for the open lab sessions afterward to perfect his new skills. He would navigate the stairs to the lab with a walker and, using one finger to type, peck out his rich, interesting, full life story, key by key. He was the light of the class, and three years later at age ninety-five he was still faithfully climbing the stairs to put the finishing touches on the memoirs of his life as a bandleader during the Big Band era.

Another subject for life enrichment of considerable interest and importance to older persons is grandparenting. Grandparenting in our culture has taken on new dimensions; what used to be simple is now overlaid with "fallout" from modern family life. Divorce; stepfamilies; custody disputes; grandchildren exposed daily to drugs, alcohol, and sex; single-family households—to name a few issues— have left many grandparents facing situations they never could have imagined. But these same situations have given grandparents more opportunity than ever to make a difference in the lives of their children and grandchildren. We can provide arenas for discussion, information sharing, and resources to give them some of the tools they need to be effective at the tasks of grandparenting.

Aging and Transition Issues

There are two crucial elements in helping persons prepare for and deal with the issues associated with aging: education and resource awareness. This area of learning has a direct effect on the lives of those served in ministry. The education component provides an overview of the complexities relating to insurance, housing and support services, legal and medical considerations, end-of-life dilemmas, and issues of family dynamics. It can provide assistance for handling immediate issues as well as help with longer-range planning strategies. The resource awareness component helps people maneuver through the confusing world of community and government resources and support. So many persons either are not aware of what is "out there" or else have difficulty navigating the system. These issues present a tremendous opportunity for churches, either independently or in a cooperative effort, to play a substantial role.

Health and Well-Being

Jesus was very interested in the physical condition of persons and spent a lot of time doing something about it. We in the church spend a lot of time visiting the sick and caring about them, but sometimes we come up short on helping people prevent illness or maintain the health that God intends for them. That can be accomplished best through education. The "normal" physiological changes that come with aging, the safe handling of medications, recognizing signals of some impending serious occurrence, and how to better manage chronic illnesses are all important subjects. Information about these and other such subjects can help people live longer and better. Learning how to keep one's home safe from hazards, for example, can be critical information in avoiding a life-threatening fall. Probably nothing concerns people in their mid to later years as much as the fear of losing their mental abilities. Teaching skills to preserve memory and helping them understand that memory loss is not inevitable can mean the difference between an involved, active life and one characterized by withdrawal and embarrassment.

It is true that hospitals and community centers hold excellent health classes. But the church can offer an environment that is more personally caring and supportive. In one church as part of a cardiovascular education program, blood pressure screening was done on Communion Sundays. People would line up to have their blood pressure checked, maybe not even so much to have it recorded, but to have that face-to-face, one-on-one encounter with someone who cares about their health.

Equipping for Ministry

We are all called to serve and we have all been gifted to serve. We need to help people at any age learn how they have been gifted and guide them into meaningful ministry with others. A key step in that process is equipping people so they are more prepared and effective. Too often we just ask for "volunteers." There is something to be done or someone to visit or an event to be organized, and we find a body to do it. Classes in Christian caregiving such as those provided in the Stephen Ministry program, for example, can change the tentative and unsure caregiver into a confident helper, able to walk alongside someone in crisis. Many older persons too would love to tutor but may be intimidated. A bit of guidance would enable them to make a great difference in a child's life—and in their own.

Practical Considerations and Strategies for Classes with Older Adults

Physical Environment for Learning

The physical environment in which the learning takes place is of notable importance when working with older adults. From the moment of entry into the parking lot, the environment should convey helpfulness and hospitality. Consideration for the surroundings and the atmosphere created speaks volumes about how highly the educational providers regard the learners. Attention to the details matters. I had a wonderfully thoughtful assistant who would not only stand waiting at the door for the participants in our weekly class, but would walk toward them, take the arm of some, and walk with them to the door. She had a sixth sense about their comfort level and anticipated their needs.

When planning the class, the location should be chosen with care. Classes held on an upper level without elevator access should be avoided whenever possible. When I first took a position of director of senior ministries, one afternoon the elder with whom I worked and I "pretended" we were handicapped. We began at the curb in front of the church and made our way through the facility with the eyes and body of a disabled or impaired older person. What a shock to discover how difficult it is to walk without handrails, to enter a facility without wheelchair ramps, to have to go some distance to a classroom, to try to get up stairs—or to even use a restroom!

The teacher can design highly relevant material with excellent content and forget to consider how important it is to create an ambiance that conveys welcome, friendliness, and comfort. The arrangement of the seating signals the tone of the class. Older adults learn better in informal settings, so if all of the chairs in a room are in straight rows (or, worse yet, are pews), the environment says that "I, the teacher, am the expert, and you are here to hear what I have say." It can even remind some of negative experiences in school and thus hinder their relaxation. Arranging the chairs in semicircles, where people can see faces instead of the backs of heads, provides a friendlier, more informal environment. The use of tables with the chairs is also very helpful, especially if any worksheets or handouts are to be used. While the use of these materials is conducive to small-group interaction and encourages discussion, people still need to be able to face the speaker. Chairs should be positioned so that participants do not have to turn any farther than is comfortable.

Consideration of Sensory Changes

We have discussed the fact that the capacity to learn is not diminished with age, but it is true that there are sensory changes in older persons that affect the learning process considerably. This is especially true of vision and hearing.

Vision difficulties increase with age in part because of some normal eye changes and also because of the presence of some conditions affecting the eye. These can include cataracts, macular degeneration, or glaucoma. Because of this, lighting in the room requires attention. Not only is it necessary to have sufficient lighting, but the elimination of any glare is especially important. Older persons are particularly sensitive to any direct glare from the windows. Any printed materials should have a clean font of adequate size and be on paper that is a good contrast to the print.

Hearing difficulties are a very real problem affecting the learning process. Only about 20 percent of persons needing a hearing aid use one. And for those who do use a hearing device, any background noise is amplified and further affects their ability to hear. Difficulties in hearing cause people to feel excluded from the group and special effort may be needed to make them feel included. Even with as few as twenty or twenty-five persons, a microphone is useful and often necessary in classroom settings.

Relaxed Atmosphere

For almost everyone, but especially with older persons, a relaxed atmosphere is necessary for learning. A warm-up activity or a group discussion question can enhance the creation of a relaxed atmosphere as the class begins. The activity could relate to the subject of the day. Sometimes the use of an icebreaker helps get people talking with each other. Some learners are quiet individuals and this should be respected. Until you know the group well, it is probably best not to call on people to answer. Information is processed a bit more slowly, so the teaching should be paced accordingly. Time constraints to complete a task are very inhibiting to elders, and if adequate time is not given it can be very frustrating. Older persons are more likely to give no answer than a wrong answer—so they can be encouraged to respond in a relaxed, non-threatening environment in which positive feedback is given.

Class Scheduling

Careful consideration should be given to the scheduling of classes. Generally, but of course not uniformly, mornings are better than afternoons because most older persons like getting an early start on the day. It is usually best to avoid the time right after lunch because we all are a little less alert at that time. Evening classes are usually less well attended because of an unwillingness to drive after dark. Shorter classes work best because of the difficulties some experience with sitting for longer periods of time.

Use of Technology

The rapid advances in technology pose something of a dilemma for teachers. On one hand Power Point presentations can deliver clear, interesting, colorful images and graphics. At the same time the use of hi-tech tends to formalize presentations and reduces the give-and-take that can be so enriching. If teachers use hi-tech equipment like projectors connected to laptop computers, it is essential to be entirely familiar with their use. Nothing dampens the interest of a class like an instructor searching for ways to correct a blank screen! Sometimes we fear that older persons are technophobes—not so! Older persons are avid users of the Internet and other advanced technologies and are not intimidated or distracted by its use in the presentation of material.

Interactive Teaching Style

Material high in meaning and personal significance to the learners lends itself to stimulating participation of class members and promotes integration of their own life experiences. An interactive teaching style is the best means to evoke this kind of participation. Even though the older adults may not have experienced much active participative learning, they readily adapt. They eagerly contribute to make it a rich experience for all in the class. Teaching this way places an added burden on the teacher, who now needs to be able to think on his or her feet, apply what one member of the group is saying to what another has contributed, and help make the appropriate connections. As the dialogue is kept going, the relevant material can be covered and the result is stimulating for everyone. This type of approach also inherently creates a less formal class.

Using More than One of the Senses

Learning is definitely enhanced by using more than one of the senses in the process. Also it should be recognized that in any given class there are visual, auditory, and kinesthetic learners, so it is best to use a variety of teaching methods. New information is best practiced immediately. Using worksheets with exercises or discussion questions greatly increases learning by stimulating more than one sense—writing and hearing, or seeing and writing. Using audiovisuals awakens the senses and learning improves as material is both seen and heard. Written outlines of material being covered are quite useful because they organize the learning and allow participants to follow along. Another useful way to stimulate various neural pathways is the use of the imagination and visualization. Whether it is visualizing a scene from earlier years or visualizing a biblical narrative, different neural pathways are stimulated and the probability of learning is greatly improved.

Planning and Marketing Programs Using Cohort Sensitivity

We all know there is no standard definition of "older" person based simply on chronological age. Also, people have a very individual self-perception as to where they fit in the range of age groups. Sometimes, though, in planning classes and programs, we lump all of the subgroups of older persons together. Thought should be given to specifically directing programs to a particular subgroup such as active, healthy older persons, those in various transitions, or those experiencing some of the frailties of aging. Some people shy away from attending "older adult" classes because of the identification with the wide age group of seniors.

The children of aging parents are a particularly important segment of a congregation that is often overlooked but can be targeted directly. They need to become informed, more self-confident, and better-directed so they can begin the necessary planning with their parents. Attractive brochures on the subject of aging parents sent directly to church or community members in their forties through their sixties could be a very effective means to engage them.

All of these details may appear on the surface to be small or non-consequential. But attention to them can make the difference between persons learning or just "being there" in a class, between whether persons are transformed or leave without being any different from when they came in.

Conclusion

Daily our culture hands us a staggering blizzard of new facts about longevity, about the aging process, and about the social impact of aging. One cannot read a magazine or view a television program without hearing about the "aging boomers." While everyone is talking about this phenomenon, few disciplines are looking broadly at the issues and generating a comprehensive approach to addressing them. It has been said that devils run off with every new idea while the angels debate what to do about it. This is a *kairos* moment for the church. The church is in a unique position to take this opportunity to be challenged creatively and lead our culture in a holistic approach to the aging phenomenon. This is "kingdom work." We can place in a holistic spiritual framework all of our theological insights, combined with our best teaching skills and informed by the most current information available in our culture. Then transformational learning in later life can impact our culture and we can be participants in what God is doing in God's world.

Questions for Discussion

1. What evidences of "ageism" have you become aware of in our culture? In what ways do we stereotype older persons? What false beliefs about older persons are evident?

2. Henri Nouwen said, "When we are primarily concerned with giving old people something to do, offering them entertainment and distractions, we might avoid the painful realization that most people do not want to be distracted, but heard, not entertained, but sustained." How do churches sometimes use distraction and entertainment as an approach to ministry with older adults?

3. In what ways can older persons themselves become involved in the design of educational classes and ministry?

4. What are some of the things that can be done to create community in a learning environment for older adults?

5. Which societal view of aging reflects best what you have observed: "pessimistic" (one problem after another) or "optimistic" (denying the realities of old age and the promotion of the successful "good life")?

6. What kinds of ministries within the church are often relegated to older adults? How can their giftedness be turned into meaningful and productive service to others?

7. How does your church plan for each element of a comprehensive transformational learning program—spiritual nurture, life enrichment, aging issues, health and wellness, service to others?

8. If you were the educator at your church, how would you design a transformational learning program with interaction among all generations?

9. Do you agree that this is a *kairos* moment for the church in terms of older adult ministries? In anticipation of the large number of boomers reaching older adulthood, how can we respond?

Notes

1. Henri J. M. Nouwen and Walter Gaffney, *Aging: The Fulfillment of Life* (New York: Image Books, 1974).

2. Lawrence C. Katz and Manning Rubin, *Keep Your Brain Alive* (New York: Workman Publishing, 1999).

3. Ronald J. Manheimer and Denise D. Snodgrass, *Older Adult Education: A Guide to Research, Policy and Programs* (Westport, CT: Greenwood), p. 44.

4. Ronald J. Manheimer, "Adult Education," *Encyclopedia of Gerontology*, vol.1, ed. James E. Birren (San Diego, CA: Academic Press), pp. 61–69.

5. M. Carolyn Clark, "Transformational Learning" in *New Directions for Adult and Continuing Education* 57 (1993), p. 47.

6. Senior Ministries, La Jolla Presbyterian Church, La Jolla, CA.

7. Jane Marie Thibault, Older Adult Advocates Conference speaker, April 2002.
8. Eugene H. Peterson, *The Message: The New Testament in Contemporary Language* (Colorado Springs, CO: NavPress, 1993).
9. Harold G. Koenig, *Aging and God: Spiritual Pathways to Mental Health in Midlife and Later Years* (New York: Haworth Press), p. 427.

Ethical Baby Boomers Face Their Aging

Steven P. Eason

I am fifty-one years old, married for twenty-nine years, with three children, ages twenty-five, twenty-two, and twenty. My wife and I both work. We have one child in college.

My father died on his eightieth birthday and my mother died when she was eighty years old, after suffering from Alzheimer's disease. For a while she lived in an assisted living facility. These words are a new language for me.

My wife's parents are divorced but neither remarried. Her dad lives alone and has had a crippling stroke. He is paralyzed on the right side and cannot speak. He has a very caring woman come in every day to help, but his benefits are running out and there are few cash reserves.

Recently I accepted a new position as pastor of a very large congregation that has grown to over 4,000 members. I remember how we packed up and left; sold a house, bought a house, contracted a mover, changed address, banks, grocery stores, gas stations, barbers, cleaners, mechanics, dentist, doctors, friends . . . everything. Our youngest will enter her junior year in high school in the fall. This is no small thing.

In the midst of all that, I wrote this chapter on baby boomers facing their aging! I have fourteen more gray hairs just since I started. I am a baby boomer and I am aging . . . fast!

This is not new, is it? Every generation has gone through midlife. Every generation has had aging parents and teenagers at the same time. But something is different. Our parents are living longer, some of us had children later in life, and the boomer generation has some unique characteristics.

Boomers came on the scene post World War II (1946–56). The United States was on a high. All was well with the world. Let's celebrate! So they did . . . and here we are, a lot of us. Roughly one out of three Americans is a baby boomer.

Walker Smith and Ann Clurman in *Rocking the Ages* give examples of how boomers did it differently from the way it was done before:

- Boomers did not just eat food—they transformed the snack, restaurant, and supermarket industries.
- Boomers did not just wear clothes—they transformed the fashion industry.
- Boomers did not just buy cars—they transformed the auto industry.
- They did not just date—they transformed sex roles and practices.
- They did not just go to work—they transformed the workplace.
- They did not just get married—they transformed relationships and the institution of the family.
- They did not just borrow money—they transformed the debt market.
- They did not just go to the doctor—they transformed health care.
- They did not just use computers—they transformed technology.
- They did not just invest in stocks—they transformed the investment marketplace.[1]

We were children who grew up in the 1950s. America was still innocent (or was more cautious about its sin). "Ozzie and Harriet" was one of our favorite TV shows. As teenagers we witnessed multiple assassinations, the violence of the Civil Rights movement, and Viet Nam. America was no longer innocent. In fact, it seemed angry. "Ozzie and Harriet," "Ed Sullivan," "Red Skelton," "Leave It to Beaver," and "My Three Sons" were all replaced by MTV and a host of real-life sitcoms. Our generation experienced a value shift. We no longer trusted institutions. The gates were open to self-expression, self-indulgence, self-gratification, self-awareness, self-preservation, self-rights, and self-promotion. It became all about self. They even call us the "me generation."

Thomas Merton clearly perceived the problem of overcoming one's ego and false self to become one's true self. As early as 1956, in *The Silent Life*, he wrote:

Although God our Father made us free, He did not make us omnipotent. . . . We are capable of becoming perfectly godlike, in all truth, by freely receiving from God the gift of His Light, and His Love, and His Freedom in Christ. . . . But insofar as we are implicitly convinced that we ought to be omnipotent of ourselves we usurp to ourselves a godlikeness that is not ours. . . . In our desire to be "as gods"—a lasting deformity impressed in our nature by original sin—we seek what one might call a relative omnipotence: the power to have everything we want, to enjoy everything we desire, to demand that all our wishes be satisfied and that our will should never be frustrated or opposed. It is the need to have everyone else bow to our judgment and accept our declarations as law. It is the insatiable thirst for recognition of the excellence which we so desperately need to find in ourselves to avoid despair.[2]

Merton's words seem to capture much of the boomer mentality. Although this egocentrism may not always be seen openly, it lurks in the shadows of all of us.

It is unfair to say that all baby boomers are egocentric, but it may be fair to say that as a generation we grew up in an environment of high expectations. Our culture marketed us as the biggest, the brightest, and the best. The future should be bright. We should be successful, even if we are not. The expectation was there. For many, a sense of entitlement crept into our sense of identity. Entitlement is a detriment to facing the challenges of aging.

The church has been ranting and raving against entitlement since Jesus argued with Mary as to whether the party needed more wine or not. "Take up your cross . . . wash each other's feet . . . the first shall be last . . ." Christianity, when defined as being "like Christ" as opposed to mere institutional religion, is all about getting the self out of the center. There is something (or Someone) else at the center.

Boomers flocked to the church when they had children, and signs indicate that many of them fall away when the children are gone. Maybe they will be back to cram for their final exam! A generation accustomed to consuming everything is prone to come to the church with the same demand for services. "We want electrifying worship services, wonderful youth programs, mission trips to foreign countries, fantastic music, dedicated staff, skilled counseling, and great preaching."

To which the church responds: "Okay, take up your cross . . ." A cross is an oxymoron when it comes to entitlement.

As a generation the baby boomers have lived more like the rich young ruler than Joseph of Arimathea. The rich young ruler wanted it all. He wanted to "inherit eternal life." He did not ask for a relationship with God. He wanted to add eternal life to his portfolio. Jesus' response to him was, "[Go and] sell all that you have" (Luke 18:18–26). Divest yourself. He could not, or would not do it. Sad ending.

On the other hand, Joseph of Arimathea was also a rich man, but his story has a different ending. He was the guy who gave his brand-new expensive hand-hewn tomb for the burial of Jesus. There is not an Easter that goes by that we do not mention Joseph of Arimathea's name.

Being rich is not the sin. Having many possessions is not the disease. Living with a sense of entitlement is what kills us, even at a young age. To become old and live by entitlement is even more deadly.

Had Joseph not given of himself, Jesus' body would have been left on the cross to be eaten by animals. The resurrection story would have had to take another twist. Although the resurrection is all about God's power and love, Joseph played a small but significant role in the unfolding of what was to be the most significant event in history. We do not even know the rich young ruler's name.

As boomers age we need to be converted from the story of the rich young ruler to the story of Joseph of Arimathea. In the transformation we will discover life in the midst of death, meaning in the midst of despair. Rabbi Abraham Heschel wrote that as we live our years of older age we sense previously missed insights. We have the opportunity to attain certain high values and to achieve wisdom inaccessible to us earlier.[3]

I had the great honor of preaching the sermon at my Aunt Gladys' funeral. She died at ninety-six years of age and had never been married. She had never been hospitalized until her final days. The old family church was filled with her friends and family. She had taught school and lived all her days in the home in which she was born.

One of my prized possessions is a framed photograph of Aunt Gladys that I keep on my dresser. It reminds me of grace. If I could only age like she did. She never complained, never focused on herself, was always interested in you, and never forgot your birthday or Christmas. She had no children, but we were all her children.

She did not own a car. Her house did not have air-conditioning. She had a big gas furnace in the middle of the living room. There was a small black-and-white TV in her kitchen. No VCR or DVD, no cell phone or fax machine, no boat or pool or computer; no club membership, no pretentiousness . . . only love, joy, peace, patience, kindness, generosity, self-control . . . fruits of the Spirit . . . God's Spirit.

Aunt Gladys did not wait to develop these traits until she became old. She intentionally yielded herself to that Spirit over a lifetime. It was not one gigantic decision but hundreds of thousands of little ones.

If it is true that boomers face their aging with an ingrained sense of entitlement, then it can only be by conscious choice that an individual moves beyond that entitlement to a place where someone wants to put your framed photograph on their dresser to remind them of grace. That does not just happen.

I had dinner with a friend of mine, a fifty-six-year-old man who has spent his life in corporate America. We were talking about retirement, the failing stock market, and all that. He said, "My plan is to retire at fifty-nine if the market is good. Then I want to do something that matters. I want to leave something behind other than just more profit for the shareholders. That's not enough."

Indeed, that is not enough, but to have your photograph on someone's dresser! See the difference? She was ninety-six years old and extremely valuable. Age cannot take that away from you. Selflessness is an antidote to deteriorating, and to a misspent life.

Ken Dychtwald, in his book *Age Power*, claims that just as society's institutions have been grossly unprepared for the baby boom, the teen boom, and the yuppie boom, we remain unprepared for the elder boom.[1] The year 2011, when boomers begin to retire, is not far off.

Boomers making demands on retirement benefits could easily break the back of the Social Security Trust Fund in the early decades of the twenty-first century. And with people living longer and longer, what will happen when boomers need ten million new nursing home beds? Entitlement does not go "semi-private." If the boomers are transformers of culture, not mere conformers, then expect major and dramatic changes. Individuality over conformity is a consistent boomer pattern. But boomers may well be the ones facing dramatic changes in the way they have experienced the world.

Boomers are aging in a different world. A survey conducted by Roper Research in 1998 for the American Association of Retired Persons is the most extensive poll done to date of baby boomers' attitudes toward retirement. The AARP reported that 80 percent of boomers expect to continue working during their retirement years. These boomers say they wish to continue in the workforce for the satisfaction work provides or for financial reasons. The poll also indicated that nearly twenty-five million boomers do not expect to be able to stop working because it will be financially impossible for them to do so. Nagging concern about adequate income and health care coverage in their retirement years means working longer. Even when boomers do retire, they do not view retirement as the end of their productivity. On the contrary, according to the survey they will seek meaningful volunteerism in new arenas of life.

When faced with our mortality, most of us want to reflect on a life that mattered. In the end, life has to have meaning. Self-indulgence leaves us empty. Have you ever known anyone who put the photograph of a self-indulgent person on his or her dresser? We admire the selfless people who are givers, Christlike people, Joseph of Arimathea kind of people.

As a generation baby boomers are going to face some unique challenges with aging. Aging does not yield to entitlement. Aging pushes the self from the center, leaving a hole of despair if there is not something to replace it. Aging does not play favorites, does not flatter you or tell you how great you are. Aging throws you into the subtraction column. Aging brings us all to a crossroads. Are you a rich young ruler or a Joseph of Arimathea? That is not a decision to be made one day, but every day. The choices we make will make all the difference.

I do not have any profound wisdom about aging. I am in the river myself. All I have is Aunt Gladys' framed photograph on my dresser as a reminder of grace, and the call of Christ to follow him, regardless of how old I am.

Questions for Discussion

1. What implications does extended life for parents and relatives have for the boomer generation?

2. Design a learning program and ask representatives of the boomer generation to sit as a panel and ask them if they would agree with the description of their generation in the chapter.

3. While it is true that some boomers return to the church when their children are involved, when the children leave, will the boomers leave again? Does the "empty nest" mean the "empty pew"?

4. In his book *Spiritual Marketplace: Baby Boomers and the Remaking of American Religion* Wade Clark Roof argues that boomers are deeply spiritual, and they seek self-authentication, intimate relationships, and improvement of family life. Does the church enhance these qualities or ignore them?

5. It is claimed that in the year 2020 the increase of health care provided by Medicare will reach $210 billion, compared with the present $105 billion. What does that mean for the boomer generation that will start retiring in 2011?

6. A member of the boomer generation states that he wants retirement to be more than "golf and trips." He seeks to find a deeper meaning for his later years. Has the church addressed this issue? If not, what ministries could be developed to speak to this need?

7. Boomers have been the "transformers of culture." What major changes do you foresee when boomers retire and confront their later years?

8. How does the author contrast the stories of the rich young ruler and Joseph of Arimathea as two lifestyles for boomers?

9. The author mentions his Aunt Gladys as a role model for graceful aging. Do you know other older people like Aunt Gladys? Explain.

10. Since boomers are not known for their loyalty and commitment to the church throughout their lives, what can the church do to provide community that all human beings need in such a way as to draw both the younger and older boomers into the church?

11. Your son, a boomer, is a successful, high-salaried attorney with a wonderful life. He has no vital relationship to the church. He tells you, "I worship God in my heart, and by serving the community, and being a good family man." What would you say to him?

For Further Reading

William and La Etta Benke, *The Generation Driven Church: Evangelizing Boomers, Busters and Millennials*. New York: Pilgrim Press, 2002. An excellent study of ways the church can reach out to boomers, busters and millennials.

David Cork and Susan Lightstone, *The Pig and the Python: How to Prosper from the Aging Baby Boom*. New York: Prima Communications, 1997. The authors discuss problems that face the economy in the next twenty years and the best way to prepare for a happy, secure retirement.

Ken Dychtwald, *Age Power: How the 21st Century Will Be Ruled by the New Old*. New York: Jeremy P. Tarcher, 1998. Chapter 3 deals with the coming "age wave" of boomers. Dychtwald describes the ways boomers have revolutionized society, the challenges they bring, and the five social train wrecks we need to prevent.

William M. Easum and Herb Miller, *How to Reach Baby Boomers*. Nashville, TN: Abington Press, 1994. Short but concise ways to strategize ministry to/with baby boomers.

Thomas C. Ettinger and Helen Neinast, *Long and Winding Road: A Spiritual Guide for Baby Boomers*. New York: Dimensions for Living, 1996. The authors focus on the spiritual issues of meaning and relevance that boomers face when they retire.

Marc Freedman, *Prime Time: How Baby Boomers Will Revolutionize Retirement and Transform America*. New York: Public Affairs, 1997. *The New York Times* calls this book "inspiring, informative and mind-opening." The author provides a new vision of aging, retirement, and the role of Americans in the twenty-first century. Despite being given a new stage of life, most Americans have shown little wisdom in using this great gift of a third age.

James V. Gambone, ReFirement: *A Boomer's Guide to Life After 50*. Minneapolis, MN: Kirk House, 2000. This book reimagines the future of boomers as a gift and possibility. Gambone urges the retirement of "retirement" and cites role models of "reFired" older persons.

Dean R. Hoge et al., *Vanishing Boundaries: The Religion of Mainline Baby Boomers*. Louisville: Westminster Press, 1995. Based on a survey of some five hundred respondents and forty in-depth interviews, this work examines the religious motivation of baby boomers. Four "churched" and four "unchurched" types are identified.

Philip Longman, *Born to Pay: The New Politics of Aging in America*. Boston, MA: Houghton Mifflin, 1987. The author deals with the present generation's insistence on entitlements and the coming boomer demand for their entitlements when pensions, retirement plans, and Social Security are in jeopardy.

Wade Clark Roof, *A Generation of Seekers: The Spiritual Journey of the Baby Boom Generation*. New York: Harper & Row, 1993.

Wade Clark Roof, *Spiritual Marketplace: Baby Boomers and the Remaking of American Religion*. Princeton, NJ: Princeton University Press, 2001.

The quest culture created by the baby boomers has created a "marketplace" of new spiritual beliefs and practices and of revisited traditions. The author charts the emergence of five subcultures: dogmatists, born-again Christians, mainstream believers, metaphysical believers, and seekers and secularists.

William Strauss and Neil Howe, *Generations: The History of America's Future 1584 to 2069*. New York: William Morror, 1991. An in-depth and provocative study of American history from a generational perspective. Four generational types reoccur throughout American history. Good treatment of the boomer mentality.

Samuel J. Tucker, *The Baby Boomers Survival Handbook for the 21st Century*. Atlanta: Atlanta Human Development Press, 1998. The authors help boomers prepare for the transitions brought on by unemployment, downsizing and retirement. The book deals with the ABCs of money management and key ways to become financially independent and debt-free.

Notes

1. J. Walker Smith and Ann. S. Clurman, *Rocking the Ages: The Yankelovich Report on Generational Marketing*, reprint (New York: HarperBusiness, 1998), p. 17.
2. Thomas Merton, *The Silent Life* (New York: Farrar, Strauss, and Girous, 1978), pp. 14–15.
3. Barbara Deane, *Caring for Your Aging Parents: When Love Is Not Enough* (Colorado Springs, CO: NavPress, 1989), p. 33.
4. Ken Dychtwald, *Age Power: How the Twenty-First Century Will Be Ruled by the New Old*, 1st trade edition (New York: Jeremy P. Tarcher, 2000), p. 77.

A Jewish View of Aging

Dwyn M. Mounger

Signs on public buses in some U.S. cities read, "Please give up this seat if an elderly or handicapped person needs it." But in similar vehicles in Jerusalem they declare, "You shall rise before the aged" (Leviticus 19:32).[1]

At first glance one might conclude that respect and admiration for older adulthood are unequivocally at the very heart of Judaism. Numerous citations from the Torah, the Prophets and other Old Testament writings, the Apocrypha, "Sayings of the Fathers," the Talmud, the Midrash, and other rabbinic commentaries might bolster this verdict.[2] And yet throughout their history Jews, like adherents of other religions, have manifested ambivalence towards aging.

The Jewish Bible

On the one hand, the Hebrew Scriptures present longevity as a blessing of God, the reward for having lived in obedience to the Torah (see, for example, Deuteronomy 6:2). Incredibly long life spans are attributed to Jewish patriarchs and leaders, especially up through the time of Moses.[3] The Torah promises ripe old age to those who, among other things, do not capture a mother bird when removing her young from the nest (Deuteronomy 22:6–7) and to those who use honest weights in measuring (Deuteronomy 25:15). Proverbs 16:31 assures the faithful that "gray hair is a crown of glory; it is gained in a righteous life" (see also Proverbs 3:1–2). And longevity is a special reward to those who keep the Fifth Commandment, to honor one's father and mother: " . . . that your days may be long in the land that the Lord your God is giving you" (Exodus 20:12; see also Deuteronomy 5:16).

It is true that the biblical texts concern themselves mainly with men, since women were considered old after menopause. However, Sarah not only is blessed with a son at age 90 but lives until she is 127 (Genesis 17:17; 23:1). Admiration and divine and human concern for the godly, aged woman reach their height in the moving story of Ruth and her mother-in-law, elderly, widowed Naomi. When, as a result of Naomi's wise advice and planning, Ruth gives birth to Obed, the local women dub the baby Naomi's own son and cry to her, "He shall be to you a restorer of life and a nourisher of your old age; for your daughter-in-law who loves you . . . has borne him" (Ruth 4:15–17). Centuries later at least one rabbi, reading that Naomi became the baby's "nurse," asserted that the Lord so restored her life that, miraculously, she was able to nourish the child with her own milk.[4]

Yet alongside these and other positive declarations about old age the Scriptures include gloomy, depressing depictions of people who have attained it. Jacob complains to Pharaoh, "The years of my earthly sojourn are one hundred thirty; few and hard have been the years of my life. They do not compare with the years of the life of my ancestors during their long sojourn" (Genesis 47:9).

> The psalmist begs the Lord:
>> Do not cast me off in the time of old age;
>>> do not forsake me when my strength is spent. . . .
>> So even to old age and gray hairs,
>>> O God, do not forsake me,
>> until I proclaim your might
>>> to all the generations to come (Psalm 71:9, 18).

On his eightieth birthday Barzillai, a member of David's royal court, whines: "Can I discern what is pleasant and what is not? Can your servant taste what he eats or what he drinks? Can I still listen to the voice of singing men and singing women?" (2 Samuel 19:35). Even David himself, greatest of the Jewish kings, recedes into loneliness and numbing cold in his declining days. Unable to keep warm, he shivers in his bed—at least until the virgin Abishag is found to cover him with her body, though they engage in no sexual intercourse (1 Kings 1:1–4).

The negative view of aging in the Hebrew Scriptures surely reaches its nadir in the grim but moving poetry of Ecclesiastes 12:1–8:

> Remember your creator in the days of your youth, before the days of trouble come, and the years draw near when you will say, "I have no pleasure in them"; before the sun and the light and the moon and the stars are darkened and the clouds return with the rain; in the day when the guards of the house tremble, and the strong men are bent, and the women who grind cease working because they are few, and those who look through the windows see dimly; when the doors on the street are shut, and the sound of the grinding is low, and one rises up at the sound of a bird, and all the daughters of song are brought low; when one is afraid of heights, and terrors are in the road; the almond tree blossoms, the grasshopper drags itself along and desire fails; because all must go to their eternal home, and the mourners will go about the streets; before the silver cord is snapped, and the golden bowl is broken, and the pitcher is broken at the fountain, and the wheel broken at the cistern, and the dust returns to the earth as it was, and the breath returns to God who gave it. Vanity of vanities, says the Teacher; all is vanity.

The Apocrypha

In the Apocryphal literature (300 B.C. to 100 A.D.) this ambivalence toward aging continues. Ben Sira notes that "to fear the Lord is the root of wisdom, and her branches are long life" (Sirach 1:20). He urges, "My child, help your father in his old age, and do not grieve him as long as he lives; even if his mind fails, be patient with him; because you have all your faculties do not despise him" (3:12–13).

The sage's admiration for the elderly continues: "Do not disdain one who is old, for some of us are also growing old. . . . Do not ignore the discourse of the aged, for they themselves learned from their parents; from them you learn how to understand and to give an answer when the need arises" (8:6, 9; see also 25:4–6).

Yet Ben Sira can also exclaim: "I hate three kinds of people, and I loathe their manner of life: a pauper who boasts, a rich person who lies, and an old fool who commits adultery" (25:2) and "O death, how welcome is your sentence to one who is needy and failing in strength, worn down by age and anxious about everything" (41:2). He also counsels, "Do not be ashamed to correct the stupid or foolish or the aged who are guilty of sexual immorality" (42:8).

The wisdom of Solomon makes no distinction between the righteous who die young and those who live to advanced years: "For old age is not honored for the length of time, or measured by number of years; but understanding is gray hair for anyone, and a blameless life is ripe old age" (4:7–9).

The Rabbinic Tradition

When one moves beyond both the Jewish Scriptures and the Apocrypha into the voluminous writings of the rabbis, at least up until the twentieth century, it becomes obvious that Jewish ambivalence towards aging and the aged persists. Until modern times no elderly class as such existed. Individuals living into their seventies and beyond were very much the exception.[5] The classical rabbinic works reflect that sociological fact. Rabbi Shimon ben Menasya (ca.165–200 A.D.) declared: "Beauty, strength, wealth, honor, wisdom, old age, gray hair [advanced age], and children befit the righteous and befit the world. . . . Grandchildren are the crown of the old." From Rabbi Yose ben Yehudah of Kefar Ha-Bavli (ca. 165–200 A.D.) comes this famous saying: "Regarding the one who learns from the young, to what can this person be compared? To one eating unripe grapes and drinking wine from the winepress. Regarding the person who learns form the old, to what can this person be compared? To one eating ripe grapes and drinking old wine."[6]

Yet Rabbi Elisha ben Abuyah, who lived in the same early period (ca. 120–140 A.D.), could make this judgment: "Regarding the one who studies when young, to what can that person be compared? To ink written on new paper. Regarding the one who studies when old, to what can that person be compared? To ink written on paper that has been erased."[7]

According to a beautiful story in *Midrash Rabbah*, elaborating on Genesis 24:1 ("Now Abraham was old, well advanced in years"), the visible signs of aging in human beings did not exist before this first patriarch. Consequently people who came to Abraham and wished to speak to him were confused. They could not distinguish him from his son Isaac. So Abraham asked the Lord to mark him with characteristics by which they could tell the two apart.

The next morning, when the patriarch awakened, he was astonished to see that his hair and beard had turned white. "Master of the universe," he said, "if you have given me white hair as a mark of old age, [I do not find it attractive]."

"On the contrary," the Lord answered, "'the hoary head is a crown of glory'" (cf. Proverbs 16:31).[8]

Traditional Judaism, recognizing that long life in itself is evidence of wisdom (education by experience), has urged respect for *all* people who are advanced in years. "He who welcomes an old man is as if he welcomed the Shechinah" (that is, the very light of the Lord's presence).[9] Moreover, the Talmud forthrightly asserts that one should honor even those who suffer from senility: "Respect . . . the old person who has lost his learning for there were placed in the ark of the covenant not only the two perfect tablets of the Law but also the fragments of the tablets that Moses shattered when he saw the people dancing before the Golden Calf."[10]

The rabbis devoted much attention to everything that might be involved in obeying the injunction of Leviticus 19:32, "You shall rise before the aged, and defer to the old." Some claimed that this law pertained to the rabbinic class—that is, to scholars, like themselves, with many years of experience—rather than to elderly persons as such. Others, however, interpreted it as a requirement to stand in the presence of all older Jews, even those who might be ignorant of the faith. The rabbis debated whether or not, if an aged person passed by more than once, one need stand each and every time. Also, should one interrupt one's study of the Torah to rise in the presence of the elderly?[11]

Maimonides (1135–1204 A.D.), arguably Judaism's greatest scholar and philosopher of all time, articulated what seems to have become the position of most devout Jews to this day:

"One should stand up for someone who is very old, even if he isn't learned. . . . One does not have to stand up fully to honor such a person, but just enough to honor him. One has to pay respect even to an aged gentile in these manners, and one should lend him a hand for support, for it is written, 'You shall stand up before the old man'—i.e., one should stand up for all elderly people."[12]

Clearly in Judaism respect for the aged is tied directly to reverence for God. The extensive rabbinic Halakah on the Fifth Commandment, "Honor your father and your mother . . ." bears this out. Noting that Leviticus 19:3 reverses the order (". . . revere your mother and father . . ."), *Kerrithoth* 6:9–28 infers that both parents "are to be equally honored and revered." Since in the Decalogue this Fifth Commandment appears just after those of the First Table (i.e., Commandments One through Four, which concern one's obligations to the Lord), the rabbis elevated it above the remainder. Therefore the bond between child and parent is "intricately bound up in the man-G-d relationship."[13]

It is hard to exaggerate the lengths to which the rabbis claimed one must go in order to fulfill the parental commandment. One must honor father and mother even if they have forsaken the Torah (*Hilchot Mamrim* 5:12ff. and 6:11; *Shulchan Aruch* 240:18). Poverty is no excuse for disobeying the commandment. "Whether you have the means or you do not, honor your father and your mother—even if you must become a beggar at the door" (Jerusalem Talmud, *Kiddushin* 1:7).[14]

Much later Maimonides could take this even further—with profound implications for the twenty-first century and its challenge of greatly increased longevity and, with it, the ravages of Alzheimer's disease. Severe mental illness in parents does not absolve the child from the duty to honor them. Even should one witness father or mother taking one's own "pouch of gold coins" and tossing them into the sea, one "should not reproach them or show distress or anger in their presence," he said. Moreover, if a son were in the act of sitting at an important assembly and the parents should burst in, tear his clothing, and beat and spit on him, their own offspring, "he should not reproach them. Instead, he should be silent and have reverence and fear of . . . the King of kings, who has commanded him thus [to revere his parents]."[15]

Should, then, one obey father and mother under any and all circumstances? No, the rabbis did draw a line if a parent should command a child to violate the Torah, such as forbidding the offspring to study it, and even if the parent should order disregard of a rabbinic precept. Under such a circumstance the son or daughter should heed, instead, the Lord's solemn voice, "Do not . . . obey . . . if it results in disobeying My words" (*Rashi* on Leviticus 19.3, *Yevamot* 5b, *Bava Metzia* 32a).[16]

Rabbi Simeon ben Eleazar argued: "If the old say to you, 'Demolish,' while the young say, 'Build,' demolish and do not build, because demolition by the old is building, while building by the young is demolition, and the example is Rehoboam son of Solomon."[17]

A study of the Jewish tradition of Eastern Europe, including the Hasidic movement, reveals that the rabbis continued to extol the elderly. Moshe ibn Yehudah HaMachiri, stressing the lifelong *mitzvoth* (commandments) to the faithful to study, portrayed old age as the Sabbath, following one's prior years that correspond to the six weekly days of work.[18] Thus it seems that especially to the elderly the prayer of Psalm 90:12 is relevant: "So teach us to count our days that we may gain a wise heart."

After the death of aged Rabbi Moshe of Kobryn, Rabbi Mendel of Kotzk asked one of his disciples, "What was most important to your teacher?"

After pausing to think, the disciple answered, "Whatever he happened to be doing at the moment."[19]

A Hasidic student once entered the room of Rabbi Yerahmiel of Pzhysha and was amazed to find him reclining, playing with his watch. Although it was nearly noon, it was apparent that the rabbi had not yet said his prayers. "You are surprised at what I am doing?" Yerahmiel asked the student. "But do you really know what I am doing? I am learning how to leave the world."[20]

Despite all these positive affirmations of aging, however, the rabbis could and did at times portray the grim realities that often accompany longevity. The Babylonian Talmud, interpreting Ecclesiastes 12:1–8, views each poetic description of disaster or dysfunction as specifically symbolizing the deterioration of a part of the body during the advancement of the process of aging.[21] Rabbi Abba declared: "Concerning his old age, a man should pray that his eyes may [continue] to see, his mouth to eat, and his feet to walk. For when a man grows old, all his functions desert him."[22] Once Caesar asked elderly Rabbi Joshua ben Hananiah why he had not appeared at a certain celebration. The rabbi replied, "The mountain is snow, surrounded by ice, the dog doesn't bark, the grinders don't grind." By this he meant that his hair and beard had turned white, he had lost his hearing, and his teeth could no longer chew food.[23]

Midrashic and Talmudic sources contain similar pessimistic references to aging, some of them humorous. The household of Rab could complain, "What I didn't lose I'm looking for." According to Rabbi Dimi, "Youth is a crown of roses, age, a crown of willow-rods." Advised Rabbi Samuel, "Open your mouth and let your food come in. Until age forty food is better, then, drink is better." A text in the Jerusalem Talmud grumbles, "Stones which we sat on in our youth make war against us in our old age."[24]

To an elderly person, "even a tiny mound is like the highest of mountains." A certain rabbi asked aged Rabbi Simeon ben Halafta, "How come we didn't receive you on the festival in the way in which my ancestors would receive yours?"

Ben Halafta answered, "You know, the rocks have gotten tall, what is near has gotten distant, two have become three, and the peacemaker of the household has ceased." By this he meant that it was difficult for him to walk either over obstacles or for very far; his legs had now become "three," one of them being a walking cane; and he no longer engaged in sexual relations.[25]

Moreover, according to the Talmud and the Midrash, old age is a time of decline both of spirit and mind. Rabbi Jonathan noted: "Solomon first wrote Song of Songs, then Proverbs, and then Ecclesiastes." Therefore, he inferred, "when a man is young, he utters words of song; when mature, he speaks in proverbs; when old, he talks of [life's] vanities." He declared elsewhere, "Old men lack sagacity, and children perspicacity."[26]

Graphically and dolefully picturing the very end of an aged person's life, *Midrash Tanhuma* says that one's disposition changes as one becomes childlike, asking for everything—existing much like a child. One sits before one's household, ignored or mocked as though one was an ape. However, when the angel of death arrives, he starts to weep and his cry pierces the world from one end to the other.[27]

And yet even the elderly can triumph over hopelessness and physical and mental degeneration, presumably through faithful obedience to *mitzvoth*. "There is old age without the glory of long life and there is long life without the ornament of age," asserts *Genesis Rabbah* 69. "Perfect is that old age which has both."[28]

Modern Judaism and Aging

From the antiquity, rich variety, eloquence, and emotional intensity of the sacred literature it is quite apparent that the Jewish tradition has much to offer the twenty-first century in the quest for vital ministry to older adults. In North America Jews, like other people, are living longer. Thus they share the common challenges that accompany this trend. Alfred Uhry's play and later the 1989 Academy Award—winning movie *Driving Miss Daisy*, about an elderly Atlanta Jewish widow and her black chauffeur, beautifully conveyed, among other things, this message.

According to studies from the early 1990s, one-third of all Jews in the United States are over the age of seventy-five and approximately 10 percent are beyond eighty-five. Those in the latter segment are increasing faster than are those in any other.[29] In both confronting the needs and utilizing the wisdom and gifts of aging people, modern Judaism draws deeply upon its venerable tradition and rituals for the "sanctification of time."[30] For the observant Jew every moment of existence is a generous gift from the Lord, a gift to be experienced with thankful blessing of the divine name. Thus old age is not a time for mere idleness, for simply longing for things past, or for hobbies and games as ends in themselves. Instead it is a magnificent opportunity for continued learning, spiritual growth, deepening communion with the Creator, and passing on a rich legacy of insights to the younger generations.

No one has more eloquently and forcefully articulated this position than did Rabbi Abraham Heschel, who was professor of Jewish ethics and mysticism at the Jewish Theological Seminary of America in New York City. His address electrified delegates to the 1961 White House Conference on Aging. Branding the pervasive American "cult of youth" as "idolatry," Heschel called old age "not a defeat but a victory, not a punishment but a privilege." "Abraham is the grand old man, but the legend of Faust is pagan."[31]

Instead of an excessive emphasis on recreation and hobbies for the elderly, Heschel pointed to "ritual and prayer" as the answer to their often empty existence spent just passing time. In keeping with the ancient Jewish stress on *mitzvoth*, he declared: "To be is to obey. A person must never cease to be." Heschel compared entrance into old age to the beginning of one's senior year in a university "in exciting anticipation of consummation." Amazingly, nearly fifteen years before the founding of Elderhostel he called for something similar: the establishment of "universities for the aged . . . where the purpose of learning is not a career, . . . but learning itself.[32]

Heschel deplored the lack of communication and interaction between old and young. "The real bond between two generations is the insights they share, the appreciation they have in common, the moments of inner experience in which they meet." He declared, "Being old is not necessarily the same as being stale."[33]

Passionately, Heschel concluded his speech in words often quoted nearly thirty-five years later. The elderly, he asserted:

> need a vision, not only recreation . . .
> need a dream, not only a memory.
> It takes three things to attain a sense of significant being.
>> God
>> A Soul
>> A Moment
>> The three are always here.
>> Just to be is a blessing, just to live is holy.[34]

In keeping with Heschel's insights, modern American Jews are developing new rituals that hold deep meaning for older people. They are experimenting with rites to mark recovery from illness and surgery, to underscore particular moments with family and grandchildren, and to ease necessary times of transition, such as entrance into a nursing home or an assisted-living facility. "Ceremonies of passage," including poetry and moving prayers of thanksgiving, sometimes of the older person's own composition, are appearing to help make special certain birthdays or anniversaries.[35]

American Jews are also exploring the richness of the concept of old age as the "Sabbath" of one's life. Observance of the seventh-day rest, among other things, compels the individual to cease creating and moves him or her to focus on the promptings of the mind rather than those of the body. Thus old age, like the Sabbath, ideally can transform a person's energy into that which supremely sustains the soul. As in Genesis the seventh day is the crown of creation, so one's elder years potentially can be a time of spiritual self-realization to its fullest.[36]

Dayle Friedman points to Judaism's "*Mitzvah* Model" as a source for a renewed vision of aging. Through faithful acceptance of religious obligation the older Jew can realize a deeper sense of self-worth and of how valuable he or she continues to be to the covenantal community. Simply to be counted as part of the *minyan*—the necessary quorum for a prayer service—is a special honor, as is leading others in reciting the liturgies and offering grace at meals. Since older people are still expected to follow *mitzvoth*, Friedman stresses that the congregation is obligated to facilitate their access fully into the worship, study, and communal life of the members, whatever architectural and other changes may be necessary. And since the elderly are valuable resources the Jewish community consequently will be greatly benefited by their continued, thorough participation.[37]

Jews of the twenty-first century are also drawing on their rich religious tradition for guidance in the perplexing ethical challenges that accompany the presence of a greatly increased number of aged people in their midst. How may one continue faithfully to obey "Honor your father and your mother" in such matters as the seemingly necessary placement of an elderly parent, against his or her will, in a nursing home or skilled-care facility? Can the venerable rabbinic tradition shed any light at all on end-of-life issues that only emerged in the late twentieth century with its enormous advances in medical science?

One major Jewish insight is the well-taken point that sons as well as daughters of parents suffering from senile dementia or other conditions that sometimes accompany aging share at least equal responsibility for their loving care. Despite the obvious fact that overwhelmingly most such caregiving in America is undertaken by female members of the family, traditional *halakah* places the accountability squarely on the male offspring. The rabbis totally exempted women from it on the presumption that their primary responsibilities were due their husbands.[38]

Such a position clearly springs from patriarchal—even sexist—stereotypes once predominant among Jews and Christians alike but uncomfortable to many in the twenty-first century. Nevertheless, it provides an excellent basis for a call to a thorough sharing of the burden by both daughters and sons today.

Ruth Langer finds in the writings of Maimonides guidance for the difficult decision to employ an in-home nurse or even to move an aged, ill parent into a care facility when he or she opposes it. "One whose father or mother has become mentally impaired should try to treat them according to their ability with pity for them," he stated. "But if he cannot stand it, because they have become too deranged, he should leave them and go, directing others to treat them appropriately."[39]

The children can be pushed too far. At the point when the conflict between them and the parent over the latter's adequate care is seriously damaging the relationship, the offspring are justified in turning over to others the necessary caregiving. However, sons and daughters need always to ensure that its quality is the best possible and that the dignity of their mother or father will constantly be respected.[40]

Jews are also persuasively addressing issues posed by the "living will," which in the late twentieth century came to be adopted increasingly especially by older Americans. With the Holocaust indelibly etched in scarlet onto their collective memory, anything that smacks of euthanasia is a particularly sensitive issue to them. Walter Jacob, while arguing that Judaism unequivocally rejects suicide and mercy killing as options, nevertheless finds the "living will" concept in keeping with the Torah and its interpretation. It is, he says, "an instrument of antidysthanonic." That is, after all chance of recovering has passed, the "a living will" enables the dying person, or *goses*, to die without undue delay.[41]

Does Judaism have anything to say to an old person who is so frail and miserable that life itself has become a great burden? Yes, modern Jews, drawing from the tradition, can gently persuade and enable that individual to let go and relinquish this weight. Dayle Friedman cites the midrashic *Yalkut Shimoni Parashat Ekev* in which an old woman complains to Rabbi Yosi ben Halafta, "I have aged too much and now my life is worthless, for I cannot taste food or drink, and I want to die."

He asks her what *mitzvah* she is daily practicing. She replies that she visits the synagogue each morning. The rabbi's advice to the old woman is that for three days in succession she stop doing so. Obediently, she ceases going to the synagogue, and on the third day she falls ill and dies.

Friedman concludes from this astonishing story that "one's evaluation of the quality of his or her life is a legitimate element in decisions about life and death, and that prolonging a life experienced as burdensome is not obligatory." This fact can be helpful not only to the aged person in such circumstances but also to relatives faced with perplexing decisions about whether or not to allow use of respirators, feeding tubes, and other medical devices on an elderly member of the family who is in *extremis*.[42]

Thus Jews, perhaps far out of proportion to their numbers, have produced literature, well-grounded in Scripture, psychology, medicine, and ethics, that can continue to influence profoundly those who confront the challenges of aging and the aged in this twenty-first-century Western world. Their religious tradition is a valuable, eloquent, arresting, and useful antidote to the tendency of modern society simply to resort to pragmatic, materialist approaches. Christians and other people of faith should join hands and voices with them in opposing that which neglects the heart, mind, and soul of the elderly.

Above all, the clear Jewish call for the senior years to be ideally the time of one's greatest spiritual and intellectual growth needs to be heard by everyone. Heschel's war cry speech to the 1961 White House Conference on Aging should be reprinted, distributed to every American, young and old, and its text reproduced in full on a permanent Internet Web site.

And yet Jews, like the rest of us in our human frailty, continue naturally to dread the physical and mental decline that can accompany the senior years. Perhaps nowhere is this mixture of admiration and dread better expressed than in this whimsical poem, inspired by 2 Samuel 11 and 1 Kings 1:1–4, from the pen of Jewish poet Barbara Holender, herself an older American and also a scholar of Hebrew and Torah—"Bathsheba Watches Abishag":

> Poor little girl,
> what are you getting out of this?
> David hardly knows you're in his arms
> warming him. Can the old man
> wake a woman even now? When I warmed him,
>   he warmed me back,
> sang me out of my marriage bed,
> bathed me in sweet sin,
> set me like a jewel in his bosom—
> a soldier's widow—wife to a king,
> mother to a king. Where can you go from here but down
> until a stone rewards you:
> "Here lies Abishag, the king's last comfort"
> but no consort. I watch you together
> hanging on, letting go.
> When his time comes, I'll mourn my conqueror,
> that sweet singer of Jerusalem,
> The Lord's anointed ruler of Israel,
> while you weep over the dust of David. Hold him for me, child,
> I can't bear to touch him.
> You are too young to know
> we do not love the same man.[43]

Questions for Discussion

1. What does the Torah teach about old age?
2. Does the pessimistic view of aging in Ecclesiastes 12:1–8 have any relevance today in light of medical/technological advances?
3. How do you account for the ambivalence toward aging in Judaism in such quotes as "Do not disdain one who is old" and "O death, how welcome is your sentence to one who is needy and failing in strength, worn down by age and anxious about everything"?
4. What is the limit placed by the rabbis on the commandment "Honor your father and mother"? What might cause a child to violate this commandment?
5. Maimonides, the great philosopher of Judaism, insisted that severe illness does not absolve children from their duty to honor their parents. The author raises the question, "How does this relate to the contemporary issues of increased longevity and the ravages of Alzheimer's disease?" How would you respond?
6. How has modern Judaism changed from the traditional Jewish view of aging? How is it the same?
7. A Jewish woman writes a letter to the editor of the *New York Times*. In her letter, referring to the Terry Schiavo case, she resents the government's encroaching on a person's right to die. Is she representing modern Judaism or her own opinion?
8. Why is the living will such a sensitive issue for Jews?
9. How does the Jewish view of aging differ from the Christian view of aging?
10. If possible invite a rabbi to speak at your church on the Jewish view of aging. After reading Mounger's chapter, what questions might you ask the rabbi?

Notes

1. Jan Schneiderman, "President's View," NCJW (National Council of Jewish Women) *Journal*, Summer 1999; available online at www.ncjw.org/news/journal-summer1999.htm..
2. See the lengthy list in Appendix I of Susan Berrin, ed., *A Heart of Wisdom: Making the Jewish Journey from Midlife Through the Elder Years* (Woodstock, VT: Jewish Lights Publishing, 1997), pp. 303–308.
3. Walter Jacob, "Beyond Methuselah—Who is Old?" in *Aging and the Aged in Jewish Law: Essays and Responsa* (Studies in Progressive Halakhah, VII), ed. Walter Jacob and Moshe Zemer (Pittsburgh and Tel Aviv: Rodef Shalom Press, 1998), pp. 2–3).

4. Ibid., p. 1, Rachel Dulin, "He Will Renew Your Life and Sustain Your Old Age (Ruth 4:15)," *Journal of Psychology and Judaism*, 20:1 (Spring 1996), p. 99ff.; Berrin, *Heart of Wisdom*, xxv–xxvi. Berrin notes, "What redeems Naomi in her old age is love, companionship, and family." See Nosson Scherman, *The Book of Ruth: A New Translation with a Commentary Anthologized from Talmudic, Midrashic and Rabbinic Sources*, trans. and comp. Meir Zlotowitz (New York: ArtScroll Studios, Ltd., 1976), p. 133.

5. Jacob, "Beyond Methuselah," p. 9, and Ruth Langer, "Honor Your Father and Mother: Care Giving as a Halakhic Responsibility," p. 21, in *Aging and the Aged in Jewish Law*, ed. Jacob and Zemer.

6. Leonard Kravitz and Kerry M. Olitzky, eds. and trans., *Pirke Avot: A Modern Commentary on Jewish Ethics* (New York: UAHC Press, 1993), pp. 67, 103, 113–114.

7. Ibid., pp. 67, 114.

8. Hayim Nahman Bialik and Yehoshua Hana Ravnitzky, eds., *The Book of Legends, Sefer Ha-Aggadah: Legends from the Talmud and Midrash*, trans. William G. Braude (New York: Schocken Books, 1992), p. 579.

9. *Genesis Rabbah* 16:6; Dulin, "He Will Renew Your Life," p. 307; C. G. Montefiore and H. M. J. Loewe, eds., *A Rabbinic Anthology* (New York: Schocken Books, 1974), p. 505.

10. Berrin, *Heart of Wisdom*, xxi; Kerry M. Olitzky and Eugene B. Borowitz, "A Jewish Perspective" in *Aging, Spirituality, and Religion* (Minneapolis: Fortress Press, 1995), p. 390.

11. Michael Rosen, "Standing for the Elder or the Elderly" in Jacob and Zemer, *Aging and the Aged in Jewish Law*, p. 105; Olitzky and Borowitz, "Jewish Perspective" in Aging, Spirituality, p. 390; Montefiore and Loewe, Rabbinic Anthology, p. 505.

12. Maimonides' *Hilchot Talmud Torah* 6:9, trans. Immanuel M. O'Levy © 1993; used by permission.

13. Ahavat Israel, "Honor your Father and your Mother: The Fifth Commandment, Parents" available online at www.ahavat-israel. com/ahavat/am/parents.asp.

14. Ibid.; see Union of American Hebrew Congregations, "Go and Study: Reverence and Honor, the Fifth Commandment," available online at www.uahc.org/goandstudy/volume3/no.5.shtml.

15. Jacob and Zemer, *Aging and the Aged in Jewish Law*, p. 28.

16. Ahavat Israel, "Honor your Father and your Mother."

17. Bialik and Ravnitzky, *Book of Legends*, p. 578; cf. Olitzky and Borowitz, "Jewish Perspective" in *Aging, Spirituality*, p. 393.

18. Berrin, *Heart of Wisdom*, xxiii.

19. Martin Buber, *Tales of the Hasidim: The Later Master*, trans. Olga Marx (New York: Schocken Books, 1948), p. 173.

20. Matin Buber, op. cit., p. 234.

21. Dayle A. Friedman, "Crown Me with Wrinkles and Gray Hair: Examining Traditional Jewish Views of Aging," Berrin, Heart of

Wisdom, p. 8; Olitzky and Borowitz, "Jewish Perspective" in *Aging, Spirituality*, p. 391.

22. Bialik and Ravnitzsky, *Book of Legends*, p. 578.

23. Jacob Neuser and Noam M. M. Neusner, eds., *The Book of Jewish Wisdom: The Talmud of the Well-Considered Life* (New York: Continuum Publishing Co., 1996), p. 180.

24. Idem., Jerusalem Talmud, *Beitzah 1*, as quoted in Olitzky and Borowitz, "Jewish Perspective" in *Aging, Spirituality*, p. 395.

25. Bialik and Ravnitzsky, *Book of Legends*, p. 578; cf. Olitzky and Borowitz, "Jewish Perspective" in *Aging, Spirituality*, p. 394; Neusner and Neusner, *Book of Jewish Wisdom*, p. 180.

26. Bialik and Ravnitzsky, *Book of Legends*, p. 578.

27. Olitzky and Borowitz, "Jewish Perspective" in *Aging, Spirituality*, p. 395.

28. Olitzky and Borowitz, loc.cit., p. 394.

29. Rabbi Richard F. Address, "Spirituality and Aging: The New Jewish Older Adult," NCJW *Journal*, Summer 1999.

30. Berrin, *Heart of Wisdom*, xxii.

31. Abraham J. Heschel, "The Older Person and the Family in the Perspective of Jewish Tradition" in *Aging and the Human Spirit: A Reader in Religion and Gerontology*, 2nd edition, ed. Carol LeFevre and Perry LeFevre (Chicago: Exploration Press, 1985), pp. 35–36. For the impact of Heschel's speech not only on delegates to the White House Conference but on American Jews and other people of faith who today seek to minister to the aging, see Thomas R. Cole, *The Journey of Life: A Cultural History of Aging in America* (Cambridge, England: Cambridge University Press, 1993), p. 242n; Richard H. Gentzler, Jr., and Donald F. Clingan, *Aging: God's Challenge to Church and Synagogue* (Nashville: Discipleship Resources, 1996), p. 30; and keynote speech by Arthur S. Flemming at the 1995 White House Conference on Aging, Washington, DC, May 3, 1995.

32. Heschel, "The Older Person and the Family," pp. 37–39.

33. Heschel, loc. cit., pp. 42–43.

34. Heschel, loc. cit., p. 44.

35. Rabbi Address, "Spirituality and Aging." For an excellent example of such a ritual see Barbara D. Holender, "A Ceremony of Passage on My Sixty-Fifth Birthday," *Reform Judaism*, XXVIII, No. 1 (Fall, 1999), p. 50; available online at uahc.org/rjmag/999bh.html.

36. Olitzky and Borowitz, "Jewish Perspective" in *Aging, Spirituality*, p. 394; Gentzler and Clingan, Aging: *God's Challenge to Church and Synagogue*, pp. 27–28.

37. Friedman, "Crown Me with Wrinkles" in Berrin, *Heart of Wisdom*, pp. 14–18.

38. Langer, "Honor Your Father and Mother" in Jacob and Zemer, *Aging and the Aged in Jewish Law*, p. 35.

39. Maimonides, *Hilchot Mamrim* 6:10, quoted in Langer, "Honor Your Father and Mother," p. 32.

40. Langer, "Honor Your Father and Mother," pp. 32–33.
41. Jacob and Zemer, *Aging and the Aged in Jewish Law*, pp. 128–129. For a view of the living will from an Orthodox Jewish standpoint, see Steven H. Resnicoff, "Physician-Assisted Dying: Halachic Perspectives," *The Journal of Halacha and Contemporary Society*, XXXVII, Spring 1999, 47–84.
42. Friedman, "Crown Me with Wrinkles" in Berrin, *Heart of Wisdom*, p. 9.
43. Barbara D. Holender, *Ladies of Genesis: Poems* (New York: Jewish Women's Resource Center, 1991), p. 27. Used by permission.

An Islamic View of Aging and Death

Harry R. Moody

A human being would certainly not grow to be 70 or 80 years old if this longevity had no meaning for the species. The afternoon of life must also have a significance of its own and cannot be merely a pitiful appendage to life's morning.

—Carl Jung

Verily, by the Afternoon, Man is in the way of Loss; except for those who counsel one another to patience and to the Truth.

—Sura 108, the Holy Qur'an

The Islamic vision of old age, as of so many other elements of Muslim life, is to be found in the Holy Qur'an (Koran) (Allen 1989). With over one billion Muslims today, the Qur'an is without doubt the most widely read book in the world. Yet, even after the traumatic events of September 11, 2001, the Qur'an, like Islam itself, remains unknown to most Westerners. Approaching the Islamic Scripture presents a problem for Western readers, even in an accessible translation. The great Persian poet Jalal ad-Din Rumi called the Holy Qur'an a "veiled book," comparing it to a bride who only reveals her beauty after the veil is lifted. To lift that veil the contemporary Western reader has many obstacles to overcome. Today, now that Islam looms larger in the mind of the West, it is more important than ever to understand the Qur'an and the Islamic vision of life, including the entire life course.

The Qur'an consists of 114 chapters or suras, and one of these is titled "Al-'Asr," translated as "Time" and also as "The Afternoon," cited in full above. This short sura describes the human condition as subject to the disintegrating power of time, symbolized by the descent of the sun in the afternoon. The late afternoon of lifetime is experienced as an irrevocable passage. Late afternoon, like later life, is a period when the light diminishes, when the day nears its end, when darkness is at hand. But this "afternoon of life," as Jung put it, must also have a significance of its own. The question is: what significance can it have?

For humanity under modern conditions the answer is usually what "Al-Asr" says it is: loss, absolute loss, the common experience of advanced age. This is hardly a new discovery, but sometimes we need reminding of it, and the Qur'an describes itself as a "reminder" to people. This fundamental truth, indeed, is one of the four "facts of existence" that the young Prince Siddartha discovered, which is what prompted him to embark on the spiritual journey upon which he would become the Buddha. Along with Buddhism, Islam begins with this ruthless, realistic acknowledgment of the common human condition.

But this sense of uniform loss is immediately qualified by subsequent verses of the same sura: the "way of loss" is absolute "except for those who have faith" (*Imam*), who counsel one another toward the truth (*al-Haqq*, one of the ninety-nine names of God), and who encourage one another to bear burdens with patience. Thus the losses of aging are balanced by a potential for inner growth and development, here epitomized by the two poles of Intellect and Will, corresponding to the virtues of Truth and Patience. We know from other verses in the Qur'an that the fulfillment of this ideal of life span development is not to be achieved within the span of a human life but is found beyond death in the encounter with God. From the Qur'an's perspective, then, old age is a sign (*ayat*), a reminder that the finite course of human life is embraced by a wider cosmic horizon.

The Qur'an repeats its meditation on old age in many different guises. Along with the intellectual apprehension of faith, there is the demand for virtue, for right action (*Ihsan*). Foremost among these right actions is the moral imperative for how the elderly are to be treated. If elders are a "sign" of our common human condition, then the old ones also include aging parents, who deserve special respect. Like Confucianism, Islam stresses filial piety or respect for elders:

> We have charged man, that he be kind to his parents; his mother bore him painfully, and painfully she gave birth to him; his bearing and his weaning are thirty months. Until, when he is fully grown, and reaches forty years, he says, "O my Lord, dispose me that I may be thankful for Thy blessing wherewith Thou has blessed me and my father and mother, and that I may do righteousness well-pleasing to Thee, and make me righteous also in my seed. Behold, I repent to Thee, and am among those who surrender" (46:15).

The age of forty mentioned here is significant. It is traditionally understood that it was at the age of forty that the Prophet Muhammad first began receiving the revelation of the Qur'an. The Prophet, like people today, had attained wealth and a certain position by the stage of midlife. Yet he was dissatisfied with worldly goods and began searching for something more. Soon he took up the practice of spending nights alone in a cave near Mecca. This awakening of a spiritual "call" in midlife is familiar to us today.[1]

As Jung pointed out, midlife is like the moment of midday when the brilliant noonday sun is at its peak. At just that point, its zenith, it begins its downward decline, the slope of the second half of life. In this verse, along with the admonishment for what we would call "care of aged parents," the human being is reminded of the need for repentance and for "surrender" (*Islam*).

There is no single sura of the Qur'an devoted to the human life course as such. But in different suras and different verses a set of common themes does emerge and a consistent message can be discerned. Some themes concern ethical relationships between parents and children, often exemplified by prophetic personalities such as Moses or Abraham. Others concern a specific life stage, ranging from the fetus (described in remarkably precise anatomical detail) to the frailty of old age. Related to these stages of life are injunctions of the religious law (*Sharia*), such as about the care of women during and after pregnancy or concerning the preparation of a will (obligatory). Finally, other verses are preoccupied with broader cosmic principles such as the meaning of time and eternity or the Final Judgment.

There is little in the Qur'an that would lead us to think of old age as a separate stage of life in the way it was understood in Hinduism, for example, as one of four stages of life (*Darshanas*).[2] In the Hindu framework there are clearly demarcated stages with distinct obligations. In Islam religious duties continue into old age as in other periods of life, and obligations are equal for men and women. Islamic societies over time developed rites of passage for major life events such as birth, transition to adulthood, marriage, and death,[3] but there are no sacraments tied to these events as there are in Christianity. Moreover, Islamic culture never developed anything comparable to the motif of stages of life evident in Western medieval or Renaissance iconography.[4]

The Qur'an offers little idealization of childhood as a distinct stage of life. There is nothing in the Qur'an comparable to the New Testament image of becoming "born again," as in the story of Nicodemus, or becoming "as a little child" by accepting faith. In the Islamic perspective faith is critical for salvation, but true faith is not opposed to rational knowledge of the adult mind. Thus the opposition between reason and faith so characteristic of Christian sensibility did not develop in classical Islam. On the contrary, the great period of Islamic civilization was one of extraordinary receptivity toward science and Greek learning.

The Islamic tradition, however, did recognize different forms of knowledge. There is a famous saying (*Hadith*) of the Prophet Muhammad, "Seek knowledge, even [as far as] in China." Along with rational knowledge of the natural sciences, Islam has recognized spiritual knowledge (*Ma'arifat*), which was cultivated by the mystical branch of Islam known as Sufism.[5]

But here again faith and mystical knowledge were usually understood as complementary, not opposed to each other. Contemporary Islamic fundamentalism, therefore, in its opposition to Western secular reason constitutes for many a betrayal of the high traditions of Islamic civilization at its peak.

From a developmental standpoint it is significant that Islam was, from the outset, a revelation given to a mature individual and directed at mature people, not in any way an idealization of the naive or childlike state. The message of the Qur'an is addressed to men and women of adult age and rational mind. The holy book constantly assumes that faith is possible for anyone with intelligence enough to see and contemplate the signs of the universe around us.

Everything that lives has its "stated term," and so has a human life. It follows for Islamic bioethics that it would be wrong to try to unduly extend life that is naturally coming to its end, but it would also be wrong to commit suicide to shorten life. Similar to Catholic doctrine, Islam would tend to approve something like "natural death." Indeed, the Qur'an repeatedly refers to old age, like death, as a natural part of the human cycle. The weakness of childhood is followed by full adulthood, then by the frailty of extreme age. Death, of course, can interrupt the life course at any time. Moreover, old age may be accompanied by its own special trials: "God created you, then He will gather you to Him; and some of you will be kept back unto the vilest state of life, that after knowing somewhat, they may know nothing; God is All-knowing, All-powerful" (16:83).

The "vilest state" mentioned here could be an allusion to the dismal spectacle of dementia, a fate not inevitable, but common enough among the oldest old. Even if mental impairment is avoided, the oldest old are likely to experience some form of chronic illness and weakness, and weakness too is part of the human condition and as such is intended by all-powerful Allah in his wisdom.

The frailty of the oldest old, the waxing and waning of an individual life, can be compared to the cycle of the growth and decline of civilizations mentioned repeatedly in the Qur'an. In the microcosm (individual life) and in the macrocosm (civilization) there is a natural cycle and a sign for those who have eyes to see.

Yet the frailty of old age, the waxing and waning of an individual life, is not the whole story. Every spiritual tradition recognizes two dimensions to human existence: the body, which obeys a cycle of decline, and the spirit, which can break free from the cycle with the gift of grace. An interesting feature of the Qur'anic view is its depiction of old age as a time of miraculous fecundity. Here the Qur'an reaches back to the story of Sarah and Abraham from the Hebrew Bible, although Abraham is also one of the most important prophets in the Qur'an. When Sarah is told that she will bear a child in old age, she is skeptical. Yet she is reminded that Allah need only command a thing by saying "Be!" and it is.

This image of miraculous fecundity in later life reminds us that old age need not be a period of absolute loss. The passage of time weakens the body and diminishes some opportunities. But our contemporary ideal of "successful aging" presents another agenda: decrement with compensation. From a spiritual standpoint, along with the decrements of age there are compensations of faith. The passage of time reveals to one who has faith the transcendent nature of life and of the universe.

Even when time has passed, it is never too late to return to Allah. The verse inscribed on the grave of Rumi reads: "Ours is not a caravan of despair. Return, return, even if you have broken your vows a hundred times, return!" Even God is described as "oft-returning" (that is, forgiving) and from the opening line of the Qur'an God is repeatedly described as the "All-Merciful" (*ar-Rahman*).

The Qur'an does not dwell on the linear stages of life because it sees all created things as caught up in a vast cosmic cycle, proceeding from their origin in God and bound finally to return again to God. It is human illusion to imagine oneself self-sufficient or independent. For the Qur'an it is not the detailed stages of the life course that are significant but rather the human being's origin and final end.

The Holy Qur'an repeatedly invokes this totality of the human life cycle as a "sign" of what is our final nature and destiny: namely, the return to God. The measure of humanity's finite term of life is just a reflection of the creative act by which the universe itself exists: "Sure We have created everything in measure" (54:49). The Qur'an constantly reminds human beings of our embryological origins: a sperm drop, a blood clot, a lump of flesh. No matter how far we travel from this point, our origin remains humble: "Has not man regarded how that We created him of a sperm drop?" (36:77).

As a creature the human being starts out life as an embryo, a "clot" as the Qur'an describes it in a sura of that title. It is surely significant that the Qur'an devotes so many verses to describe this embryological transformation but none at all to the stages of adult life as such. It is as if, against the background of birth and death, all stages of life are collapsed into an instant. According to the Prophet Muhammad, this world is no more than a single hour.

Nonetheless, the last stage of life, old age, has also a meaning of its own, as Jung suggested. Old age is important because, at the end of the journey of life, old age and death bring to light what is the basic human situation at all times: namely, complete dependency upon God and God's mercy. It is only when one is ungrateful or forgetful that this existential fact is forgotten. The last stage of life, like the first, becomes important as a "reminder" (*Dhikr*) of what is always the fundamental cosmic situation.

One contemporary version of idealized old age stresses autonomy and independence above all things. For such a stance the fact of death constitutes the ultimate proof of dependency. Themes of death and dying are prominent in the Qur'an as well as in Islamic traditions and sacred law.[6]

The Qur'an is completely unsentimental in its description of death. Resurrection and judgment are promised, but no one, not even the prophets, can escape death. Death is an expected fact of life, and the sacred law (*Sharia*) requires believers to prepare in advance for death: for instance, to plan for disposal of property. The Qur'an offers detailed instruction on the law of inheritance.

However, if death is a natural event, it is also a symbol of something else. From the Islamic standpoint aging and death are not to be construed as purely natural events but also as "signs" of the divine order of the cosmos. In turn, the last stage of life from an Islamic point of view assumes a positive character as a period of personal transcendence.

This opportunity for transcendence in the midst of loss, enunciated in the sura "Al-Asr," is a fundamental theme of all the later suras of the Qur'an. What appear in the text of the Qur'an as "later" suras were chronologically the first ones to be revealed. These suras convey the theme of absolute divine transcendence with stark power and the austere rhythm of final judgment. Some of these suras are "The Expanding" (dealing with the rhythm of the spiritual journey), "Power" (the realm of the Spirit), "The Unbelievers" (tolerance), "Sincerity" (God's incomparable nature), "Daybreak" (the problem of evil), and "Mankind" (temptation and the need for guidance).

Again and again in these suras a fundamental existential and psychological issue is at stake: namely, the recurrent tendency of human beings to think ourselves guiltless or not responsible for our actions, to project blame outside ourselves, and at the same time to imagine ourselves wholly independent and self-sufficient. In fact, both the psychological tendencies of projection and invulnerability are aspects of the same condition, a kind of narcissism[7] that spiritual practice seeks to overcome. Narcissism becomes a particular threat in old age inasmuch as repeated losses can become a narcissistic wound that on the one hand aggravates isolation, self-pity and bitterness, or on the other hand removes illusions of self-sufficiency. The experience of aging and the imminence of death, then, can open up the possibility of final accountability for one's actions, which we sometimes witness in the process of life review in old age.

Aging and mortality can be positive occasions for self-knowledge, in accordance with a *Hadith* favored by the Sufis: "He who knows himself knows his Lord." Indeed, death in Islam is not merely a biological fact but acquires a deeper, mystical meaning in accordance with a statement by Ali, son-in-law of the Prophet, Fourth Caliph, and fountainhead of the Sufi tradition: "Man is asleep. At death, he will awaken." Ali's statement converges with the injunction of the Prophet: "Die before you die." This intentional or spiritual death constitutes the extinction of the ego or in psychological terms, the overcoming of narcissism. The process is described by mystics in similar terms the world over, and the account given by Sufism parallels what we find in yoga, in Zen, and among the Jewish and Christian mystics. Thus in the Sufi tradition death takes on a completely different meaning from that for the ordinary person:

"He who deems death to be lovely as Joseph gives up his soul in ransom for it; he who deems it to be like the wolf turns back from the path of salvation.

"Everyone's death is of the same quality as himself, my lad; to the enemy of God an enemy, to the friend of God, a friend. . . .

"Your fear of death is really fear of yourself; see what it is from which you are fleeing!"[8] It is well known that Islamic sacred art avoids figurative imagery or the depiction of discrete recognizable forms. Islamic art prefers calligraphy or the arabesque to any kind of portraiture. Indeed, Islamic sacred art, like Qur'anic Scripture, tends toward the extinction of any object that might become an idol or serve to veil the ego from Absolute Reality. Sacred art, like meditation, is ultimately a contemplation of the Void, as the Buddhists might put it. Here again death acquires an important symbolic meaning. From the Islamic or Sufi perspective death is not to be seen as the end point of a temporal career as much as the discovery of the reality of extinction, or "no self" (*Fana*), which is a traditional theme of mystics both in Islam[9] and Christianity.[10]

For the mystic, who lives in what Meister Eckhart called the "Eternal Now," each moment of life, along with the total life course itself, becomes a sign pointing toward our origin and destiny in God. But the sign takes on different appearances depending on the perspective we adopt. Human time can be represented symbolically by the circle or the line: one figure closed, returning on itself, the other open and unbounded toward the future. Both the circle and the line are symbols of infinity, but the meaning is different in each case.

Modern secular existence dwells almost exclusively in the domain of linear time, the line indefinitely projected out into the future, whether individual or collective. In contrast to this modern linear-narrative self as perpetually moving toward the future, the Islamic mystics understand human time and the cycle of life itself as a circular movement in which both spiritual and physical death signify a return to God as origin and destiny. The Islamic mystics like Rumi, Attar, and Junayd again and again went back to this spiritual perspective on the meaning of death as a "return" to the origin.[11]

The idea is entirely Qur'anic, as expressed in the following verse, recited traditionally by pious Muslims whenever a death is announced: "Verily, we belong to Allah and unto Him we are returning."

To sum up, then, the Islamic vision of aging and death: First, it is utterly realistic about the human condition and devoid of sentimentality or evasion. Here the Islamic view is in sharp contrast with the practices and attitudes of modern culture, in which death is a taboo topic. The denial of death in modern times represents, from an Islamic view, a pathological condition, a flight from reality. Old age, the afternoon of life, is a time when this illusion falls away and we see that we are finite creatures, creatures who will die. Is it surprising, then, that the modern outlook entails not only a denial of death but a denial of aging as well?

The significance of old age, indeed of the human life course itself, is simply that of a window through which we glimpse the reality of our human condition. That reality, the Qur'an assures us, is not simply loss and disintegration but something more. That "something more" amounts to hope and faith. Faith is not to be understood as a childlike suspension of intelligence but rather as a fulfillment of intelligence.[12] The message of revelation is a message "for those possessed of minds." The ultimate question is the oft-repeated query of the Qur'an itself: "Are there any that will remember?" Perhaps in this question, more than any other, lies the greatest challenge to modern culture with its repeated tendency to banish old age and death, to forget or cover up what is always our cosmic situation as mortal, dependent human beings. The challenge is simply this: Can we find a way to integrate aging and death into a vision of the course of life as a whole? Can we find a way to remember and then to say yes to life?

Questions for Discussion

1. Since most Christians are unaware of the basic beliefs of Islam, invite a Muslim from the community to discuss these beliefs. If this is not possible, ask the pastor or Christian educator to do this, relying on such guides as Houston Smith, The Religions of Man.
2. Why do you think Westerners have not considered reading the Qur'an?
3. Is there a relationship between the Third Commandment and the Islamic commandment about filial piety?
4. Why is age forty such a turning point for Muslims? How can you relate that to Jung's view of middle age, discussed in Chapter II?
5. How does the Qur'an use the story of Abraham and Sarah to illustrate "the marvelous fecundity" (productivity) of old age?
6. In an adult class on world religions, ask one of the members to tell what the poet Rumi said about old age.
7. Islam teaches that old age and death open up "the possibility of final accountability for one's action." Can you see a connection between this view and the Christian view of faith review?
8. The author implies that in Islam death is more of a reality than in Western culture, which still denies death and considers it a taboo subject. Discuss this different perspective.
9. For Islam, old age involves not only a period of absolute loss, but also a time for the compensations of faith. How does this speak to the denial of aging in America, or our preoccupation with the view that growing old is always a fun time?
10. Discuss the saying of Ali, "Man is asleep, but at death he will awaken."

Notes

1. Harry R. Moody and David Carroll, *The Five Stages of the Soul: Charting the Spiritual Passages that Shape Our Lives* (New York: Doubleday, 1998).
2. Sudhir Kakar, "The Human Life Cycle: The Traditional Hindu View and the Psychology of Erik Erikson," *Philosophy East and West* 18 (July), pp.127–136.
3. Frances Robinson, *Atlas of the Islamic World Since 1500* (New York: Facts on File Publications, 1987).
4. Elizabeth Sears, *The Ages of Man: Medieval Interpretations of the Life Cycle* (Princeton, NJ: Princeton University Press, 1986).
5. Eva de Vitray-Meyerovitch, *Rumi and the Sufism*, Editions du Seuil, 1977 (Sausalito, CA: Post-Apollo Press, 1987).

6. Thomas J. O'Shaughnessy, *Muhammad's Thoughts on Death: A Thematic Study of the Quranic Data* (Leiden: E. J. Brill, 1969); Jane I. Smith and Yvonne Yazbeck Haddad, *The Islamic Understanding of Death and Resurrection* (New York: Oxford University Press, 2002).

7. Mark Epstein, *Thoughts Without a Thinker: Psychotherapy from a Buddhist Perspective* (New York: Basic Books, 1995).

8. Rumi, *Mathnawi*, trans. Nicholson, 1970, p. 62.

9. Seyyed H. Nasr, *Islamic Art and Spirituality* (Albany, NY: State University of New York Press, 1987).

10. Bernadette Roberts, *The Path to No-Self: Life at the Center* (Albany, NY: State University of New York Press, 1991).

11. William C. Chittick, *The Sufi Path of Love: The Spiritual Teachings of Rumi* (Albany, NY: State University of New York Press, 1983).

12. Frithjof Schuon, *Understanding Islam* (Bloomington, IN: World Wisdom Books, 1998).

Ethical Issues in Aging

Isabel W. Rogers

Choice-Making

Dennis the Menace and his pal Joey are strolling down the street eating ice cream cones. Says Dennis, in his lofty wisdom: "It's easy to know right from wrong, Joey. Wrong is when everybody *yells*."

That is a wonderful child's-eye view of ethics, but we adults have learned that making moral decisions is not quite that simple. The more years we live, the more situations we face in which there really are few easy answers, few really satisfactory answers. We live and make our decisions in a world of tremendous complexity.

A century ago things seemed less complicated. Change did not come so rapidly; society had time to work out clear patterns of right and wrong, and individuals could work with those patterns as they faced moral choices in their own lives. In our day, however, we keep encountering decisions that are simply unprecedented.

Technological changes constantly confront us with wholly new situations. For instance, how are we to protect children from pornography on the Internet without destroying the freedom of adults? In 1906 there was no Internet, and no one dreamed of such a possibility. Demographic change has likewise brought unprecedented choices. The fast-growing population of the elderly poses problems we have never had to face or think through before. How shall we care for loved ones whose lives have essentially ended but who go on "living"? In 1906 people died of pneumonia or scarlet fever or tuberculosis; they rarely lived long enough to be struck down by our degenerative diseases of old age like Alzheimer's.

The result is that in our time clear, simple answers to moral issues are hard to come by. And because that reality is uncomfortable to live with, people often turn to some authority—the Bible, perhaps, or the church—seeking final, authoritative solutions that will excuse them from thinking and asking questions. And then the temptation is to brand as heretical or even non-Christian the people who keep on asking the disquieting questions.

We need to remember that there never has been total unanimity about how to make moral decisions. Down through the centuries there have been three classic ways of approaching moral choices— different from each other, but all authentically Christian, all biblical. People who differ with each other in their approach may come out with different decisions, so we need to recognize that equally conscientious Christians can deal with issues thoughtfully and responsibly but disagree on the outcome.

Let us look briefly at ways of coming at moral choices—any moral choices—and then keep these in the background of our thinking as we discuss some of the issues related to aging in our society.

The American theologian H. Richard Niebuhr uses three metaphors to explain these patterns. He speaks of the human being as craftsperson, who makes things according to a design; as citizen, who seeks to do his duty, to be obedient to law; and as answerer, who gives appropriate responses to actions upon him and around him. We will explore each in turn.[1]

The craftsperson—seeking good outcomes

A cabinetmaker has a picture—on paper, or in his mind—of the table he wants to produce. He assembles tools and materials and then sets out to make a table that matches what he has pictured. His actions are designed to move him toward a goal.

There are many thinkers, says Niebuhr, who use this image to describe one way of coming at ethics. They ask the question, What results do we seek? What is the good we are aiming for, or the evil we want to avoid? Then, having ascertained the goal, we seek to do those things that move us toward the goal rather than away from it. One judges the action by asking about its *results:* does this action bring about the good we seek? And no matter how sincere our intentions or motives, the moral quality of what we do is determined by the good it produces or the evil it prevents.

Legislators in one state, debating the state's assisted-suicide legislation, warned of tragic consequences that might follow the legislative decision. Some said that to approve the law would open a Pandora's box of evils: it would cheapen human life, and it would give opportunity for family members, with inheritance in mind, to persuade elderly parents to take their own lives. Others argued that because advanced technology can now force people to keep on "living" when suffering has made life unbearable, to refuse to pass the legislation was to condemn many to a dehumanized existence.

The question here is, What will be the results—what the good we can achieve, what the evil we can avert?

Now, people will not always agree on what results we ought to seek or how to achieve them. That means, of course, that even people who agree on this approach may still differ in their concrete decisions. Moreover, nobody can possibly anticipate all the potential consequences of any given action; the network of human causality is far too complicated for that to be possible. But the point is, one way to make moral judgments is to figure out what we are aiming for and how we can move toward it. This can be called an ethic of *results*, or an ethic of the *good*.

The citizen—obeying the law

A second group of thinkers, says Niebuhr, organize moral reflection around the human being as one under law. We live out our lives having to answer to rules and laws, from "Eat your spinach" to "Pay your income tax." This provides a symbol to help us understand the moral life: one has to figure out what is *right*, and then do it, regardless of consequences.

Here is a woman who conscientiously files her tax return and pays the full tax, even though many of her friends have devised ways to dodge their fair share, and indeed they laugh at her for being naive. It is clear that what she does has no effect whatsoever on her friends; they are not persuaded by her example to change their way of doing things. She does what she does simply because her conscience tells her that it is her duty, whatever the results might be.

In this pattern a person does what he or she does because it is right, period. Actions are judged not by the good they produce or the evil they avert, but by the rightness of the act.

Christians, of course, find their ultimate duty in God's law, revealed in the Bible. But there are problems here. It is not always easy to take a quite general commandment from the Bible—say, "You shall not kill"—and interpret it for our day. Is this an absolute prohibition of war? Christians certainly do not all agree on that. Is this an absolute prohibition of capital punishment? Honest Christians have always debated that.

Moreover, many specific biblical injunctions simply do not relate to twenty-first century life. In Exodus 23:19 the writer commands, "You shall not boil a kid in its mother's milk." Most of us would wonder why anybody would want to do that, anyway!

This approach to ethics, however, is the way of choice for many Christians. They seek to do the right, as they discern the right—whether it does any good or not, even if it is costly for themselves and others. This can be called an ethic of *duty*, or the *right*.

The answerer—doing what is fitting

Niebuhr discerns a third group, who find the best way of coming at ethics in the notion of *response*. What are we like in our moral living? We are like persons answering questions addressed to us or meeting challenges and giving responses. It is like driving a car, constantly responding to what is happening all around us. The road turns, we turn the steering wheel; a car comes out of a side road ahead, we lift our foot from the accelerator, alert to see what the other driver will do.

Many thinkers argue that this is the kind of thing we do in our moral life. Making moral choices is not so much a matter of ideals and goals or of laws as it is of people, needs, relationships, and happenings. Our task is to find the *fitting* thing, the *appropriate* thing, to do in the situation. We respond to prior actions—someone has acted upon us—and we anticipate further action and response.

A couple has been out for the evening and upon their return, just as they walk into the living room, the older of two children hauls off and strikes the younger. Wise parents do not leap to judgment and immediately punish the older one. They ask the baby-sitter, "What is going on here? Who's been doing what?" (It may well be that the younger child has been goading the older one all evening long, and the older one is finally striking back.) The parents seek to respond in an appropriate way, given the dynamics of what has been happening.

For the Christian, of course, the central question is, "What is *God* doing in our midst, and what must we do in response?" And we seek to respond to God, fitting our response in the whole network of human events.

Obviously this is immensely complicated. We will never grasp all the complexity of what is happening and the meanings that lie behind what people are doing. But the fact is that we act in this responsive way more than we realize. If we are responsible people, we cannot ignore what is happening around us, and we must seek to do the appropriate things.

Here we have three ways of approaching moral choices. One is concerned with *results*—how can we bring about the most good? The second is concerned with *duty*, or *law*—what does my conscience tell me is the right thing to do, whatever the results may be? The third is concerned with the appropriate *response* to what is happening, always seeking to do what is fitting.

It is important to say again that all three of these are Christian, all three biblical. We need to recognize, then, that responsible Christians may come at decision-making from any of these approaches, or any combination of them. And almost inevitably there will be differences among us in the choices we end up making. It behooves none of us to condemn those who disagree on particular moral issues, as though we were Christian and they were not. Rather, we need to listen carefully to each other, knowing that we can learn from others and have our own perspectives broadened and deepened.

What we are talking about here is *ethics*—the enterprise of reflecting on our moral choices. "Morality" refers to the actual pattern of the choices we make; "ethics" is *thinking about* those choices. Every society, every group, every person operates according to some morality, some pattern of choices. When we stand back from those choices, reflect on them, talk about them, we are engaging in ethical discourse.

As we talk ethically, then, about choices related to the experience of the elderly, we face questions that are often agonizingly complicated, with few assured answers. We need the best thinking of all of us, in all our diversity, as we seek to serve the God who cares for us all.

Choices

The decisions encountered by those of us who are in our later years or who have responsibility to care for older family members are diverse and often deeply troubling and painful. In this brief space we can explore only a few of those choices, so we will look at three clusters of issues that seem to be of widespread concern in our society.

Long-term care for the vulnerable aged

An out-of-state friend called. Her mother is in an assisted-living facility, her acuity gradually fading with Alzheimer's. The mother has been receiving antipsychotic drugs to calm her fears, but the medications were making her sleep most of the time, day and night. So the nurse, sensing that her patient was not having much of a life, suggested that they wean her from the heavy dosage to give her more time of consciousness. The inevitable result: wakefulness and alertness particularly at night, when she restlessly charged up and down the halls, plaguing the staff with her fears and complaints.

The administrator, alert to the problems for the staff and fearing for the safety of the patient, called for a return to heavier sedation; the patient needed to sleep through the night.

My friend on the phone, a perceptive and realistic person, mused about that. "I care about Mother's welfare, and I want for her those longer periods of alertness. But the administrator holds the power—power to ask my mother to leave if she causes too much trouble. Then what will we do? So—whose side should I be on?"

The question is a perennial one, and an unanswerable one: whose welfare should predominate in those medical decisions? That of the elder person? Of the medical staff? Of the patient's family? This conflict over values arises again and again; it is an example of many of the issues faced in long-term care of the elderly who are in slow decline.

1. *The first, hard question to arise must be faced by the family: Can we care for this loved one at home, or does the person need to go into institutional care?* Already the family is dealing with radical changes in relationships, with accustomed roles upset. The "children" (now middle-aged) have through the years depended on their parents for wisdom and support; now it is the older person who has become dependent. A myriad of dislocations are developing in the family's structure of intergenerational responsibilities.

A great majority of families opt for home care as long as possible, and though some can have professional help, most often care is provided by the family or close friends—twenty-five million men and women at last count. Many times the central issue is money. Unless the aged parent has sufficient income, many families have no real choice: they *must* keep that parent at home because they find the cost of institutional care beyond their reach. And further painful choices follow. Children still at home need medical care and education and clothes; many a family simply cannot cover all these expenses plus the cost of elder care even if both parents work in the marketplace.

The cost goes far beyond the monetary. A heavy price is often paid in personal stress and strained family relationships and, in many cases, hours that are not available to give to the needs of the children or the marriage.

Even when money is not an important issue, however, placing elders in institutional care against their expressed will is still a heartbreaking choice. This raises early on what is one of the most basic conflicts in all long-term care situations: the elderly person's need for autonomy and dignity in personal decision-making over the need for others to decide what is best for that person's long-term welfare. In many cases it would in fact be more beneficial for the patient to be in an institution with professional care. It would likely benefit the family or friends to be freed of the responsibility of physical caregiving, as well as reduce the stress and even danger for the elder. But if the elder resists, what about that autonomy that is part of our very humanity?

Dealing with that requires asking the question of competency. Is this elder person competent to handle the realities of living? If not, others will feel that they must take on the decision-making on the elder's behalf. But assessing competency is not a simple task. At its core, competency is understood to refer to the ability to manage one's own person and to manage one's own property. More specifically in the medical context, the question is, does the patient have sufficient cognitive ability and sufficient emotional strength to understand proposed treatments and their consequences—in other words, is the person able to take a responsible part in decisions about medical care and treatments?

That can be difficult to determine. The level of competency can fluctuate in an elderly person—from one time of day to another, from one social context to another. It is certainly affected by general health, or the physical disorders the person suffers. Institutionalization itself can sometimes have what can only be called a stupefying effect.

All of this adds to the complications in deciding between home care and institutional care. Given a genuine desire to respect the elder's independence, how serious must the incompetency be before loved ones feel compelled to take over the decision-making? And if the elder does stay at home, at what cost is that to the family and the family's relationships?

2. *When that competency is very clearly and very severely diminished and the elder person must move to institutional living, a whole host of new problems arise.* The decisions may be made predominantly by others, but those decisions will still reflect the difficult tensions between two concerns: First, what is in the patient's best interest? The priority here is placed on the patient's welfare, often as medical professionals determine that welfare. Second, what would the patient want? What would be the patient's decision if the patient were still competent to make decisions? Oftentimes family members or close friends take the lead in determinations of this kind.

One way to preserve something of the older person's autonomy is to discover ahead of time what that person's values are—that is, provide an opportunity for the elder to make choices before impairment develops. An older adult may well have lived a good, full life, developing wisdom through rich experience. Through the years the person has been working out values and living by them. Families and care professionals can work at ascertaining those values, especially in the early stages of mental deterioration. In this way they can develop criteria for making judgments later on, when the older person is unable to participate.

Many in the medical profession call this "substituted judgment." It enables care providers to follow what they think to be the authentic desires of the patient and in this way to preserve something of the patient's autonomy at a time when the individual cannot personally make the decisions that are needed.

This would call for discussions before a crisis arises, enabling a patient to make choices about what kind of care should be given when his or her mental faculties become impaired. Health care providers could take responsibility for discussing with patients the kinds of choices that might come up in the future. Members of the patient's family or dear friends generally (though not always!) know best what the person's values are, and they need to engage in frank discussions with the patient, painful though that can be. In those discussions the elder can bestow a wondrous gift on the younger family members or friends—the gift of trust. The decisions to come will be difficult and often laden with guilt for the adult children. The parent who says, "I trust you to do the best for me because I know you love me" can help to ease the burden their loved ones will have to carry in the future.

Legal instruments like a living will or a durable power of attorney might seem like abstract and impersonal documents; they need not be, however, for they can enshrine the very personal values of the individual who has made them, enabling that person to participate, in a way, in medical choices to be made in the future. Advance directives of various kinds can express the older adult's hopes and concerns for the future and give a kind of "informed consent" for medical treatments—or the withdrawal of medical treatments—at a later time.

What is best for the patient's welfare? What would the wishes of the patient be if he or she were able to express them? The tension between those concerns will not go away, and decision-making will not be simple or painless, no matter how many preparations are made in advance. But the potential conflict between the patient's welfare and the patient's autonomy can at least be somewhat mitigated if all the people involved are willing to talk together, realistically, about future possibilities.

Terrie Wetle of Brown University's Department of Community Health summed up the point of this issue some years ago. She noted that discussing these considerations would make the issues surrounding them clearer. Although decision-making will remain difficult, open discussion and consideration of the ethical issues and the values that undergird them will enable better decision-making and will result in a better life for the patient and greater satisfaction for those providing care.[2]

Hard Choices at the End of Life

In the late 1980s the medical community was rocked when a young medical resident frankly admitted that he had helped a patient to die. Her suffering was intense; her death was imminent; she begged for relief. He gave this account of his action:

> I injected the morphine intravenously. Within seconds her breathing slowed to a normal rate. Her eyes closed and her features softened. She seemed restful at last. The older woman stroked the hair of the now sleeping patient. I waited for the inevitable next effect of depressing the respiratory drive . . . the breathing slowed . . . became irregular, then ceased. It's over, Debbie.[3]

This may very well happen often, but few talk about it. It reflects the kind of crisis being faced by increasing numbers of people in our time, and it confronts us with decisions that often the old rules do not seem to fit. Kenneth Vaux has called for an ethic that transcends reason and convention, one that is rooted in the situation of the patient on one hand and in "the ultimate ground of being" on the other. He said that the crises of end-of-life decisions bring us in contact with mysteries of life and death and face to face with "the human impulses of risk, guilt and sacrifice."[4]

The precipitating factor in all this, of course, is what Joseph Fletcher has called the "protracting capabilities" of modern resuscitative medicine, the ability to prolong the life process artificially.[5] Even when the body fails, physicians can bring the patient back to life, using machines that enable the body to function.

Polls indicate, however, that many, many Americans recognize that such treatments are not always beneficial. Especially with older people, they can often simply prolong unbearable suffering. There has developed in the past decade or two a broad consensus supporting the notion that elderly people in great suffering and facing imminent death should be allowed to die. This does not mean approval of such action as that taken in Debbie's case, where the resident actively hastened his patient's death. It is, rather, widespread support of withholding "extraordinary treatment"—any treatment in the absence of which a person would almost surely slip into death. A majority of people would probably consider it morally acceptable, for instance, to take a patient off a respirator if the physician has determined that death is both imminent and inevitable.

The ideal so often expressed is "natural death." When the body is unable to sustain itself and it will most certainly not recover that ability, then there is no moral requirement that we use extraordinary means to sustain it. The physician is to keep the patient as comfortable as possible and then, in a sense, stand back and allow nature to take its course. It is the sense of "a right to die"—the right to choose to die rather than suffer through endless treatments that cannot stave off death for more than a short while. And since in the majority of such cases the patient is not able really to make the choice, it is assumed that families and friends can act, seeking to carry out what the patient would want.

Whatever the extent of public support, however, these are not always simple decisions. For one thing, what is a "terminal condition"? Alzheimer's disease can last through long agonizing months and years. At what point in the disease does one "allow the patient to die"?

Another complicating factor is that "natural death" may not be quick and easy. We remember that when Karen Ann Quinlan, after long public debate, was unhooked from the respirator, she lived on for almost ten years. Ending treatments does not guarantee an easy death.

Differentiating between *allowing to die* and *causing to die* is still a matter of great concern. Withholding extraordinary treatment and seeking only to keep the patient comfortable is certainly not the same as ending that life by injection, as the young physician did with Debbie. The distinction, however, can be a shaky one, and families and physicians facing that decision properly feel genuine moral anguish. On the one hand, the reality is that when we turn off a respirator, it is our action that hastens the death. But on the other hand, if it was the disease that caused the breathing incapacity, then one could say it was the disease that took the life. We are dealing with the impenetrable mystery of life and death, and we face these choices, as Kenneth Vaux put it, with "risk, guilt, and sacrifice."

Perhaps the most difficult and painful choice of all comes when one asks, "What treatments are to be ended?" Does this include nutrition and hydration? Do we remove the tubes providing food and drink? How could providing basic sustenance be considered "extraordinary treatment"?

Many who give much thought to this question would say that treatment is treatment, and giving food and drink in an artificial way is as "extraordinary" as enabling a person to breathe. Yet the long moral tradition in Western culture requires that we feed the hungry and give drink to the thirsty. For Jesus this was one of the basic duties of citizens of God's kingdom (see Matthew 25), and medical tradition has always required that the physician give comfort and care when a cure is impossible. Many have reminded us that we cannot know what goes on inside the mind of an unconscious person or what it is like to die for lack of fluids.

All these considerations make it imperative that this whole question be approached in genuine humility, with a deep sense of caution.

One hopeful development is an increasing concern for the comfort of the dying patient, engendering widespread discussion of "palliative care." Where there is no possibility of cure, medical facilities can focus on relieving the effects, especially the pain, of an incurable illness. The term "palliative" comes from the Latin word for "cloak"—referring not to covering up treatment that is inadequate but rather to protecting a patient from the most painful aspects of an illness that is incurable. It has been suggested that often patients want to die because their pain is not being properly controlled or no one is working with them to end despair and isolation and restore hope.

The columnist Ellen Goodman wrote approvingly of a state board of medical examiners that disciplined a doctor for undertreating pain in his patients. The physician had once prescribed Tylenol for a man dying of cancer, and he had refused morphine for an eighty-two-year-old man with congestive heart failure (he feared that the patient would become addicted!). In the past, said Goodman, doctors were penalized for giving too much medication, but now the health community is recognizing that patients have a right to pain management. "We have finally embarked on a long-delayed discussion about the need for palliative care, for compassionate treatment, for understanding the real experience of illness; physical pain affects attitudes about living and dying."[6]

Goodman titled her column, "Easing Pain Is Doctor's Responsibility." Indeed, and it is the responsibility of all of us, each in our own way. At a conference in Toronto on palliative care a spokesman reported: "All we're saying is that this fear that someone is crossing the line and getting into euthanasia is really detracting from a far more important issue, which is that people shouldn't die in pain. . . . Everyone is trying to improve the quality of the life of patients before they die."[7]

Indeed, "quality of life" is more and more being considered to include not only freedom from pain but also genuine comfort and human dignity as life ebbs away. It is the need for warm baths and cleanliness, for personal care—shaving, having nails trimmed. It is having the chance to mend hurtful relationships, forgiving and being forgiven. Personal desires like these are more and more being included in advance directives. They reflect the reality that dying is not merely physical; it is emotional and spiritual as well. It is the whole person who is passing through the event of death.

Medical technology has brought us to a new day. It is giving us wondrous possibilities of healing, and where that is not yet possible, the gift of longer lives. But through the ages technological progress has always been a two-edged sword; bane and blessing come as twins yoked together.

We need to face realistically the limits to what medicine can do for the debilitating diseases of old age. But we all have the possibility of working together—patients, doctors, families—to make it possible for a person's last days to be marked by human dignity, by hope and peace and love.

Responsible Choices in Sexuality

"My life has been very lonely." That is one of the realities of the later years, for old age is a time of losses. Retirement brings the loss not only of an assured role in society but also of the colleagues who enriched each day's work. The friends who were always available for recreation times now are becoming ill, or are dying. And most devastating is the loss of a spouse to death or debilitating disease. The warm mutuality of two lives intertwined has ended, and feelings of isolation are inevitable.

The deep human need for companionship poses all sorts of dilemmas for older adults and their families and friends. For instance, what happens to the relatively healthy person whose spouse develops Alzheimer's or some form of dementia? Is the healthy spouse then barred from intimacy with others—especially when that intimacy might include physical expression? Or what about the surviving spouse when the other has died, but who for financial or other reasons is not able to remarry? People in these situations are all around us. How shall we act compassionately and nonjudgmentally toward them, keeping in mind both our Christian commitment to faithfulness in marriage and our recognition that few moral questions come to us with clear, simple, black-and-white responses?

The reality of sexuality

One source of confusion is our tendency to think of "sexuality" in only romantic or even erotic terms, when the reality is that being male or female is an integral part of our very constitution as human beings, and it colors all of our responses to the world around us. The biblical writers celebrated the goodness of the body and of the physical life, including the sexual dimension. "Male and female [God] created them," says Genesis 1. And "God saw everything that he had made, and indeed, it was very good."

Now it is as bodies that we make contact with the outside world, contact that depends on our senses—primarily sight and hearing and touch. We look at our neighbors and establish communication with them. We listen to the words they speak, and we speak in response, and each knows that the other is *there* and responding. Perhaps it is touch that most closely links us with others; a touch can give us a sense of connectedness as nothing else can.

This means that if God creates us as bodies that are male or female, then it is as sexual beings that we are related to our neighbors—*all* our neighbors, not just those of the other sex. To love is to reach out, to be connected to others, to be involved in other lives, and this is manifested in a whole range of bodily expressions, all the way from a glance and a nod to the oneness of sexual intercourse.

Clearly, then, sexuality is not just one part of our being, a part of us that can disappear with age; we are sexual beings from birth to death. The *kinds* of communication may change, but there will always be a need for some kind of intimacy, for some sharing that makes us know we matter.

Let us look at two settings in which the need to be related, to be in communion, can raise problems for older persons.

Life in an institution

In almost any series of interviews done among older adults in institutional care, the universal human need for intimacy comes through loud and clear. Listen to some comments from a fine video documentary.[8] Older persons speak of the need for touch and companionship, the need to be held and stroked:

"I show my sexuality in companionship. Most of all, I need the reassurance of a hug." "It's having a confidante who will listen and not turn away." "It's the need for closeness and caring, and I get it in all sorts of different ways." One widow talks about being with a male neighbor (with no thought of marriage). "We like to link arms with each other as we walk down the hall. That way we can *feel* the closeness. It's comfortable."

When older persons enter institutions they do not leave these feelings behind. But oftentimes the yearning for intimacy is construed as pushing for romance, and people all around raise their eyebrows. "My widowed mom is keeping company with this married man," wrote "Geraldine" to Dear Abby. "Isn't a man whose wife has an incurable illness considered married?" The implication is clear:

Mom has no business finding closeness with a man who has a wife, even an incapacitated wife. That route to happiness for Mom must remain closed.

Institutions themselves often seem to ignore these needs of their patients. Patient privacy can be almost nonexistent; staff members tend to enter rooms freely, without knocking. Even in a "proper" marriage, a visiting spouse can meet insurmountable barriers to intimacy. Unless the institution provides a "privacy room" for such couples, the security of privacy is unobtainable.

The other side of the equation, of course, is the institution's responsibility to protect its people—patients and staff alike—from abuses of sexual freedom. Unwanted physical advances, even crude language and provocative behavior—these things can threaten the web of security in the institution's life. The administrative staff is likely to err on the side of safety, and the affectional needs of the elders can go unfulfilled.

Many institutions caring for the older persons are church-run institutions, and many, many church people have loved ones living in them. What is our responsibility in our congregations? To what extent do we help each other—in Sunday school classes or study groups or wherever—to understand the larger questions of sexuality, the relation of sexuality to our capacity to reach out to others and to love them? To what extent do we talk honestly about the "Geraldines" who find companionship with a married man? Do we face together the situation of the man—still married, but having really "lost" his wife to Alzheimer's—being cut off from the closeness and affection she had brought?

Ours is clearly an aging society, and the number of older people in institutional care can only increase. Our capacity for love and intimacy does not end in old age; we need to find ways for that ability to be expressed for the enhancement of the humanity of us all.

Older adults at home

Most older persons, of course, do not live in institutions; it has been estimated that at least 90 percent are still at home, living in their own homes or with their adult children. But even there widowed or never-married older adults still can face opprobrium when they find intimacy with other elderly persons.

The widowed person often discovers that adult children resist any suggestion of a new close relationship for their parent. They have difficulty accepting the notion that their mother or father might develop a new affection, and what if they should express that in some physical way? This new relationship could lead, they think, to unfaithfulness to the dead spouse. This could rouse criticism in the neighborhood, to the embarrassment of the whole family.

Even if the couple's affection deepens into enduring commitment and remarriage comes into the picture, financial complications can arise. Adult children may, of course, worry about what a new spouse might do to their inheritance. But beyond that, finances can make marrying impossible.

Here is a couple in their seventies, each of whom has been widowed for a decade, and they have been dating, comfortably and happily, for a couple of years. Marriage would be a joyous outcome, but money intervenes. The woman's husband left her well provided for through his company's pension system, but that pension would be forfeited should she remarry.

What are they to do? Do they seek the warmth of shared lives by simply living together? Or shall we insist that if they cannot marry, they must remain to some degree apart, since cohabitation is legitimated only by marriage?

One complication in all of this is that as hearing and vision dim, touch can become perhaps the primary avenue of connecting with others. Older adults often develop a genuine "skin hunger," a yearning to be nourished by the touch of other people. An affectionate hug, an arm around the shoulder, and a hand on the arm when walking—these are ways of affirming that a person is there and is a human being. "We like to link arms with each other when we walk down the hall. That way we can feel the closeness." The need for touch is lifelong, but it becomes more acute when a person is gradually being cut off from other links to people.

Touch can come dependably and comfortably within the intimacy of marriage. But there are a wide variety of other relationships where life-giving touch can be a reality. Here a congregation can be a community of real nurture. A commitment to true intergenerational ministries and relationships can bring people warmly together, with such reality that they know they belong to each other and to God.

We are inescapably sexual beings, finding our connection with the world through our bodies, male or female. But that connectedness is much larger than its expression in romance with the other sex. It drives all the rich interrelationships of human life, and for that we can be immensely grateful to the God who has created all things and called them good.

Letha Dawson Scanzoni has pointed out that "we are sexual beings until the day we die." Each one of us, whether or not we continue to express our sexuality genitally, will continue to feel that we are enveloped in God's love. We can appreciate God's gifts and share God's love, care, and joy with others. After all, intimacy is precisely this.[9]

Choice-Making in Trust

"Wrong is when everybody YELLS," says Dennis the Menace. Well, we grownups realize that making moral judgments is considerably more complex than that, and we know that even when we have done our honest best, we still may not have made the wisest decision.

When we come to our decisions in some of the crises associated with aging, we find ourselves again and again struggling with the problem of guilt. Here are adult children, or a spouse, believing they *had* to move an older family member into institutional care and knowing that the person is deeply unhappy. Convinced that they had no alternative, they still feel racked with guilt. Here is a physician who calls for the cessation of extraordinary treatment for an aged patient, and the patient's family agrees. But afterward they keep reliving that decision; was there not any other possibility?

How, then, do we deal with the ambiguity, the uncertainty of our choices? How can we live with the possibility that perhaps we should have done otherwise than we did? There are resources in our faith on which we can draw, resources that enable us to face courageously the risks involved in making these moral choices.

The Support of the Christian Community

Jesus said to his disciples on the night he was to die, "When the Spirit of truth comes, he will guide you into all the truth" (John 16:12). It is clear, however, from all that the New Testament says about the work of the Spirit that it is not to individuals that the Spirit reveals "all the truth"; it is to the church. The Spirit's work is to draw us into community—the Christian community; in that life together we share with each other our insights into God's will and strengthen each other to do that will.

So it is that we individual Christians who face painful moral choices pray earnestly that God will guide us to do the divine will. But at the same time we recognize that God's guidance comes to us partly through the fellowship of believers in our congregation. So we seek the counsel of those with whom we regularly share worship and study and ministry.

It is incumbent upon the congregation, then, to take seriously its responsibility to be an agent of the Holy Spirit. As the proportion of older members rises in most congregations, it becomes all the more urgent that our churches structure opportunities for people to study together and pray together about the moral crises we have been discussing in this chapter.

There could be informal study groups, set up as needed, in which people could read together helpful books and articles and help each other with the choices they face. There could be short-term courses of study in adult Sunday school classes, courses organized to help people think through in advance some of the decisions that will almost surely confront many of them. There could be church supper programs or weekend retreats—the possible venues for such sharing are myriad.

Providing possibilities of these kinds would reflect our clear conviction that we individual Christians do not face our crises by ourselves. We are members of the body of Christ, and in that body we seek the truth together.

Our knowledge of the forgiveness of God

Martin Luther observed that because we are sinners living in a sinful world, even our most conscientious actions will be tinged with sin; we cannot ever claim to have done the perfect will of God. Therefore, said Luther, "Sin boldly!" We *must* choose, we *must* act; we cannot hold back out of fear of sinning. So we go ahead and do what we must do according to our best understanding of God's will. Fully aware of our sin, however, we rely on the forgiveness of God.

It is the assurance of that forgiveness that empowers us to take risks and act courageously. We know that our relationship with God depends, not on the purity of our obedience, but on the grace and mercy of our God. This means that we need not keep on accusing ourselves of being unloving when we have done the best we know how for the ones we love. We need not wake up in the night, going over and over in our minds those choices we made, asking ourselves if there had been any other possibilities. We can turn these anxieties over to God in the sure knowledge that God is gracious and that we are God's children.

Our trust in God's sovereignty

It is still a reality, of course, that though we rest in God's grace and do not accuse ourselves, a choice we made could cause pain and even broken relationships, and we cannot always undo these unforeseen consequences, grievous though they be. Then we need to remember that our God is not only a forgiving God but also a sovereign God who can turn even the wrath of us humans to praise. The apostle Paul affirmed it in Romans 8:28: "All things work together for good for those who love God"—*all* things, not just the happy events of our lives.

To speak of God's providence need not mean that God causes the bad things to happen. God gives us freedom, and God does not step in to prevent us from using that freedom foolishly. So it is not that God *wills* dire things; rather, God uses them in carrying out divine purposes. Out of whatever happens, a sovereign God can bring good.

Leslie Weatherhead wrote some years ago that God's divinity means that there is nothing that can defeat God or ultimately frustrate God's plans. God is able to bring good out of what appears to us as sheer evil.[10]

So we do our conscientious best. We face the hard choices that our own aging or the aging of our loved ones thrusts upon us. We make the wisest decisions we know how to make, and then we leave the outcome in the sovereign hands of God. Such trust empowers us to minister faithfully to those we love.

Questions for Discussion

1. H. Richard Niebuhr identified three approaches in making ethical decisions: "What are the results?" "What is right?" and "What is the fitting response?" Choose one of the following issues of old age and show how all three approaches might be valid.
   A. Moving an aged relative to a nursing home.
   B. Deciding about "heroic measures" for a loved one who did not have a living will.
   C. Two church members in their eighties living together outside of legal marriage.

2. A woman comes to a pastor for counseling. She is torn between caring for her aged mother, for teenage children, and for a husband who complains he is being neglected. As a pastor, how would you counsel her?

3. You are in a church school class on "Between Generations" and discussing a case in which a cranky grandfather who lives alone needs to be placed in a personal-care center. He refuses to go and has the right to make that refusal. How would you help him make that decision if possible?

4. If your father, who has Alzheimer's disease, is in a nursing home and does not recognize his family, and if your mother is comparatively healthy, active, and fully engaged in living her life, how would you feel if she began going out frequently with a widower she has known for several years?

5. Your father and mother are in a nursing home in separate rooms in different sections of the building. Your mother has had a stroke but has no other debilities and is confined to a wheelchair. Your father is able to walk around, has no dementia, and wants very much to spend some intimate time with his wife, who wishes the same. The facility has no private place for them to be together. Both share rooms with other residents. If they were members of your congregation, what could you do to help them?

6. Is a person who is brain-dead but whose other functions are working still a person? What about persons with dementia? Is a person without memory still a person? When does a person stop being a person?

7. In the famous Terri Schiavo case some who would have reinserted the feeding tube maintain that removing it is tantamount to "judicial murder." Some even insist it was a "modern-day crucifixion." Do you agree or disagree? Why?

8. You are walking the track with a physician and the issue of living wills arises. She says, "I am not a Christian, but I can't understand why some Christians demand 'heroic measures' if they believe in a better life beyond death." How would you answer her?

9. A conservative Presbyterian minister ignores an aged couple in his congregation who live together outside of wedlock. He never visits them or makes any effort to welcome them into church life. What would you say to the persons? To the pastor?

10. A lawyer who sits on the session or board of a church is quite concerned with ethical questions regarding power of attorney, placement in nursing homes, and living wills. He wants the church to address these issues. What plan of action would you recommend?

11. Discuss how you would answer the question that is common in times of crisis, "Why does God allow bad things to happen to good people?"

Notes

1. A good, lucid discussion of all this can be found in George Chauncey, *Decisions! Decisions!* (Richmond: John Knox Press, 1972), pp. 76–88.

2. Terrie Wetle, "Long-Term Care—A Taxonomy of Issues," *Generations* (American Society on Aging), Winter 1985, p. 34.

3. Discussion of the "Debbie" case is found in *The Journal of the American Medical Association* 259:2 (1988), p. 292; 260:6 (1988), pp. 787–89.

4. Kenneth L. Vaux, "The Theological Ethic of Euthanasia," *Hastings Center Report* (Special Supplement), January/February 1989, pp. 20–21.

5. "Ethics and Old Age," *Loma Linda University Ethics Center Update*, June 1988, p. 2.

6. *Richmond Times-Dispatch*, September 13, 1999.

7. *Richmond Times-Dispatch*, September 16, 2002.

8. "Growing Old in a New Age, Part 4: Love, Intimacy, and Sexuality," *The Annenberg/CPB Collection*, P. O. Box 2345, S. Burlington, VT 05407-2345.

9. Letha Dawson Scanzoni, *Sexuality: Affirm Sexuality as God's Gift, Act Wisely About Sexual Feelings* (Philadelphia: The Westminster Press, 1984), p. 110.

10. Leslie Weatherhead, *The Christian Agnostic* (Nashville: Abingdon, 1965), pp. 212–213.

Pastoral Care of Older Persons

T. Ronald Vaughn

As I survey the chapter titles of this book, I am aware of the fact that each will likely accomplish two things: one, present new and helpful cognitive data, and two, offer direct or indirect suggestions for the use of such data in ministry to, for, and with older adults. Insofar as that is the case, each article is in actuality about "pastoral care of older persons." I am not able to predict or to summarize anything presented by others, because I have not had prior access to their writings. Rather, I will offer some independent reflections on the theme, based on my own background in both ministry and secular employment. I will lean more toward theory and theology, with little attention to individual or programmatic implementation. I am confident that all the articles taken together will be a rich source of ideas and information about pastoral care among this special population.

My Background

I come to this task from a journey that warrants mention because many of my perspectives derive from observations and assessments formed in a particular environment of bivocational ministry. For more than seventeen years I served small and midsize congregations (sometimes more than one) while simultaneously being employed in health care. I worked in a state psychiatric hospital, a regional acute-care medical center, and in long-term care facilities. In the first two settings I served in both clinical and administrative roles, then for several years was administrator of three skilled-care nursing homes totaling four hundred beds. Predictably, the vast majority of the nursing home residents were older adults. A substantial number of those with whom I worked in the psychiatric and acute-care settings were as well. Thus on a daily basis for many years I "earned my living" caring for third-agers with emotional or physical problems severe enough to require an inpatient setting. As a needed balance I was at the same time presented with a typical blend of well older persons in each of the churches I served.

Incidentally, the health care settings were non-confessional. I was not paid to be a minister or a chaplain in either of them. I had, therefore, the unique opportunity to reflect on the content and implications of Christian theology as a "secular employee" who was also an ordained minister. An important addition here is the fact that I was also able to interact with and to observe professional clergy "in action" as they visited and ministered to patients and residents in each setting.

Much of what I write here is the result of ongoing consideration of this personal material and of subsequent ministry to older adults in two churches I have served since I returned to full-time parish work. These comments will be free-ranging but maintain a basic unity in line with the article's title. I intend them to apply equally to ministry among frail and infirm elderly and to ministry to the vast majority who are active, vibrant, and unimpaired.

An Unfolding Challenge

When I began my ministry the shelf of available books and materials on Christianity and aging was indeed short. It is one of the unacknowledged triumphs of the church that the last three decades have seen the resource data in this area multiply exponentially. There are many reasons for this, the dominant one being the ongoing search for implications from the increase in average life expectancy. What does the existence of a burgeoning population of elderly persons "speak" to the church, and what, in turn, does the church "speak" to it? In fits and starts the church has valiantly undertaken to address this social reality, but by most accounts it has only partially succeeded in producing effective results. I maintain that the definitions of and models for pastoral care of older persons are evolving, and that the process has been in many ways painfully slow. A more positive way to state this would be that the entire field is in its infancy. Perhaps that reality must inform our comfort level even at this historic juncture. We do not yet have "all the answers" and have likely not even asked many of the right questions.

The health care field and the church have run in parallel lines in responding to needs of older adults. As a licensed nursing home administrator, I am very much aware that the entire long-term care enterprise is of recent origin, largely created in America by the passage of the federal Medicare/Medicaid laws and their accompanying regulations. Many critics have noted that the resultant care model, now ensconced in law, is woefully flawed, and while few would dispute that, the emergence of better ideas for care and service has been less than impressive. The industry should be on the cutting edge for creative and novel approaches, but, alas, governmental bureaucracy and oversight have spawned an unfortunate stagnation and inertia. We all await the conceptual revolutions that will radically alter care for the frail and infirm elderly. We can hope those change agents are now on the horizon.

In similar fashion the church has taken tentative steps in its awareness of and pastoral response to this growing population. It has worked extremely hard to come to terms with the interrelated complexities of human aging. In this it has had to learn from other areas and disciplines, all the while attempting to articulate and define pastoral care models dealing with the whole person in the entire human life span.

As governmental red tape creates inertia in health care, so too denominational prioritizing affects ministry to older adults. A few church bodies are leading the field in research, publication, and material development. Some seminaries are actually requiring course work in gerontology or older adult ministries. Most denominations, however, have yet to come to grips with the staggering significance of this demographic change and are, therefore, sadly deficient in effective response. This situation must be remedied, and ecumenical cooperation is imperative for future success. Despite preliminary findings and uncertain boundaries, Christian churches must work together in this unfolding challenge. Surely these efforts will be blessed by the God of all phases of life.

Clergy Discomfort

One of my early observations as an employee in a psychiatric hospital was the infrequency of area clergy visits to patients. I wondered if perhaps I was simply not around when those visits took place. After consulting with social workers and hospital chaplains, I was confirmed in my initial observations. There were, and are, many reasons for this, and not all of them are indicators of a significant social phenomenon among religious professionals. However, I later made the same discovery as a nursing home administrator. As a member of ministerial associations in the cities where these facilities were located, I inquired further among colleagues about visitation and pastoral care practices for parishioners in nursing homes. Many clergy were quite willing to admit that it was difficult for them, spiritually and psychologically, to visit residents in that environment. Their expressed reasons for this were the typical listing one might expect. My summarization would be this: pastoral care for nursing home residents is difficult due to the intense concentration in one location of ill and infirm persons and the accompanying components of their care. I would add that the long-term care setting suggests a terminus, an end place, what many crudely phrase, "where old people go to die."

I also suggest that some of the same reasons are used for infrequent visits to psychiatric facilities: the overwhelming number of persons there with various diagnoses of severe mental illness. Most church workers are not trained to respond to the level of physical or mental illness found in these settings and therefore may be perfectly content to relate only tangentially to the entire situation. That is quite understandable and entirely reasonable. Wise practitioners know their limitations even as they insist on the best of care for their clients from more experienced, more highly trained professionals.

If a statistician could quantify all the reasons given for lack of clergy visitation, the list still might omit what I perceive to be a foundational ingredient for any discussion of pastoral care for older persons. My baseline observation is that many clergy struggle with older adult ministry due to extreme personal discomfort with the whole notion of human aging and ultimate demise. If this is in any sense true and accurate, an extension of the principle would lead to the revealing conclusion that just as individuals experience discomfort, so do groups of individuals, so do congregations, and so do denominations. The corollary to this is undeniable: we tend to avoid or to minimize contact with what makes us uncomfortable.

In ministry to older persons are we tentative, sluggish, or inadequate because we are made uneasy by the profound ideas and stark realities of human aging? Are older adult ministries low denominational priorities due to value judgments based on these aversions? I am convinced that it is so even if my personal conclusions are drawn from data largely accumulated in institutional settings.

I am well aware that most persons reading these pages are not often involved in ministry in such places. Are my observations relevant to pastoral care situations in congregations, in small groups, or even one-on-one? To that I now turn while answering with a resounding "Yes!"

An outline of pastoral care

Conceptually this article is unfolding in a building-block fashion. I have said that the age wave boom has essentially created a new form of ministry and that the church is still seeking to find its bearings amid the plethora of new things it is learning. We can be grateful that preliminary data is being distilled and made available to the church in various forms. As a result many good things are happening, many ideas are being used and discarded, and many adjustments are being made. I have alleged that a significant factor in all of this is a pervasive discomfort with human aging and decline. This point is not an indictment so much as an observation— certainly not original with me, but convincingly verified by my own limited experience in both health care and parish ministry. Assuming the essential correctness of my conclusions, I offer the following suggestions as an outline for the pastoral care of older persons.

The first requirement is the practitioners' development of personal comfort with aging—their own and that of others. This seems to be the primary demand in all fields of professional endeavor. Pastoral care and Christian ministry are not exceptions to the rule. Clearly we develop comfort with any topic, discipline, field, or activity through having an interest in it. But secondarily we develop that comfort, often grudgingly, by the sheer necessity of having to do it. The need to render effective, intelligent pastoral care for older adults is a stunning social reality, and a self-evident imperative for our day.

This being the inevitable case, it is worthwhile for caregivers to engage in some basic self-awareness as it relates to aging matters and to their actual hands-on work with these persons. How, indeed, do we "feel" about that prospect and reality? How great is our comfort level? How uncomfortable are we? Are we accepting of our own aging and our own mortality? How do we acquire needed skills for successful ministry? It is of paramount importance that we be able to answer these questions and make every effort to do so honestly.

For a taste of this kind of self-disclosure, join me in a simple exercise. Make a quick turn back to Contents page of this volume. Scan the words in the article titles. Notice that many are heavily laden with emotion-producing potential: late life, transition, retirement community, nursing home, depression, life's dark places, Alzheimer's disease, abuse. The terms also serve as mental connectors to other words that do not appear, but could. That list might contain dysfunction, loss, death and dying, loneliness, funeral, lingering illness, fragility, and more.

I purposely conducted this experiment several times as I reflected on the tone and content of my contribution to this book. I read the article titles deliberately in order to discern my own affective response. Some of the words and phrases intrigued and excited me. Some had a highly negative effect. My guess is that readers may have had a similar experience with what are clearly emotion-charged words and phrases. In our stream-of-consciousness thinking, each word creates a derivative, and for every word there is likely a mental picture. For every picture there is a host of affective response.

Sorting through all the material of this personal awareness is essential for appropriate pastoral care of this age group. There are many ways to accomplish it, and help is available from several places. It gives a baseline knowledge of "where we are," and it can be prescriptive for what, if anything, we need to do in order to "fix it"; that is, for better preparing ourselves for this purposeful Christian activity.

I state this again as more than a caveat: Ministry to and pastoral care of older persons is not confined to work among the frail and incapacitated. I state this since the sociological, political, and even theological discussions of aging often turn on the notion of the observable deficiencies of the group. This emphasis almost always highlights what I term the "three D's"—deficient, disease, and dysfunction. It says that since aging persons are deficient, they "need" various and sundry things for any semblance of meaningful life. They "need" government-funded prescription drugs, health insurance, special housing, transportation, retail discounts, specialized medical services, etc. Even if for the best of reasons, a cultural mind-set has been created that equates aging with lack, inability, need, and, curiously, entitlement. Is this necessary, accurate, or just? How did this kind of thinking attach itself to aging populations? Asking the question will assist in transitioning to my second suggestion in an outline for pastoral care.

From media to music to medicine, cultural stereotypes seem to dramatize the negatives of aging. Buying into this *schema*, service providers in many disciplines are therefore predisposed to assume that their best input is an attempt to ameliorate these defined needs. That becomes, in a nutshell, the *modus operandi*, the "way to do it." Pastoral caregivers must tread very carefully here, and Christian theologians must be enjoined to do their best thinking at this crucial crossroad. I will now demand that theology offer the redemptive antidote to this viewpoint, which I declare to be a particularly unfortunate characterization. I am saying, in short, that the self-aware caregiver must be armed with the proper theology of aging.

Here is why. If we accept the cultural mind-set, we then define pastoral care as something we "do to" or "apply to" or "exert upon" elderly persons. In so concluding we become entrapped in one of the most egregious forms of ageism. This is true whether the "clients" are bedridden and incoherent or well and youthfully active.

I understand Christian theology to present a fundamentally different alternative. My phrasing would be that pastoral care of any age group or any individual person is based on the caregiver's personal identification with and empathic understanding of the other modeled on the agapic ministry of Jesus of Nazareth.

The crucial distinction between these two approaches was illustrated to me only days before I wrote these paragraphs. Attempting to see a parishioner in a rest home, I discovered that she was out for a physician visit. Leaving her room, I encountered another resident, who inquired, "Are you a pastor?" I responded that I was, to which she remarked, "How nice of you to visit old folks like us." A few comments followed, and I left the building. I took with me the abiding impression that she had viewed my presence in the facility as an extraordinary thing, and that I was to be applauded for appearing in that difficult environment in order to do ministry. Well aware of other meaning and innuendo that could have been packed in her words, I heard the message that visitation to the elderly in a rest home was commendable, even meritorious. My strong reaction was to affirm that had I visited under any guise other than my Christian self-conscious identification (however faulty) with and empathic understanding (however inadequate) of my parishioner, I would have been guilty of crass condescension.

The cultural stereotypes are insidious and must be vocally protested and strongly resisted. Both young and old can "buy" into them. They create a dichotomous condition of thinking that produces an "us over against them" mentality. "We" minister to "them"; "we" broker or offer pastoral care, as a product or commodity, to "them." And, of course, the entire process, as we do it, is worthy of special consideration, in spite of our personal discomfort with the rendering of that care. It is a mind-set that must be ferreted out, labeled, and dispelled. Christian theology shows us how.

The Christian answer

It is my understanding that stereotypes that demean older persons may well be a European and American creation. If so, I am heartened by the inclusion in this book of several articles about views on aging from other cultural perspectives. I hope they will give cues and clues about where things have gone wrong, and also ideas and suggestions about how to combat these disgraceful perversions. Multicultural material can make a needful impact in this regard. It is one useful tool in redefining both human aging and societal response to it. Other disciplines, such as psychology, sociology, anthropology, and medicine, make their contributions as well.

The entirely redeeming resource is the Christian tradition in which we look for:

1. an accurate self-understanding
2. the correct theology of aging
3. the complete model for ministry, Jesus of Nazareth
4. the most suggestive outlines for definitions of pastoral care of all persons

Another article in this book deals with the theology of aging. I simply state here, with emphasis, that the locus of understanding and addressing all issues related to life in every one of its stages must be the theology of the church. While we welcome and applaud input from all friendly sources, the church must be very clear about its foundational underpinnings in this matter. Only theology can propose, even in the face of dying and death, a new life for the individual in a realm beyond time. It must declare that such a prospect is not an innate human potentiality but a free gift from a loving God. This is the ultimate completion of the "life cycle" of the human species, and belief in such a doctrine has everything to do with one's views on aging and end-of-life matters.

The church asserts that Jesus of Nazareth offers the most complete model for ministry. The Gospels must be studied and restudied for knowledge of this crucial material. My conviction that all ministries involve the caregiver's identification with and empathetic understanding of other persons, which is accomplished through agape love, is modeled for us in the life of Jesus. His self-understanding was partly derived from the servant motifs of the Old Testament, and while they had Messianic implications for him, those same themes yield ministry implications for us. Perhaps Paul captured the essence of Christian servanthood in his reflections on Jesus in Philippians 2. He begins the pertinent section with, "Your attitude should be the same as that of Christ Jesus" (v. 5, NIV). The great kenotic passage follows, endorsing the "pouring out" of self for the sake of the other. While we are nowhere commanded to be "little Jesuses," we are instructed to model the use of our unique gifts and talents upon the life of the Son.

Finally I suggest that the Christian theology of aging combined with the observed ministry of Jesus may well yield effective outlines for pastoral care models. I do not mean, of course, that from such conjoining will emerge a catalog of "New Ideas For Senior Groups" or a handbook on activities for "Golden Oldies." That kind of material is readily available. I do mean that if we grasp some of the fundamental concepts in theology we can begin to faithfully keep Paul's command about a new attitude. New attitudes automatically lead to creative new action and activity. Jesus himself suggested that there was more than one way to offer a cup of cold water. Perhaps with a new and better informed attitude we can likewise turn a salad luncheon for seniors or a trip to a theme park into genuine pastoral care in the name of Christ.

I am extremely optimistic about the future. If the proper foundations can be laid, then the rising edifice of ministry will be an amazingly effective thing, where all persons are organically connected and pastorally nurtured from cradle to grave. In our time of God's providence, this excellence and competence is exceedingly possible. It is the nature of the church to make the possible real.

Questions for Discussion

1. This chapter states that even "helping professionals" may have difficulty visiting in nursing homes or psychiatric facilities. Is that difficult for you? Why? What is the hardest part?

2. You are a deacon in your church, and the session has reorganized the ministry teams. They have asked deacons to visit members in nursing homes. You have never been in a nursing home and are petrified to visit a member there. What do you do? How do you begin?

3. Regardless of your present age, how do you feel about getting older? Do you have fears? Name them. What excites you, or gives joy about growing older?

4 . Can you name a person of both genders who models the kind of older person you would like to become? Why did you name these persons?

5. As a church visitor how can you "identify with" and "empathetically understand" older persons, particularly if you have watched their aging?

6. A seminary professor of pastoral care saw no need for including pastoral care of older persons as a vital component of his courses. Do you agree? Why or why not?

7. What biblical passages help you think of pastoral care among older adults? Consider your favorite stories or verses of Scripture that might teach about human aging or relate to older people.

8. Scholars tell us that Jesus of Nazareth lived on this earth less than thirty-five years. Discuss how Christianity might be different had he lived to a ripe old age before his death. What implications do you see for pastoral care?

9. The contemporary church still focuses on youth ministry. You have been asked to serve on a pastor's nominating committee of an eight hundred–member church with a high number of older persons. Would you consider ministers with special training in pastoral care of older persons? Or is this just the responsibility of retirees who become parish associates? Explain.

10. The senior minister has asked you as the associate pastor to design two types of pastoral ministry for older adults. One for the active sixty-five- to seventy-five-year-olds, and the other for the frailer seventy-five-year-olds and older. How would you begin? How would you find resources for both age groups? For those seventy-five and older?

For Further Reading

Butler, Michael and Ann Orbach, *Being Your Age: Pastoral Care for Older People*. London: SPCK Press, 1993.

Clebsch, William A., *Pastoral Care in Historical Perspective*. New York: Harper Torchbooks, 1967.

Cohen, Gene D., *The Creative Age*. New York: Harper/Collins, 2000.

Kimble, Melvin A., "Pastoral Care" in *Aging, Spirituality and Religion: A Handbook*, eds. Melvin A. Kimble, Susan H. McFadden, James Ellor, James Seeber. Minneapolis: Fortress Press, 1995.

Kimble, Melvin A., "Pastoral Care of the Elderly," *The Journal of Pastoral Care*, 16b(3), 1987, pp. 270–279.

Koenig, Harold G., *Aging and God*. New York: Haworth Press, 1994.

Koenig, Harold G. and Andrew J. Weaver, *Counseling Troubled Older Adults*. Nashville: Abingdon Press, 1997.

Maitland, David Johnson, Aging: *A Time for New Learning*. Philadelphia: The Westminster Press, 1987.

Meiburg, Albert L., "Pastoral Care with the Aged: The Spiritual Dimension" in Gerald L. Borchert and Andrew D. Lester, eds., *Spiritual Dimensions of Pastoral Care*. Philadalphia: The Westminster Press, 1995.

Valliant, George E., *Aging Well*. Boston: Little, Brown and Company, 2002.

Life in a Retirement Community

Samuel M. Stone

A Community for Living

The decisions regarding a retirement community truly are among the toughest you will face in your entire lifetime. Not only are there the complex issues revolving around whether or not to take the leap and, if so, when and where. There is also the often missed realization that the questions arise at a time in your life when you are least well equipped to assess yourself objectively and to think clearly about how best to approach the final phase of your mortal existence.

This exploration of life in a retirement community will take seriously the difficulties in making the decision by offering a wide range of information and suggestions for consideration. In the end there will be the acknowledgement that the decision involves as much reflection on how you see yourself—your own self-understanding—as it does an investigation of what a particular retirement may or may not have to offer as you approach a new phase of life.

Unless you have a close friend or family member who entered a retirement community and spoke well of the experience, chances are you will not be inclined to think favorably of this option for yourself. A number of other options will spring to mind in an instant—stay put, move to a resort location, wait until you have to decide, simply set aside a decision until the time comes, or rely on the kids.

The stay put option is the one elected when, among other reasons, you find it very hard to separate yourself from a neighborhood and a house filled with a lifelong collection of things and memories. The very notion of packing and leaving or, what is worse, deciding what to do with four thousand five hundred square feet of stuff that will not fit into an apartment of little more than eight hundred or maybe eleven hundred square feet may be deterrent enough. Moving to the beach, or near a golf course, or to the mountains sounds a lot better. Once there, you speculate, all of those things that you never had either the time or the inclination to do previously will suddenly spring to life. Convincing, yes?

You never know what is going to happen, so why not wait until you really have to decide? As long as your health is good and you are managing pretty well on your own or with just a little help from your spouse, why hurry? You can always wait until you no longer can get up the stairs, but even then you could turn the den into a bedroom and stay a little longer. This line of thinking, of course, is a close relative to the notion that you will know when the time comes. Do not ask just how this wisdom will appear, but you are confident of being in charge of your own life.

For a large segment of older adults one of the last options is to rely on the kids. The reasons are legion: the grown children have not been all that reliable up to now; they do not have the time or the room to handle their parents; they live halfway across the country and never stay in one job or location for long; putting up with the grandchildren, as lovable as they are, for more than three days would be impossible; and on and on. In the end clear-headed older adults are quick to say, "I do not want to be a burden to my children" and "I want to be in charge of my own destiny."

While the options mentioned can be challenged and made to appear lightweight, the truth is that some of them can become realistic and workable alternatives, given the right circumstances and the right individuals. The fact that only about 5 percent of all older adults in the United States elect to enter a retirement community says that there are alternatives, a lot of alternatives. But how good are they? Do they address the realities of living longer, as so many Americans do, and consequently developing the need for care and assistance at some point? If being in charge of your own destiny is a criterion of value in your later years, then how can this be accomplished?

So let us get serious about some of the truly thoughtful aspects of considering life in a retirement community. For those who are inclined to think in terms of a meaningful existence in the older adult phase of life there are aspects of a retirement community that are especially appealing. The word community says a lot. More to the point, the reality of a vibrant, interactive, engaged community of exceptionally caring persons can and should be at the heart of the retirement community that you select. For a retirement community to appeal to you it should consist of persons who share with you many of life's greatest concerns, persons who have experienced many of the same challenges and achievements, and yet somehow also persons who know when to be at your side and when to respect your desire for privacy.

There is little doubt that hard-core loneliness and a deep sense of isolation are a fact of life for many older adults. The fact of being alone and the emotional void of loneliness become a reality as a spouse dies, as close relatives become more incapacitated or move farther away, and as you lose touch with former co-workers, neighbors, or church members. Retirement communities provide an effective response to these and many similar painful circumstances through immediate access to a selection of new friends and neighbors, instant companions at meals, and activities tailored to your interests and capabilities.

In the thinking, even if unspoken, of every individual or couple entering a retirement community is a serious health consideration. Often it is a recent episode that provides a scare and an added incentive to get serious about ensuring that there will be help available when it is needed. (More will be said on this topic later.) Most retirement community residents cite this as the single most significant influence in the decision to enter a retirement community.

Health considerations are not only a matter of available physicians, hospitals, and nursing care, but also the everyday matters of nutrition, exercise, socialization, learning and staying alive intellectually, being an active volunteer and giving back to the larger community, and of course spirituality and participation in the life of the religious faith of your choice. All of these dimensions of a vital older adult are positive aspects of life in most retirement communities. They can be available where you reside now, but will they remain so as your life circumstances and condition change?

A retirement community should provide for you not merely a safe place to reside in your final days but more specifically a vital community in which you live to the fullest some of your best years.

Transition from "I'm not ready yet" to "I waited too long"

The marketing staff at any retirement community will tell you that the sentence and truly the sentiment most often expressed is "I'm not ready yet." What does this mean? Ask yourself that question. You have said it, or at least thought it, so spell it out. Make a list of what readiness implies and what must happen to make you ready to enter the retirement community that is just right for you.

Readiness implies a time factor. There is a time, now, when you are not ready, but there will be a time, in some vague or not so vague future, when presumably you will be ready. Also implied are certain hurdles to be crossed or overcome—these may include getting rid of or doing something with all of those belongings you have accumulated; it may include some notions of independence and resistance to giving up freedom; and it may include an image of yourself as being different from those who are called older adults.

Saying that you are not ready may be a coded message that in reality is saying, "Don't force me to make decisions: I am in charge of my own destiny." For those accustomed to making critical decisions in their careers or in their family life, this can be a powerful force, despite how loudly the clock is ticking or how swiftly the years are eroding the ability to maintain control effectively.

A positive and most constructive way out of the blind alley of control often is found in the discovery of a popular rationale for action: "I do not want to be a burden to my children." Some carry this line of thought to an extreme as in the gleeful bumper sticker, "I'm spending my children's inheritance."

One way or another, family considerations enter the picture to influence readiness. Sometimes it is at the encouragement of the children, those in the so-called sandwich generation, wedged between still raising their own children and starting to become concerned about aging parents or aunts and uncles. It can be a very tough role for adult children to play effectively. It happens, but seldom is greed on the part of the children a factor, or certainly not a prominent factor. More often it is the genuine concern of a well-meaning child that is rebuffed by a stubborn and shortsighted older adult. The situation becomes all the more desperate when yet unseen signs of an impending dementia condition distort the thinking process of an older adult.

Another truly healthy way out of the control blind alley is for you as the older adult to assert responsibility, to take charge in the sense of looking squarely at the readiness issue in order to examine and know its parts, and then plot a realistic course for yourself. To be worth its salt, this course must include the realities of illness, disability, financial limitations, need for care, and your own demise. The other side of the ledger should include the numerous ways in which this final phase of your life can be new and exciting, vital and engaging, and filled with so many of those experiences that you denied yourself along the way, for whatever reason.

Readiness ceases to be resistance when it begins to be preparation. Sadly, the second most frequently expressed sentiment, heard by all retirement marketers, is "I regret waiting too long."

Financial Considerations

The choices available to you when considering the options for retirement living will be influenced, of course, by the costs, your assets, and what will be affordable for you. While there has been a tendency for certain types of retirement communities to be developed to appeal to a wealthy clientele, persons who demand larger units with more amenities, lush landscaping, and elegant dining rooms with the latest in trendy meals, good options still exist for persons of more modest means and for those who are willing to put the effort into research and exploration.

One reliable way to learn about the fees charged by retirement communities is to seek consumer protection information from the appropriate state agency, often a department of insurance, that maintains up-to-date lists of various types of facilities with sufficient information on the fees charged and the financial condition of facilities to enable you at the very least to develop a list of places for further investigation. There are also federal and state government Internet sites (listed at the end of this article) that report performance data on the licensed nursing facilities associated with many types of retirement communities.

Similarly most retirement communities will ask you, upon applying for admission, to provide enough information about your personal finances in order to determine your ability to meet contractual obligations to the facility in the long term. The forms used and the questions asked are typical of those asked by banks years ago when you applied for a car loan or similar credit. In other words, the financial tests for admission are not strenuous, but reasonable. After all, you want the assurance that all of the other residents have the ability to meet their obligations because the viability of the facility and the stake that you may have in it depend on everyone doing their fair share financially.

There are a number of older retirement communities, especially among those that are religiously or fraternally affiliated, where the fees remain much lower than in the newer, more upscale facilities. Just to offer a rough estimate of affordability, it is fair to say that in the early part of the twenty-first century most retirement communities are expecting, for example, a single person to present evidence of solid assets (those that can be converted to cash readily) of at least three hundred thousand dollars and a reliable annual income of at least thirty thousand. If you fall below this hypothetical benchmark, the good news is that you may still be a candidate, especially for those facilities that include in their mission providing financial assistance should you begin to exhaust your resources. These same facilities very often will also be certified Medicare and Medicaid providers, the latter giving you assurance that the facility has access to resources to sustain you with nursing care even if you become impoverished.

The option of being dependent upon Medicaid in old age and in a nursing home is repugnant to some and wholly unthinkable to others. Nevertheless, the realities of aging in America today are such that many of us are going to live longer and may well live beyond the reach of our best-laid financial plans. If we have the misfortune to be seriously disabled and in nursing care for many years, few people can sustain for long such annual costs as forty-five thousand to seventy-five thousand dollars per year. The thought of protecting an inheritance for your children fades quickly in such a circumstance. These considerations have increased the popularity and, indeed, the practical necessity for anyone except the very wealthy to invest in long-term care insurance, beginning at an early age.

Be clear in your understanding that Medicare, especially when paired with supplemental insurance, provides some valuable financial help for older adults with respect to physician care, hospitalizations, and therapies, but Medicare is not a long-term care provider—offering only partial reimbursement for up to one hundred days of care in a certified skilled-nursing setting.

Once you have identified a few retirement communities that meet your particular criteria—starting with affordability and location—then you want to look closely at every aspect of security within that facility that you can image. You want to know that the place is safe—in terms of structure, fire protection, vandalism, surrounding neighborhood, nearby development trends, reputation, character of management, board leadership, corporate affiliations, and of course finances. Most states require retirement communities to publish annually and provide to prospects some form of financial disclosure statement that has been reviewed independently and authorized for distribution. You want to become satisfied on your own that the facility has the necessary reserves and is solvent for the long haul.

One easy inquiry to make concerns the occupancy levels. If a facility consistently maintains occupancy levels at 95 percent or above in the independent or residential areas, you have a fairly reliable clue that all is well. This factor alone is not sufficient evidence, but it will be indicative of the health and strength of the facility.

Among the many financial considerations relative to retirement communities one of the toughest points is to think in a new way about your assets and how you will invest your resources in your older adult years. The key point is that life in a retirement community, financially speaking, is more an insurance decision than a housing decision. This is a simple but difficult concept for many to accept. Dominated by capitalism as we are, many of our working years are devoted to building and amassing assets. The better retirement communities take seriously the realities of the aging process, and everything is oriented toward focusing on the services and care that we need as those outward signs and trappings of success and status become less meaningful and less relevant in our lives. Payment of the entrance fee buys insurance and assurance.

Types of Retirement Communities

So far retirement communities have been discussed without defining types and varieties of such facilities. New facilities appear seemingly overnight and are promoted widely in the media. There is little wonder that many people are confused by all of the picture-perfect claims as they begin to shop the retirement community market. It will not be possible to capture all of the differences and nuances, but here are some broad distinctions that may help you distinguish one facility from another:

Continuing Care Retirement Community (CCRC): Typically these facilities have large independent areas (cottages and apartments) and, on the same campus, comprehensive health care sections, including licensed assisted-living and skilled-nursing, often with Medicare and Medicaid reimbursement available for the latter. Most are nonprofits, often religiously affiliated, but for-profit corporations have expanded into the field. With few exceptions, the financial arrangements begin with an entrance fee, having various refund formulas, and continue with monthly maintenance and service charges.

Assisted Living (AL) with Retirement Housing: These largely for-profit AL facilities (a significant upgrade of the older rest home model) began to appear in the 1990s. They offer an intermediate alternative between the larger CCRCs and the traditional nursing home facilities. Usually there is a monthly rental fee plus fees for additional services.

Assisted Living with Memory Loss Focus: Another version of the newer for-profit AL facility appears as a single building, varying in size and scope, with particular attention given to dementia care (Alzheimer's disease and other forms of memory impairment).

Nursing Homes and Rest Homes: Usually owned by for-profit corporations, free-standing nursing homes dot the landscape in cities and rural areas across the nation—some twenty-two thousand facilities. These typically offer licensed skilled-nursing, assisted-living, and/or rest home services, and with few exceptions they are providers of Medicare and Medicaid assistance.

In the context of this article the term "retirement community" refers to those facilities in the first two of the four types described above, but chiefly the first, the CCRCs, because in their continuum of living accommodations and services they provide at an exceptional quality level the full gamut of what an older adult may require in the final years of life.

At the same time there can be very good reasons for individuals to prefer any one of the four broad options. Particular circumstances will influence or dictate a decision of one over another. The driving force may be immediate needs, financial considerations, or location, especially proximity to significant relatives or other caregivers. Rest assured, there are good places to be found in each type, and they can be found when sufficient time and diligence is devoted to the task of searching for them.

Nevertheless, given the means and the benefit of advance preparation, a retirement community, whether nonprofit or for-profit in concept and structure, is likely to be the better or ideal route to follow. Procrastinators of the "I'm not ready yet" variety will find that the options narrow and become largely unattractive in the absence of advance planning and decisive action.

Generally speaking, the best retirement communities sustain occupancy rates well above 95 percent. The choice of available units is limited on a given day so that an active engagement with the marketing staff is necessary over time in order to gain the most desirable placement. Seldom is it possible to enter directly into the assisted-living or skilled-nursing sections in most retirement communities without first becoming a resident in an independent or residential unit.

A shortcoming of the facility typing attempted here is that a number of descriptors have been omitted in the interest of presenting the highlights. One such item is the place of dementia care in the facilities mentioned. While in only one of the headings is dementia care specified (as memory loss), in fact such services are provided in one form or another in all four types of facilities. Some AL facilities have made this the exclusive or primary focus, and almost all nursing homes, whether free-standing or as an integral component of a CCRC, have a special care, memory impairment, or Alzheimer's unit—using one of these or still other names essentially for the same service.

Memory loss is experienced by almost everyone over the age of fifty-five, and some form of dementia or old age senility is a fact of life among older adults, brought about by a variety of physiological factors and to date evading cures or remedies. Each retirement community and nursing home must, of necessity, develop approaches, programs, and even special units to address the consequences of dementia. In part this includes an educational process for family members and fellow residents to help them accept those unfortunately afflicted and their condition with grace, kindness, and patience.

Dealing with dementia is a challenge for everyone involved. Whether or not this is a part of your personal concern, you will do well to consider this phenomenon as you explore retirement communities. Knowing how dementia, along with other illnesses prevalent among older adults, is understood and approached should be a part of your comparison shopping.

Living with Fewer Burdens

What is it like living in a retirement community? One of the all-time favorite answers to this question was given by a resident who, when asked, said to a prospective resident, "It is like being on a really nice cruise ship all of the time without ever getting seasick."

This resident's freely and joyfully expressed sentiment summarized her experience. More than that, it showed her surprised delight in finding this phase of her life to be far more satisfying and uplifting than she had expected. By implication she gave credit to the place, with all of its services and accoutrements, and to the community of fellow residents for giving her life new dimensions and the possibility for new meanings.

Throughout our lives we have heard the sage advice that change of place will not necessarily lead to change of problems. At various stages and in regard to certain events or miscues, it is certainly true that we cannot effectively run away from our problems, nor morally should we attempt to do so.

This would not, it seems, be the appropriate analysis to apply to us as we make the transition into older adulthood. This phase of life is not in and of itself necessarily fraught with problems, nor should we necessarily become a problem for ourselves or others. As older adults we are not seeking an escape, a cover, or a cure.

Rather, what we need as older adults is a realistic and optimistic approach to life that says, yes, there are new and different challenges ahead. But there are just as many genuine opportunities for intellectual and spiritual growth, for having rewarding and satisfying experiences, and for contributing to the larger community, which has, after all, made it possible in many ways for us not only to survive but also to prosper and to reach the age of wisdom and relative abundance.

In seeing her life now like being on a cruise ship, our happy resident was saying that she felt more secure and more content than before. There is less about which she might be anxious, less cause for worry, fear, or concern. Many of the burdensome practical demands of daily living are erased, such as home maintenance, yardwork, housekeeping and cleaning, meal preparations, and shopping. Life is simplified with respect to paying bills, taxes, and insurance.

There is a trade-off for sure. Certain freedoms and liberties associated with living in one's home of many years are traded for a congregate or, to use an even uglier word, institutional way of life, but there are solid gains in independence from many unknowns, uncertainties, and impediments, things that put a heavy yoke around the neck of any home and property owner. The weight of such baggage is all the greater as we age and need to focus on those things in life that have the most importance.

As much as we fight for our independence and resist, as we say, "giving up our freedom," the reality is that loneliness is a big negative factor plaguing the lives of many older adults, especially those who cling to a past that is long gone. The simple fact of never having to eat alone, of there always being a fellow resident available with whom to share a meal, watch a movie, play a card game, discuss a book, or just talk for hours at a time, if you wish, is an enormous balm to heal a sad and lonely heart.

Retirement communities always feature their activities programs in their marketing literature. Talk of activities and staff activity directors, however, repels a significant number of prospective residents. Images come to mind of the camp counselor, dressed for the occasion with clipboard in hand, maybe even a whistle around the neck, and standing at the steps to the bus or the door of the lounge or auditorium primed for the next event on the monthly activity calendar.

Scenes close to this image do occur, but far more central to life in a retirement community today is the reality of options. Residents come, not to conform to another person's or institution's notion of what is best for them, but to live and realize, insofar as possible, their own expectations for their individual lives. In other words, the life of a resident in a retirement community is much the same as life elsewhere—but better, freer, and less encumbered. There are residents who continue to travel extensively, maintain vacation homes, work part-time or even full-time, earn an income, follow their investments, engage very actively in a wide range of volunteer work, devote time to their family, friends, civic and church obligations, and more.

Activity calendars are published and distributed, filled with events, outings, lectures, concerts, and more—and this is very important—suggested, planned, and largely led by the residents themselves. Residents totally run the facility's library, convenience store, greenhouse, and whatever else the residents in collaboration with the staff decide is desired and in the best interests of all concerned.

Retirement communities, especially the nonprofits, in a sense belong to the residents. Ownership and ultimate legal responsibility lie in the hands of the volunteer board of directors or trustees, but everyone associated with the enterprise recognizes the financial and, if you will, life's stake the residents individually and collectively have in the viability and success of the venture. This gives the residents reasons to have representation on the governing board, a voice within the committees, and a hand in decisions affecting every aspect of the well-being of the facility.

The channel for this kind of resident involvement in most instances is an association of all of the residents and a council or similar body elected by the residents to represent their collective interests and to engage management directly in matters both big and small. Residents generally will say, "We have no interest in running the place, we've done that, but we sure do want to know what is happening." This is a nice way of saying that it is the residents' money and personal security, by and large, that is at stake. At the same time, the residents' association is a two-way channel available as well for management on its own and on behalf of the governing board to advise, inform, and build a healthy, wholesome collaborative spirit at the core of the community.

Savvy administrators and staff see themselves as facilitators helping the residents realize many, if not most, of their expectations. The residents are clients and customers, expecting certain promised services to be delivered, an expectation that is more often than not exceeded in most facilities. Ultimately the staff may be called upon to fulfill a guardian's role as a participating caregiver, along with others, but this is at a time when the individual resident's life within the community is ending, not beginning.

When asked why they came to a retirement community, residents invariably will say, "I came because of health care," that is, they came because they wanted assurance of having available when they need it a range of health care services—access to a physician, clinic services, emergency call, consultation and help, and the levels of care, from assisted-living through skilled-nursing. All of the social interactions with the resident community and the activities are nice and important, but when the chips are down, it is the provision of sophisticated, skillful, and compassionate care at the upper levels that really counts.

Marketing personnel try hard to attract younger (sixty-five- to seventy-five-year-old) residents who are more likely to be in good health and able to enjoy fully an active retirement, but too often the new residents arrive knowing that significant disabilities already are taking a toll and prompting the need to know that spaces and services will be available. Whether from the first day or after years of what administrators call aging in place, residents are well aware of declining abilities, and they anticipate that life in a retirement community ultimately means receiving care and having end-of-life concerns recognized and competently addressed.

Levels of Care

Retirement communities are organized in their buildings and personnel according to levels of care, primarily in three steps: independent, assisted-living, and skilled-nursing. The physical structures comply with codes and regulatory requirements that are distinctive for each level, and the capabilities of the staff, both in type of skill and degree, vary across the continuum of care. For example, the same maintenance technician may repair an air-conditioner in an apartment one hour and in a skilled-nursing room the next, but the work of the dietician and cooks and certainly the caliber of nursing staff attending to resident needs change from level to level.

Transitions through the levels of care are critical points in the life of every resident and their closest family members or caregivers. Provision is made in the contract and policies of every retirement community for the transfers and changes in levels of care. Ideally a resident will come to the realization that he or she needs more help. A sudden or dramatic change in one's health condition may force this realization or bring to the surface a long-term declining condition. By whatever means it arises, the question becomes the focus of attention for the resident, the closest family members, the responsible person with a health care power of attorney, the resident's physician, and certain members of the facility's staff, notably the medical director, director of nursing, a social worker, and the administrator.

While in many respects a decision in regard to a change in the level of care is a technical issue, the fact that it brings forth such a concentration of expertise and persons of great significance in a resident's life illustrates the kind of thoughtful attention that is given to critical details in the life of each resident, one at a time, day by day, within a retirement community. The privacy and integrity of each resident is respected, but in a discreet and confidential manner a great many of life's issues—some trivial beyond belief—are given whatever time and attention they may require to sustain a resident's well-being or, if you will, a daughter's contentment.

One of the principal ways that retirement communities give objectivity to the transfer decisions is by use of the more or less universally accepted "activities of daily living" (ADLs)—which include one's ability to perform the functions of dressing, grooming, bathing, eating, toileting, and transferring (or ambulation). Orientation or cognitive awareness and functioning are often included, along with the ADLs, as critical factors in assessing a resident's status. Normally it is experienced registered nurses and social workers together who make these assessments, and in licensed facilities they must be confirmed by orders from the resident's personal physician.

Finding and keeping a competent personal physician has become in recent years a difficult matter for older adults, wherever they may live. The reasons for this are the subject of many books, studies, and articles. A part of the picture is the finding of a physician who has the training and patience to resonate with the needs and expectations of older adults in matters of their own health and treatment. Another element has to do with the economic realities of medicine today, including managed-care guidelines and Medicare reimbursement rates.

Retirement communities often can afford its residents some decided advantages when it comes to finding and keeping competent physicians and in doing even more in regard to the provision of professional medical services. Licensed nursing homes, including those within CCRCs, must ideally retain as a medical director a physician with credentials in geriatrics or internal medicine. Moreover, the medical director must be able to guide and advise the facility staff and have the desired attitude and manner best suited to gain the confidence and trust of the residents.

The medical situation today being what it is, residents in retirement communities are very fortunate to have the benefit of access to a facility-retained physician who often takes as his or her own private patients a large percentage of the residents, who are seen directly at the facility. The services of the physician may include rotations with other physicians or nurse practitioners within the practice. Even if the duties are on occasion delegated, the advantages of the priority access and exceptional quality of care are of great value to any resident.

Like the hospitals, retirement communities expect, even require, residents to have and maintain up-to-date wills, living wills, and power of attorney documentation both for health care and for financial and legal decisions. Unless they are admitted to a hospital, these are matters of considerable importance that procrastinators could allow to slide, but retirement communities help residents bring them into focus. One of the subtle characteristics that retirement community residents have in common is that they have more often than not been able to recognize the reality of death and the finality of life in a way that replaces fear with comfort and assurance.

Some Quality Indicators

What is it that you want to know about a retirement community? Before even visiting it, you should read the facility's marketing literature thoroughly. Try to understand what they say they provide and do, and also look for what you feel is distinctive about each facility. There is more that retirement communities, especially CCRCs, have in common and significantly less that sets one apart from another. However, among administrators in the retirement field it is said, "When you have seen one CCRC, you have seen one CCRC." It takes a careful reader and a sharp observer to discern the notable differences.

Notice in the facility publications whether there is an accreditation seal. If there is, this can say a great deal in advance about a facility. For the nonprofit CCRCs, for example, the Continuing Care Accreditation Commission is the national accrediting entity. This commission is sponsored by the six thousand–member American Association of Services and Homes for the Aging based in Washington, D.C.

Currently more than five hundred twenty of the over three thousand CCRCs in the country are accredited, so it is a relatively small number of facilities that have elected to participate in the voluntary program and have been judged by peers at five-year intervals to be fully in compliance with a set of standards pertaining to governance and administration, financial resources and disclosure, and resident life, health and wellness.

Many states require CCRCs to provide any prospective resident a financial disclosure statement that provides information in considerable detail pertaining to the key points of facility ownership, board membership, management, operations, and financial stability. Major sections of the annual independent audit are included. Typically this document is reviewed by a state consumer protection agency, often within a department of insurance, and authorized for release before it can be distributed publicly. The same state agency may also have available lists of retirement communities and information on their status relative to state and federal laws and regulations.

There are a number of Internet sites that contain survey or inspection results and similar comparative data, particularly on nursing homes. Five major national agencies with the addresses, telephone numbers, and Web sites are listed as references at the end of this chapter. Of course from these Web sites there are links to mountains of related information across the country.

When you visit a retirement community to see for yourself, there are a number of items recommended for your list of what to notice: of course the appearance of the grounds, the condition of the buildings inside and out, the level of cleanliness everywhere, and the social atmosphere (friendliness, attitude, responsiveness, and so forth) in evidence among and between both residents and staff.

Be sure to inquire about the management history and structure of the facility. Is the facility owned or managed by an outside entity, or is it a stand-alone or community-based organization? Whatever the structure, it is helpful to understand and be satisfied with who is in charge and how critical financial and management decisions are made. It would be wise to meet the executive director and/or administrator and to know their tenure within the organization.

It is vitally important that you eat a meal at the facility or, at the very minimum, visit the main dining room and learn all that you can about the menus, the meal program and its options, and the quality of the food. Of equal importance, you should meet and talk privately with residents—learn from them their experience in the facility and assess their levels of satisfaction. It is also important, though you may be reluctant to do so, to visit the health care portions of the facility to see, hear, and smell for yourself what is taking place in the care of the facility's most dependent residents.

Location may be of importance to you. Indeed, often it is the most important factor when a prospective resident, for example, is considering relocating close to a particular son, daughter, or other family member. If location is not that big a factor for you, you still want to keep in mind proximity to vital services, such as hospitals and physicians, shopping and service centers, public transportation, cultural venues, and other attractions of special interest.

Whether the facility is church-related or otherwise religiously affiliated may be a factor of importance to you. What difference does it make? As far as the facilities and services per se are concerned, it may not matter that much. There are church-related CCRCs that do not employ or provide the services of a chaplain or minister, and there are community-based CCRCs that feature such persons on their staff and have a prominent role for them within the organization. Does this factor alone say anything, or is it marketing at work? As with church-related colleges, there are church-related CCRCs for which the meaning or value of the kinship varies considerably from one to another.

From my own perspective I will say that ties to a church-related or religiously affiliated organization can be of great significance when the facility and its parent organization pointedly trace their origins to that faith community and continue to derive their inspiration and volunteer leadership from that source. When the mission is viewed as a ministry and when the administrative leadership self-consciously see and identify themselves as engaged in a caring ministry, then the affiliation has body and soul. The community in which I am employed is far from being a monastery and does not pretend to be a congregation, but the residents see themselves as brothers and sisters in Christ reaching out to each other to form a vibrant and vital community, which by itself has tremendous appeal.

Questions for Discussion

1. By what process do we become more serious about readiness, and consequently more realistic about seeing ourselves as older people more objectively?
2. What are the factors in communal living that are repugnant and what factors have decided appeal?
3. How do we reconcile the awareness of our own declining abilities with the insistence on independence and not being a burden to others?

4. Is this notion of a new and different phase of life just a simple way of saying that death is just around the corner?

5. What can the church do to encourage persons to plan ahead for the possibility of entering a retirement community or care facility? What kind of programs could be offered to assist in this difficult transition in a person's life?

6. What kind of support can be offered by the church for leaving one's old home place, for moving into new facilities, for downsizing personal belongings, and for building a new community within the new environment?

7. Could the church offer a seminar or program using members who are already living in a retirement community to give "an inside view"?

8. If possible, organize a field trip for members to a local retirement community for an on-site tour.

9. How can the church maintain the vital connection between the faith community and persons who live in a retirement community, especially for those who can no longer travel to the church for worship?

10. Name some ways that the skills and talents of older persons can continue to be utilized by the church, even the talents of those who are in assisted-living, or nursing home facilities?

Resources

American Association of Homes and Services for the Aging (nonprofit)
2519 Connecticut Avenue NW
Washington, DC 20008
(202) 783-2242
www.aahsa.org

American Health Care Association (for-profit)
1201 L Street NW
Washington, DC 20005
(202) 842-4444
www.ahca.org

Assisted Living Federation of America
11200 Waples Mill Road, Suite 150
Fairfax, VA 22030
(703) 691-8100
www.alfa.org

Continuing Care Accreditation Commission (nonprofit)
2519 Connecticut Avenue NW
Washington, DC 20008
(202) 783-7286
www.ccaconline.org

Centers for Medicare & Medicaid Services (CMS)
(agency of the federal government)
www.cms.gov
Presbyterian Association of Homes and Services for the Aging
222 Park Place
Waukesha, WI 53186
(800) 633-4227

For Further Reading

Amarnick, Claude, *Don't Put Me in a Nursing Home.* Deerfield Beach, FL: Garret Publishing, 1996.

Buckman, Robert, *I Don't Know What to Say . . . : How to Help and Support Someone Who Is Dying.* New York: Warner Books, 1997.

Furman, Joan and David McNabb. *The Dying Time: Practical Wisdom for the Dying and Their Caregivers.* New York: Dell, 1991.

Gubrium, Jaber F., *Living and Dying at Murray Manor.* New York: St. Martin's Press, 1975.

Lustbader, Wendy, *Counting on Kindness: An Explanation of Dependency.* New York: Free Press, 1991.

McInnis, Pauline, *The Nursing Home Companion.* Washington: Devon Books, 1993.

Morgan, Richard L., *With Faces to the Evening Sun: Faith Stories from the Nursing Home.* Nashville: Upper Room Books, 1998.

Selin, Peter S., *Nursing Homes: The Family's Journey.* Baltimore: Johns Hopkins Press, 2001.

Simmons, Henry C. and Mark Peters, *With God's Oldest Friends: Pastoral Visiting in the Nursing Homes.* Mahwah, NJ: Paulist Press, 1996.

Thomas, William H., *Worth Living: How Someone You Love Can Still Enjoy Life in a Nursing Home—The Eden Alternative in Action.* Acton, MA: Vander Wyk and Burnham, 1996.

Tisdale, Sallie, *Harvest Moon: Portrait of a Nursing Home.* New York: Henry Holt and Company, 1987.

For Further Information

For a list of nursing home state ombudsperson offices see Peter Selin, op. cit., pp. 253–258.

For useful suggestions on helping parents make the transition to a nursing home see Linda Boatman, "Helping Your Parent Make the Trasition to a Nursing Home," *Presbyterians Today*, March 2000, p. 15.

Going Outside the Camp: Ministry in the Nursing Home

Richard L. Morgan

"Very truly, I tell you, when you were younger, you used to fasten your own belt and to go wherever you wished. But when you grow old, you will stretch out your hands, and someone else will fasten a belt around you and take you where you do not wish to go" (John 21:18). When Jesus spoke these words to Peter there were no nursing homes.

In fact, the average length of life was only thirty years at the most. Today in America alone there are over two million people living in nursing homes. These words of Jesus speak clearly to this growing population. And that population will increase dramatically in the next few years as people eighty-five years and older, the group most likely to need long-term care, is expected to triple to almost nine million by the year 2030. Currently a sixty-five-year-old has a 43 percent chance of entering a nursing home at some point in his or her life.

At times older persons find themselves in a nursing home against their will. They feel abandoned by their families and face a painful journey through loss, change, and diminishment. Alienation and boredom are the effects of life lived totally in an institution. Nursing home residents confront critical spiritual challenges including empty and *routined* time, meaninglessness, and separation from their faith community. A "Blondie" cartoon depicts Dagwood's boss, Mr. Dithers, commenting on reading about health care and nursing homes. He asks Dagwood, "When I am 90 years old, and in a nursing home, will you come to visit me?"

Dagwood replies, "Oh, for heaven's sake, Boss. You're not that much older than I am . . . I'll probably be in there with you."

Mr. Dithers slumps on his desk and cries, "Oh no! The stories are already bad enough, and now you tell me *that*!"

A report ordered by Congress and prepared by the Department of Health and Human Services concludes that more than 90 percent of American nursing homes have too few workers to take proper care of patients. It further states: "It is currently not feasible for the federal government to require that homes achieve a minimum ratio of nursing staff to patients—as experts recommended—largely because of the cost."[1] Our concern is the ministry of the church to these oft-neglected residents of nursing homes. The author of the letter to the Hebrews described Jesus' ministry as "suffer[ing] outside the city gate" and challenges Christians to "go to him outside the camp" (Hebrews 13:12–13). The church needs to design new ministries to go "outside the camp," to reach out to residents in nursing homes, who are often considered outside the bounds of the church's ministry.

I have been in enough nursing homes for enough years to become a part of—a participant in—a world of unexplained noises and strange sights, odd appearances and mysterious events, which at their heart are the most mundane of things. Nursing homes hold all the force and drama of life and death and the movements between, made manifest in earthly banality.[2]

Stages of Adjustment

Morton Bard and Dawn Sangrey have identified three adaptive phases of the nursing home resident.[3] The three stages are: (1) impact; (2) recoil; and (3) reorganization.

During the *impact* stage the resident faces the initial emotional and spiritual adjustment of being in a new environment. I well recall one elderly woman we brought to a nursing home. After the death of her husband she had been accustomed to a good life in a comfortable apartment, but now as she glanced around at her one-room home, with its blank walls and confining look, she gasped and said, "Has my life come to this?"

The *recoil* stage is the phase when residents struggle to adjust to their new environment and reorder their life in the new setting. During this phase residents seek to find some meaning for what appears to be their final residence. Other residents, facing their death, often ask the same question, "Why has the Lord left me here so long?"

During the *reorganization* stage residents reorganize their activities and seek to find purposeful living in the new community. In my earlier book, *With Faces to the Evening Sun: Faith Stories from the Evening Sun,*[4] I followed stories of nursing home residents from settling in through weeks of adjusting to their new community until finally they felt at home. I have known residents who have not succumbed to depression or despair, and who use their time to serve one another. They push a wheelchair for a neighbor, help the activities director, or feed someone who cannot hold a spoon.

Ministry in the nursing home needs to be aware of these stages.

Meeting Emotional and Spiritual Needs

One of the most glaring needs of residents in a nursing home is maintaining their identity. I recall one resident who came to a group I was leading and when I asked her name, she replied, "My name? Same as it's always been!" She said more than she knew. In a place where people often become depersonalized or patronized, she was affirming her identity.

Another obstacle that faces nursing home residents is the boredom of routinized time. People who live in nursing homes live in an environment characterized by rigid time routines. There is a time to get up, a time to eat, coffee time, and bedtime. There is craft time, bath time, and time for taking pills. The time is kept by people in white uniforms. There is a sameness about it all, and interruptions in the routine are rare. Parts of the day may be marked off by meals, as a nursing home resident remarked.[5] "We go from one meal to the next. That's about it." Time seems like a treadmill—it moves, but nothing happens. The temptation is to become a prisoner of the deadly routine and let one's life revolve around which chair to sit in, or where to sit and stare. The present seems all the time that exists. As Dayle A. Freedman points out: "The past is absent. There is no one who shares one's personal history, and there is nothing which evokes it. Staff members relate to the impaired person before them, and the older person experiences a loss of his or her past."[6]

Furthermore, there is little hope for the future. The nursing home residents know that this will be their last home, the final stage of their life journey. Death awaits them. Yet there is often little recognition of this; when residents die, doors are shut and in secrecy their bodies are whisked off. Seldom are other residents given the opportunity to mourn the loss of their friends. Denying residents the right to know when others die blocks their own grief process. As Shakespeare wrote, "He who lacks time to mourn lacks time to mend." Despite the rhetoric that residents need to be shielded from the death of others, they need to know so they can mourn.

Residents face a serious loss of community. Visit any nursing home and quietly observe how few residents interact with each other. One woman remarked that prior to entering the nursing home, she was the life of her community and church. She derived a great deal of energy from people and was in constant interaction with others. But at the nursing home she mostly just stared at the walls. When she tried to talk with others they stared at her as though she was crazy. Residents soon play the game, stay by themselves, and try to be "good" patients.

Little opportunity exists for forming friendships or bonds with others. Tracy Kidder's book, *Old Friends*, offers a striking contrast to this lack of community. Lou Freed and Joe Torchio are strangers thrust together as roommates in Linda Manor, a nursing home, where they are relegated to live out their final days. Lou and Joe develop a friendship that transcends all the indignities and the impersonal life of a nursing home. But that story is a rare exception to the rule.

One of the basic needs of residents in a nursing home is to discover meaning in their lives. They feel a serious loss of self-esteem and a gnawing sense of uselessness. I can still visualize my old friend Oscar, walking aimlessly through the halls of a nursing home, and pleading, "Give me something to do!" These people are major victims of our society's demands that work alone gives us worth. We are judged by what we do or give, not by who we are. Nursing home residents face an even greater threat to their being because they have to be dependent on others for everything, "counting on kindness" as Wendy Lustbader puts it.[7]

Another major issue for nursing home residents is being cut off from their faith community. Like the ancient Hebrews, transported from their faith community in Jerusalem to the strange world of Babylon, they find it hard "to sing the LORD'S song in a foreign land." So those ancient people of God, paralyzed with despair, "sat down . . . and wept when we remembered Zion. On the willows there we hung up our harps" (Psalm 137:1–2, 4).

Too often the mainline churches have made ministry to the nursing home a low priority. Clergy often avoid consistent visitation. As one clergyman told me: "I hate to go into those places. It makes me feel utterly sad that I might have to go there someday. But I go once in a while, and get it over with!" Sporadic attempts are made by groups in the church, usually women of the church, to visit the residents, and bring cheer and hope. But all too often these visits are meaningless and make residents feel they are only valuable at holiday times. We have all heard stories of parishioners who complain, "No one at the church visited me."

Everyone who enters a nursing home feels that admission means they are going somewhere to wait to die, the last stop on life's journey. Yet all too often there is little pastoral care for them related to the end-of-life issues. It is rare when someone takes the time to talk to residents about their fears of dying or what happens at death. In a nursing home almost every week someone dies, often with no word or wave of farewell. These deaths, when residents become aware of them, cause them to worry about their own dying.

These are some of the basic spiritual and emotional needs of nursing home residents, and it is the mission of the church, the caring community, to find ways to meet these needs in the spirit of the one who "suffer[ed] outside the city gate."

Ministry Beyond the Camp

When we think about nursing homes most of us shy away from even picturing ourselves there. That is one place we would rather not go. Our hope is that we can end our days in our familiar home, surrounded by all we know and love. It is a frightening prospect for one who has spent a lifetime fighting to be in control, to lose that control. How do we minister to people in a nursing home?

By a Ministry of Presence

This means simply "being there" and visiting with the resident. You may not know what to say or how to answer all their questions, but your presence is all that they need. At times it is holding their hand in a time of loneliness or fear, or sitting in silence by their bedside, or attending to some of their needs. At times you may have to listen to their stories. When older persons tell stories it is not a symptom of dementia; by telling the same stories over and over again they are affirming that in a changing world some things are constant.

Henry Simmons and Mark Richards have outlined helpful steps in pastoral visitation in their book *With God's Oldest Friends*. After a *greeting*, they say the visitor needs to speak a word. This is followed by *sharing communion*—"the person needs to know for that moment that she matters, that God loves her, and that you are there for her."[8] The last step is simply *ending the visit* with a kind word or a prayer or a blessing. There is simply no substitute for visiting persons in a nursing home, ever mindful of Jesus' words, "I was sick and [you] visited me" (Matthew 25:36 KJV). Ruth Harris Calkin has written a powerful poem about visiting in a nursing home, titled "I Wonder":

> You know, Lord, how I serve you.
> With great emotional fervor in the limelight.
> You know how eagerly I speak for you
> at a woman's club.
> You know how I effervesce
> When I promote a fellowship group.
> You know my genuine enthusiasm at a Bible study
> But how would I react, I wonder,
> If you pointed to a basin of water
> And asked me to wash the callused feet
> Of a bent and wrinkled old woman,
> Day after day, month after month,
> In a room where nobody saw, and nobody knew?[9]

By Support Groups

There is often little communication among residents in a nursing home.[10] Feelings of isolation and abandonment prevail. Groups offer a helpful way to build community and form friendships. These groups may focus on Bible study or life review. Miriam Dunson's helpful book *A Very Present Help*, offers ten studies of the Psalms. This study, based on Dunson's experience in leading Bible studies in a nursing home, connects the Psalms with the needs and situations of older persons.

In my book *Remembering Your Story*[11] I offer one hundred questions that could be asked of a group of residents to prompt them to remember their stories. A revised *Leader's Guide*, based on many groups in health care centers, provides exercises and helps for anyone wishing to lead such groups. Often these groups become long-term support groups.

One story illustrates the power of groups. A few days earlier Ruby had left her home, no longer able to live alone. She seemed forlorn and woebegone, so the social worker brought her to a Bible study group. Pauline read the story of Jesus coming to the disciples at three in the morning during a violent storm. They had struggled against adverse winds and felt overwhelmed and defeated. Jesus got into their boat and calmed their fears.

Pauline turned to Ruby and said, "I know it's hard to leave your home and come here. I know it seems strange here, and you feel overwhelmed by it all. But we're all in the same boat here. We'll help you to get through this."

Ruby mustered a glimmer of a smile and replied, "But the sea is so great and my boat is so small."

"I know," replied Pauline, "but never forget, Jesus is with us in the boat."

A glimmer of hope peeked through Ruby's gloom.

Support groups provide a common bond, and since older people often have a strong faith this can be a rallying point.

Through the Rituals of the Church

David Oliver points to the need for the church to bring the worship of the church to residents. He laments the fact that "the volunteer . . . is anxious to be finished and on his or her way. The message does not always relate to the life-world in which residents find themselves, nor does it reach a large number of persons."[12] He believes that if a sufficient number of persons from the church were regularly in the home, possibilities for developing a faith community in the home would be better. Simmons and Richards suggest how the church can offer rituals in the home.[13]

"Room Blessings for New Residents," a "Service for Upholding a Resident Moving from Independent Living to Health Care," and a "Memorial Service for Residents" can be found in my book With *Faces to the Evening Sun.*[14] In vivid contrast to the routinized life one has in a long-term facility, religious life provides a sense of significant time. Today, instead of a time of monotonous boredom, meaning can exist in relationship to significant moments in religious history. For nursing home residents who cannot attend their home church and feel cut off from their faith communities, religious life offers a unique opportunity for experiencing community. Sharing in worship forms close bonds within the nursing home.

By Helping Residents Face Dying and Death

Eugene Bianchi has well written that the paradox of faith is the strange notion that death is "a final celebration of life." He calls us to anticipate what may be the greatest grace of our lives that can occur as we approach death—the celebration of what has been and what now is. Our entire life is a preparation for this moment. "To celebrate is to rejoice for having experienced life with its pains and joys, to be glad that we have helped our survivors to preserve and nourish the beautiful, fragile gift of life into yet another season."[15]

Except for a hospice hospital there is no other place where death seems more present than in a nursing home. Many residents perceive this place as the last stop before death. Yet even here residents can be denied discussing their feelings about death.

We fear the final parting of persons we love, and facing their dying means we have to confront our own. Dying is no longer a natural part of living and has become a taboo subject. An awkward silence surrounds death, leaving a void for the dying. Although we say we do not discuss death because we do not want to upset the old person who is dying, it may well be that we are afraid of our own dying.

In their study "Nursing Home Residents' Perception of the 'Good Death'" Florence Gelo, Linda O'Brien, and Bonnie O'Connor conclude that the majority of people being interviewed define a good death in terms of freedom from pain and suffering. They also indicate that religious faith and prayer are important to them in coping with death and dying.[16] Although most of these residents affirm a genuine faith in God, some did broach the topic of having to face God's judgment and punishment, suggesting some anxiety. Pastoral care should include exploring these fears and anxieties instead of never mentioning the subject.

My experience has been that the person who is dying is willing to talk about it, at least to some extent. People who are dying have told me many things—that they are ready, or they are not. Sometimes they are frightened or want to review their lives; others talk about their sadness at leaving their families or about wondering what lies beyond. However, sometimes the resident may not want to talk about it. The visitor can elicit some feelings about death by asking such questions as "What do you think about your condition?" or "Can we talk about what is happening to you?" or even more directly, "Do you think you are dying?"[17]

By Helping Residents to Serve

Most people perceive nursing home residents as passive recipients of care. Many are there to be served, kept active, and entertained. Seldom do we realize that some residents are still able to serve and care for others. Nothing affirms residents of nursing homes more than making them feel useful and needed.

Conclusion

Whatever form ministry takes for residents in a nursing home, we must never forget that these are God's children, not just frail demented survivors of life. We need to be sensitive to the needs of those who are often left in abandoned corners of God's world and frequently avoided or forgotten.

Henri Nouwen has reminded us of an old legend in the Talmud. Rabbi Yoshua ben Levi came upon the prophet Elijah and asked, "When will the Messiah come?" Elijah replies, "Go and ask him yourself."

"Where is he?" asks the rabbi, and "How shall I know him?"

"He is sitting among the poor covered with wounds."[18]

An old lady died in the geriatric hospital near Dundee, Scotland. It was felt that she had nothing left of any value. Later, when the nurses were going through her meager possessions, they found a poem. Its quality and content so impressed the staff that copies were made and distributed to every nurse in the hospital. One nurse took her copy to Ireland. Later it appeared in the Christmas edition of the news magazine of the North Ireland Association for Mental Health. Now it wings across the Internet.

An Old Lady's Poem

What do you see, nurses, what do you see?
What are you thinking when you're looking at me?
A crabby old woman, not very wise,
Uncertain of habit, with far-away eyes?
Who dribbles her food and makes no reply,
Who seems not to notice the things that you do,
And forever is losing a stocking or shoe . . .
Who, resisting or not, lets you do as you will,
with bathing and feeding, the long day to fill . . .
Is that what you're thinking? Is that what you see?

Then open your eyes, nurse, you're not looking at me.
I'll tell you who I am as I sit here so still
As I do at your bidding, as I eat at your will.
I'm a small child of ten with a father and mother,
Brothers and sisters, who love one another.
A young girl of sixteen, with wings on her feet
Dreaming that soon now a lover she'll meet.
A bride soon as twenty—my heart gives a leap,
Remembering the vows that I promised to keep.
At twenty-five now, I have young of my own,
Who need me to guide and a secure happy home.
A woman of thirty, my young now grown fast,
Bound to each other with ties that should last.
At forty, my young sons have grown and are gone,
But my man's beside me to see I don't mourn.
At fifty, once more babies play around my knee,
Again we know children, my loved ones and me.
Dark days are upon me, my husband is dead;
I look at the future, I shudder with dread.
For my young are all rearing children of their own,
And I think of the years and the love that I've known.
I'm just now an old woman . . . and nature is cruel;
'Tis jest to make old age look like a fool.
The body, it crumbles, grace and vigor depart,
There is now a stone where once was a heart.
But inside this old carcass a young girl dwells,
And now and again my battered heart swells.
I remember the joys, I remember the pain,
And I'm loving and living life over again.
I think of the years all too few, gone too fast,
And accept the stark fact that nothing can last.
So open your eyes, nurses, open and see,
Not a crabby old woman, look closer, see ME!

This poem by an unknown Scottish lady in a nursing home reminds us to look beyond what age does to people to see their young souls within.

Viktor Frankl found meaning in a Nazi concentration camp, and he wrote that meaning can be found in three ways: (1) by what we give (in terms of creative deeds), (2) by what we take from the world (in terms of our experiencing values), and (3) through the stand we take toward a fate we can no longer change (an incurable disease, an inoperable cancer, or the like).[19] These three aspects of meaning in human life—what we give, what we experience, and what attitude we take—relate to the nursing home. In this place often described in negative terms as a warehouse for the elderly, or a modern leper colony, residents can find meaning as they reach out to help others, as they reflect on the values of their lives, and as they face the frailties and problems of aging with courage and heroism.

A junior nursing student from Arizona State University, Angel Akins-Cash, wrote the following poem, which resonates with anyone who does ministry in a nursing home.

Through Her Eyes

Through her eyes, she said so much.
Through her eyes, my heart she touched.

I felt days of laughter, and days of tears,
Through her eyes, days turned into years.

Her whispering eyes spoke so loud.
Telling the story of a woman, so proud.

Through her happiest moment and her darkest hour
She takes me with her through eyes of great power.

I experience days of yesteryear
I go with her calmly—no shame, no fear.

I taste the moment of years gone past.
Times by the sand of the hourglass.

I hear of a love that they had together.
Now only in her heart, it lives forever.

She smells the roses, she hears the wind,
Through her eyes, she lives again.

On this never-ending journey, she takes me.
Through her eyes, I learn to see.

I see days turn into years, and years turn into days.
Right before me, out her life plays.

But these years have passed and are here no more.
Happened before my time, but I've seen them before.

I know through her eyes, a lesson was learned.
Through her eyes, my world has turned.

Through her eyes, wisdom did pour.
Those sweet eyes, I have no more.[20]

When there are caregivers like this student nurse who go beyond the necessary ministries of healing to seeing the eyes of the heart of residents and relating to them with compassion and love, life will get better for God's oldest friends in these places of mercy. Simmons and Richards write: "Nursing home residents have much to teach us. If we are unafraid to draw close, we have much to learn. . . . The lessons have a pointedness that gives new meaning to religious convictions that all life is holy, and is part of God's gift. . . . The nursing home resident who has learned anew to thank God for this life can be a powerful teacher and witness."[21]

The apostle Paul confronted the Christian church, at that time mostly Jewish in nature, with the challenge of going outside its boundaries to include Gentiles. The church became an inclusive fellowship, where "there is no longer Jew or Greek, there is no longer slave or free, there is no longer male and female, for all of you are one in Christ Jesus" (Galatians 3:28).

Sallie Tisdale reminds us that residents of nursing homes are outside the camp, removed from the mainstream of society, and separated from the faith communities. "Standing apart . . . almost parenthetically removed from its environment, the nursing home becomes a kind of tribal village, a place of misfits."[22] If this is so, and increasingly this is the image still imprinted on the minds of those who shy away, the church has a new challenge—to meet the needs of the new Gentiles outside its boundaries.

One recent development that promises hope for nursing homes is the Eden Alternative pioneered by William Thomas. The core concept of the Eden Alternative is quite simple: "We must teach ourselves to see the environment as habitats for human beings rather than facilities for the frail and elderly."[23] The Eden Alternative shows how companion animals, the opportunity to give meaningful care to other living creatures, and the variety and spontaneity that mark an enlivened environment can succeed where pills and therapies fail. The Eden Alternative is a step in the right direction to remake the experience of aging across America and around the world. Still, nothing can take the place of the church being vitally involved in ministries of visitation, pastoral care, and worship.

On one occasion I was leading worship at a nursing home during Holy Week. I was trying to get the residents to remember the sacred events of Jesus' last week on earth. When I asked questions, all I received were blank stares and uninterested glances. Desperate to get someone to respond, I asked, "Surely some of you can remember one of the words of Jesus from the cross?"

A dear old lady smiled at me and replied, "Yes, it is finished! And so are you!"

I was finished, but the challenge remains.

Questions for Discussion

1. Check out the local nursing homes in your community, and arrange a visit for members of the church. Before the visit ask members of the group to talk freely about their feelings about visiting a nursing home. Ask them to be honest.

2. When you visit ask the activities director if he or she is interested in volunteers from the church to visit residents, read to them, take them for walks, or help with other activities.

3. When the group returns have a debriefing session in which you discuss their reactions to the visit, including the effect it had on the residents and the visitors.

4. After visiting a nursing home meet and discuss the kind of ministry the group could provide. A ministry of presence, providing occasional worship services, Bible studies, or a sing-along are some of the possibilities.

5. Many residents in nursing homes never get to their own church. Another opportunity for ministry would be to take tapes of worship services to them, or talk about the worship so residents feel as though they have been in church.

6. Through the care committee of the church establish a family caregiver group so members can make weekly visits to the nursing home.

7. Recruit youth in the church to visit residents and to record their life stories. Richard Morgan's *Remembering Your Story* has a one

hundred–item questionnaire that could provide questions for the interview.

8. Ask the session or board of the church to consider the possibility of a support group at the church for family members who have a relative in a nursing home.

9. How can a ministry to nursing home residents be personal—not just dropping off fruit, flowers, or cookies at the receptionist's desk?

10. If your church has a child day care try to arrange a visit by the children to a nursing home or make that a field trip for a church school class.

Notes

1. Robert Pear, "Odds of Good Care for Elderly Slim," *The New York Times*, February 2002.
2. Sallie Tisdale, *Harvest Moon: Portrait of A Nursing Home* (New York: Henry Holt and Company, 1987), xiii.
3. Morton Bard and Dawn Sangrey, *The Crime Victim's Book* (Secaucus, NJ: Citadel Press, 1986).
4. Richard L. Morgan, *With Faces to the Evening Sun: Faith Stories from the Nursing Home* (Nashville: Upper Room Books, 1998).
5. Jabor F. Gubrium, *Living and Dying at Murray Manor* (New York: St. Martin's Press, 1975), p. 166.
6. Dayle Freedman, "Spiritual Challenges of Nursing Home Life," in Mel Kimble et al., *Aging, Spirituality, and Religion* (Minneapolis: Fortress Press, 1995), p. 363.
7. Wendy Lustbader, *Counting on Kindness: An Exploration of Dependency* (New York: Free Press, 1991).
8. Henry Simmons and Mark Richards, *With God's Oldest Friends* (Mahwah, NJ: Paulist Press, 1998), p. 32.
9. Ruth Harris Calkin, "I Wonder," reprinted from *AGEnda*, No. 85, October 1998.
10. Tracy Kidder, *Old Friends* (New York: Wheeler Publishing Co., 1993).
11. Richard Morgan, *Remembering Your Story* (Nashville: Upper Room Books, 2002).
12. David Oliver, "Will the Real Nursing Home Scandal Worsen in the Future?" *Journal of Religion and Aging* (1987), p.158.
13. Simmons and Richards, *With God's Oldest Friends*, pp. 76–88.
14. Richard Morgan, *With Faces to the Evening Sun*, pp. 183–190.
15. Eugene Bianchi, "Death Preparation as Life Enhancement" in *Affirmative Aging*, ed. Joan E. Lukens (Harrisburg, PA: Morehouse Publishers, 1995), p.131.

16. Florence Gelo, Linda O'Brien, and Bonnie O'Connor, "Nursing Home Residents' Perception of the 'Good Death,'" *Journal of Religious Gerontology* 10 (1997), p. 22.

17. Robert Buckman, *I Don't Know What to Say: . . . How to Help and Support Someone Who Is Dying* (New York: Little Brown and Co., 1989).

18. Henri Nouwen, *The Wounded Healer* (New York: Doubleday, 1972), p. 183

19. Viktor Frankl, *The Doctor and the Soul* (New York: Vintage Books, 1965), xiii.

20. Used by permission of the author, Angel Atkins-Cash.

21. Simmons and Richards, op.cit., p. 101.

22. Tisdale, op. cit.

23. This is the mission statement of the Eden Alternative.

Elder Abuse: Don't Ask— Don't Tell

Miriam Dunson

The abuse of older persons is one of the best-kept secrets of all time. It is unpleasant to talk about. It is not only unpleasant to talk about; it is agonizing to talk about because its reality strikes at the heart of our notions of love, home, and family. However, talk about it or not, elder abuse happens. Today's families are stressed perhaps more than earlier generations by social, economic, and personal issues. If a family is living happily and then an older relative comes to live with them and has to be cared for, the entire family structure is stressed and abuse happens, sometimes intentionally and sometimes unintentionally.

Older persons are afraid to tell about abuse from a caregiver for fear that if they tell there will be no one to care for them, and for fear that the next step will be the much-dreaded nursing home. Adult children or other caregivers become abusers in an effort to deal with their own frustrations and angers for feeling trapped in a situation that is unpleasant and for which they are not properly trained. Therefore no one tells. No one outside the caregiving context knows about the abuse, or if they do know they "don't want to interfere." Thus the abuse goes on, and nothing is done about it.

Because of this fact it is difficult to come up with any accurate numbers concerning elder abuse. However, the National Aging Resource Center on Elder Abuse estimates that two million cases of abuse and neglect occur in American households each year.[1] Others who have studied the situation indicate, however, that only one in fourteen incidents is reported.[2] The nation has begun to recognize child abuse and much is written about this form of abuse. However, not as much publicity or attention has been given to the rights of older persons who are cared for by family members or paid caregivers. Many who are in nursing homes or other care facilities are cared for by nurses and aides who are overworked and underpaid and who are under great stress in an effort to meet the needs of too many older adults in their care.

However, the fact is that abuse does happen, far more than is shown by any figures that might be found, and in places where you would not expect to find such abuses. According to the March-April 2002 issue of *Aging Today,* published by the American Society on Aging, some efforts have been made by the National Center on Elder Abuse (NCEA) to deal with these problems. The NCEA director, Sara Aravanis, was quoted as saying at the First National Summit on Elder Abuse held in Washington, D.C., December 4, 2001, "Elder abuse and neglect deserve an organized national focus" and "The graying of America demands that there be a concerted effort to deal with these pervasive problems."[3]

Ricker Hamilton, protective program administrator at the Department of Human Services, Maine Bureau of Elder and Adult Services, has stated that federal funding has been scant when compared to funding for other types of abuse prevention programs. He said elder abuse programs receive .08 percent of federal dollars targeted at preventing abuse, whereas child abuse programs receive 93.35 percent and those serving victims of domestic violence receive 6.7 percent. Reporting on the First National Summit on Elder Abuse, Mary Joy Quinn wrote: "Noting that older Americans constitute about 13 percent of the U.S. population, a percentage projected to double by 2030, [Hamilton] said it is appropriate to enlarge the pie and allocate more funding for elder abuse programs without taking away from any of the other groups."[4]

The summit produced twenty-one recommendations to address the issues of abuse on the national level. These four seemed most crucial:[5]

1. Develop and implement a sustained national strategic communications program to educate the public on elder abuse. Encourage the Centers for Disease Control and Prevention to recognize elder abuse as a public health issue.
2. Work for the enactment of a national elder abuse act to raise national awareness and to focus federal resources on elder abuse.

3. Increase awareness of elder abuse within the justice system so that it becomes a higher priority crime-control issue.
4. Create a national adult protective services resource center to train and certify adult protective services workers at all levels.

However, these are only recommendations to a government that is already deeply involved financially with many other priorities, such as homeland security, the turmoil in the Middle East, the U.S. economy, and other important issues. It is unlikely that issues pertinent to older adults will be addressed in the very near future, nor will they reach a high priority for our nation during the next decade or two. The question remains: What happens to all those being abused in the meantime? Who can help?

One answer to the question is the church. There is no other institution or organization that has such full access into the homes or care facilities as does the church through its pastors and other church visitors. Therefore it seems that some of the most urgent actions to be taken at this time to fill in the gaps where there are needs not being met would involve the church. Education of visitation teams, of students in seminaries, and of pastors through continuing education about how to recognize the signs of abuse and what to do when abuse is identified is crucial in order to properly address the matter of elder abuse.

In developing a program for the education of the congregation, there are many questions: Who are the abused? Who are the abusers? Why does abuse happen? How are older persons abused? What can be done by the church to prevent and stop elder abuse? These are questions that every congregation needs to be discussing, followed by action in every way possible to stop this quiet, hush-hush agony experienced by so many older persons.

For congregations that wish to begin these discussions, the following are some helps and suggestions.

Who Are the Abused?

According to one source, victims of abuse are mostly in the "old old" category, and the vast majority are female. Their ages range from seventy-five years to beyond. Persons at highest risk of abuse are the dependent older adults, and since dependency increases with age, abuse also increases with age. Women live longer than men and therefore experience abuse more than men. Especially vulnerable are people with Alzheimer's disease or other dementias who sometimes behave violently or aggressively toward others.[6]

What Are the Different Kinds of Abuse?

Sometimes abuse of older persons is not recognized because it is not defined properly in the minds of those involved. A working definition would include the fact that elder abuse is the mistreatment or neglect of an older adult and is usually by a relative or other caregiver.[7] Most elder abuse takes place at home, and in 90 percent of known cases a family member is the abuser.[8] However, abuse also takes place in nursing homes and other care facilities.

There are many kinds of abuse:

1. *Physical violence:* Hitting, slapping, forcing sore arthritic joints to move in painful ways, confinement, lacerating, burning, restraining, pushing, and shoving. A ninety-eight-year-old woman in a nursing home was beaten on the head with a spoon because she had trouble swallowing. Signs of this abuse were obvious when blood began to creep down her neck just underneath the skin. Her niece observed the damage, the victim told her story, and the guilty nurse's aide was convicted.[9] However, many cases are not observed, or even if they are the abuse is not reported.

2. *Threats of violence:* Constantly saying, "If you don't . . . I will . . ." or "The next time you do that, I will . . ." Victims can live in fear of violence even if violence never happens. In the movie *Trip to Bountiful* the character played by Geraldine Page was a good illustration of this kind of abuse. She lived with her son and daughter-in-law, and the daughter-in-law had set up many rules for her mother-in-law to follow, such as Don't sing hymns while you sweep the floor, Give me your Social Security check on the day it arrives, Stop hiding things in your bedroom, and so on. The daughter-in-law would end each rule reminder with, "If you don't do that, I will tell your son!"

3. *Verbal abuse:* name-calling, shouting, using dirty language, speaking out in anger. "Stop talking, you don't make any sense." "You are worthless." "You are an old tightwad geezer." "Don't talk so loud, you annoy me."

4. *Financial exploitation:* misuse of the funds of the older adult, stealing, con games, using assets or property of an older person for personal gain. In Kentucky in 1992 a lawyer was sentenced

to six months in jail for billing a ninety-year-old woman $825 a day, supposedly for visiting her three times daily in a nursing home before her death, a total of $145,000. He claimed to have visited her 585 times during the 195 days before she died, whereas the nursing home records showed that he visited her only three or four times during that period of time.[10]

5. *Emotional abuse:* engaging in actions that cause fear, grief, anxiety, anguish by demeaning, name-calling, insulting, ignoring, humiliating, threatening, isolating, and so forth. The emotional abuse is often the result of verbal abuse, especially as related to the worth of the person. An example of this abuse is seen when the adult child takes the parent to the doctor's office. The parent is in good health, with all mental faculties in place, but because the person is old and in a wheelchair, the receptionist speaks over the head of the parent to the adult child as if the parent is not present or not a person.

6. *Active neglect:* intentionally not providing for the needs of the older persons, intentionally giving no attention to personal hygiene, no attention to bedsores, skin abrasions, and other conditions that need attention, denial of food and medication. Keeping a dependent person clean and with good personal hygiene is a difficult task at times, and it is easy just to let it slide. An aide was heard saying to a resident in a nursing home who needed to go to the bathroom, "Just go ahead and let go, honey, I'll clean you up later . . . I'm busy now." This kind of neglect can easily lead to loss of dignity, loss of self-control, loss of personal respect.

7. *Passive neglect:* unintentionally not fulfilling the caregiving responsibilities, causing distress without conscious or willful intent. Both in a home caregiving situation and in a nursing home setting, it is possible that there is so much to do, so many facets of the caregiving, that without meaning to do so, the caregiver lets neglect happen. In the home this may mean that professional home care is necessary to improve the situation or a decision made for a care facility. If in a nursing home, pressure needs to be placed on the administration to provide sufficient staff to meet the needs of the residents or arrange the schedule around the residents rather than the convenience of the staff.

8. *Self-abuse:* The person lives alone and does not feel well much of the time. He or she does not feel like cooking, so doesn't eat

well; does not feel like cleaning, so the house is messy and dirty; does not feel like bathing or doing the laundry, so is not personally clean or dressed in a neat and clean manner. A woman lives in a mobile home where she has lived alone for fifteen years since her husband died. She is not well, but she insists on continuing to live alone and take care of herself. She has no children. To enter the mobile home a visitor must walk through a wire fence entrance area that contains two dogs that are never taken outside the fence. The odor is almost unbearable. Inside the mobile home there is a narrow path about twelve inches wide, leading from the kitchen to the bedroom to the bathroom, winding between stacks of newspapers, magazines, old clothes, paper and plastic bags, bottles, and trash about five feet high. The bed is dirty, the dishes are dirty, the clothes are stained, the shoes are in shambles. This woman lives in the midst of the "stuff" that she has saved for years and from which she does not wish to part because she "may need it sometime."

9. *Prescription drugs taken but not needed:* An article in the Louisville newspaper *The Courier Journal* stated that close to a quarter of all Americans sixty-five or older have been given prescriptions for drugs they should not take.[11] Some of the drugs can produce amnesia and confusion, and others cause serious side effects, such as heart problems or respiratory failure. The article goes on to say that there is no need to prescribe these drugs for older people, either because safer alternatives are available or because the drugs are simply not needed. This is another kind of abuse caused by medical services.

Who Are the Abusers?

Family members, usually adult children, are the most frequent abusers of older persons. Caregiver stress is the most common reason for abusing the care receiver. There may be many other stresses going on in the life of the caregiver than the stress that comes from the actual caregiving. There may be stresses of divorce, job loss, loneliness, feelings of being trapped, anger because of finding oneself "the one" in the family who has turned out to be the caregiver, and many others. However, perhaps the greatest stress comes from the relentlessness of the day-to-day care. *The Harvard Health Letter* as far back as 1995 stated that on average families keep a highly dependent older family member for many years at home, doing the bathing, feeding, dressing, and toileting, and so it is easy to have the system break down.[12] Sometimes drugs or alcohol are also involved in the life of the caregiver, and if the caregiver is dependent financially upon the care receiver, this leads to even more abuse.

Elder abuse is not only found in homes and carried out by family members, but unfortunately it is quite prevalent in nursing homes, carried out by nurses and aides. In a testimony before the U.S. Senate Special Committee on Aging an official of the General Accounting Office, Leslie G. Aronovitz, stated: "Almost one-third of nursing homes in the United States have been cited for deficiencies involving actual harm to residents or placing them at risk of death or serious injury. The testimony stated that nursing homes care for approximately 1.6 million older adults and disabled persons.[13]

Much of the problem in nursing homes is created by short staffing, overworked nurses and aides, and rapid turnover in the certification program for nursing aides. Many times as soon as the trainee becomes a CNA (Certified Nursing Assistant), he or she moves on to a better-paying job. Another problem is the low salary rate for both nurses and aides in the nursing home. The aides, in particular, do the hardest work (lifting, changing beds, and so forth) and the most unpleasant work (changing diapers, smelling the smells), and yet their pay is the lowest, often only minimum wage. When they are on a strict time schedule day after day, hurrying to care for an entire hall filled with people needing their special care, they can begin to cut corners, become frustrated, and become unable to give the care that is necessary for each resident.

What Can the Church Do?

Doctors are often the only non-family members with opportunity to observe the lives of older adults and intentionally watch for signs of abuse and neglect. And they can work with other professionals to ensure that suspected cases are followed up. However, one non-family member who always has a welcomed entrée into the homes of older adults is the pastor. Pastors, if trained in awareness, can play a critical role in identifying and preventing abuse. It is interesting to note that research indicates that clergy as a group are the ones who have the greatest opportunity to encounter abuse in the home or in the nursing home, but they are also the group rated least effective in addressing these issues and are among those less likely to refer abuse or neglect cases to helping agencies.

With government funds being funneled into other areas and with the needs of older persons seen as a low priority by many government officials—and yet at the same time increasing rapidly—it behooves the church to be aware of what is happening in the lives of older adults and to seek ways to address the issues. The following are steps a congregation can take to enhance care of older adults in their congregations and beyond.

1. Educate the pastor, the visitation committees, other volunteer visitors, and in fact the entire congregation about how to recognize the signs of abuse and about what the laws of the state require after abuse has been identified.

2. Include in the educational program of the church an emphasis that encourages healthy lifestyles among its members of all ages, helps identify behavior that is abusive, and provides ways to avoid abusive behavior. Included in this emphasis could be a focus on violence, healthy handling of stress, dealing with anger, and managing conflict.

3. Provide a support group for caregivers and respite care for care receivers in order that both can have a break at least once a week from their routines.

4. Explore what services are available from agencies in the county, such as the Area Agency on Aging, Home Health Care Services, Dial-A-Ride Programs, Meals on Wheels.

5. Explore the possibility of employing a parish nurse to serve on the staff of the church and monitor the health of members of the congregation, especially those who are homebound and in nursing homes or other care facilities. There are several models for parish nurses, such as a cluster of churches employing such a person, or medical persons in the congregation forming a committee to provide at least some of the services needed.

6. Help each homebound person to develop a "buddy system" with a friend outside the home who will contact them by telephone or a visit at least weekly, send cards on special occasions, and be a faithful friend.

7. Include books in the church library on the process of aging, elder abuse, nonviolent behaviors, anger, depression, stress, and caregiving.

8. Develop a list of the care facilities (retirement homes, nursing homes, personal care homes) within a fifty-mile radius of the church that includes the cost, requirements for acceptance,

services provided, levels of service available, and how many residents or units there are in the facility. This list should be kept current and placed in the church office so that when an older person can no longer be cared for by a caregiver, the family does not have to begin from "square one" in finding a suitable place.

9. Ask the pastor and the visitation committee to develop a working relationship with a mental health professional who has comprehensive knowledge of services for older adults in the community and can assist in formulating a plan of action when abuse is identified.

10. Church members can help prevent abuse by making regular visits. Older adults who receive visitors regularly are at less risk of being mistreated.

11. Educate the congregation concerning the negative attitudes toward older people and people who have disabilities.

How can a care committee be educated about elder abuse?

A good way is to share information gleaned from personal experiences. Ask the committee to discuss the following issues and questions:

1. Identify the issues related to abuse.
2. What are the most common experiences they have observed or heard of?
3. Have they ever confronted a situation of elder abuse and whether or not to report it?
4. Have they felt caught in the middle of a relationship where there is spousal abuse?
5. What is the role of the care committee member?
6. What is pastoral care in cases of elder abuse?

Planning a training program

1. Raise awareness concerning abuse as a motivation for learning. Use videos, testimonies of victims, speeches from experts in the field.
2. Study each different kind of abuse, and discuss ways to address each according to the need. Invite persons from local care facilities and professors in nursing schools to speak to these issues and to lead discussions.
3. Provide training in dealing both with the victim and with the abuser. Invite lecturers or use small-group sessions with local

trained people as trainers or facilitators. Include books and other written material. Learn about the local resource people and agencies that may bring their expertise into the situation.

4. Use local experts to serve on a panel to discuss the different ways of dealing with elder abuse.

5. Facilitate interaction among the participants with the aim of planning for future involvements in elder abuse issues. Seek commitments from the participants for future involvement in advocating for the victims of abuse.

Care for the Caregiver

Elder abuse is indeed an atrocious and unacceptable action on the part of the caregiver whether that person is a family member, an employee, a nurse, or someone else in the role of caregiver. However, just as agonizing and unacceptable is abuse of the caregiver. Caring for an older relative who is dependent upon the caregiver for all of the activities of daily living can be one of the loneliest and most thankless responsibilities in a person's life. It can also be a moving, satisfying, growing, and fulfilling time.

If the care receiver is being cared for by a family member, it does not matter how much or how little the caregiver does for the family member, there will be guilt involved. If the caring requires twenty-four hours a day, seven days a week, the caregiver can become overburdened, exhausted, and depressed because of the demanding character of the work in a confining situation. Caregivers may begin to set limits on what they will and will not do and very often begin to feel guilty about all that they are not doing for their family member. There is a thin line between doing too much and overdoing, and doing too little and feeling guilty.

If the parent is in a care facility and the son or daughter is working full time, especially if there are children involved, the adult child still finds himself or herself in a balancing act between guilt over not doing enough and resentment over being pressured to do too much. The sandwich generation is a reality today and adult children find it difficult to strike a happy balance.

Resentment and guilt can also be found when, for example, a daughter is the caregiver because she is single and/or perhaps lives nearby and the other siblings are married, have their own families, and live some distance away. Resentment emerges because the daughter did not intend to live this important time in her life career taking care of her parent while the other siblings are away living their own lives as they wish. Guilt emerges because the caregiver loves these same siblings toward whom she is feeling resentment. Resentment can increase when the other siblings come to visit and the parent shows a great deal of attention to and love for them while giving little or no attention, praise, or thanks to the daughter who is the caregiver.

As much as we would like to deny it, the fact is that many older people abuse their caregivers. The fragile, sick older person is not without the power to be quite abusive. This can come in the form of focusing exclusively on themselves and using what control they have left to them to destroy their relationship with the caregiver. Sometimes the person has always been difficult to be around, even as a younger person, and this only increases as he or she gets older. Others continually feel angry about what is happening to their body and take it out in rage on the most convenient target—most often the caregiver.

Self-care for the caregiver

Caregiving requires a deep and constant caring for the self. This is hard when we find ourselves in conflict as we weigh competing demands. The possibility always exists that the needs are greater than the capacity of the caregiver to fulfill those needs. In this case the caregiver must make that known and seek a solution to the situation before becoming overwhelmed.

Care for the caregiver cannot be postponed until all other claims are met; it must happen all along the way. Especially is this hard for the adult child to do. This is a place where the church can be of great help. Giving respite care so the caregiver can have an afternoon off each week, or a full day if possible, can be invaluable for the physical and emotional health of the caregiver.

Many women spend their lives in caregiving—for children, parents, spouse, friends—and find their identity in this role. A young woman once asked an older woman, "What is life's heaviest burden?" The older woman answered, "To have nothing to carry."

A caregiver needs to strike a balance between constant care for the self as well as for the care receiver. This can make the care itself stronger and provides opportunities for greater closeness with the loved one.

Self-care includes permission to enjoy the ordinary comforts and pleasures of life even when someone we love is suffering. Denying self-care does not reduce the other's suffering. It only limits the self's ability to bear it.

The caregiver's self-feelings should be distinguished from feelings for the other person. We can become too sensitive to the distress of the loved one. We need to keep a separate sense of self: This is your suffering, not mine, and I do not help you by suffering it myself.

Widen the circle of support for caregivers. If we believe that all the help we need should be provided by family members and that they could give it if they were unselfish, better organized, or emotionally strong enough, we will destroy the possibility of receiving the kind of care we need. It is a mistake to view help given by those other than family as a sign that the family has failed. Another, more useful, way to view the situation is to see it as a widening of the circle of care. It is an acknowledgment that we are all one body, dependent throughout our lives on the gifts of others, as they are on ours.

Caring and nurturing are traditionally seen as women's work and have been discounted and treated as costly distractions from the world of business and commerce. In this way society has neglected one of the most basic works of caring. Practically speaking, this means that a woman must maintain her regular job performance while a loved one needs her to shop, cook, take them to appointments, and so forth. Businesses in the future will need to seek to find ways to support those who find themselves in this kind of situation.

Richard Morgan has provided four strategies for caregivers to care for their own needs:[14]

1. Believe that you can only bear burdens *with* others, not *for* them.
2. Extricate yourself from the dance between guilt and anger.
3. Activate the "Mary" side of your personality and make time for your soul.
4. Remember, your best is good enough.

What makes caregiving possible at all is a personal network of help and support, including the following:

- Someone at work to cover for you so you can visit a friend or parent in the hospital.
- A friend who will check on a parent when you are out of town.

- A neighbor to answer your call when there is an emergency.
- One church has a "love bank"—you deposit in the bank according to your gifts and time—making visits, cooking meals, balancing checkbooks, driving people to appointments, doing household tasks. You turn to the bank for some of the same things when you yourself are in need.

Conclusion

When our parents and grandparents die they leave a very empty space. We discover there is no one ahead of us to mark the trail, to buffer us against the struggles. It is a very lonely feeling. We gradually come to realize that we now play that role.

When I was a much younger person I could look around the church and the community and identify the "spiritual giants"—leaders I could look up to, admire, follow, and believe. There came a time when I realized those giants were not there anymore. What had happened was that they were gone, and now I was becoming the older generation. The question arises: Why am I not the giant that I saw them to be? At some point we inherit the legacy, become the keeper of traditions, care for those parents, grandparents, and "spiritual giants" that we adored as children. We become the guardians of the family values, the providers of continuity, which includes the responsibility of caring for the older members of the family. It is our privilege and responsibility to do this. It sometimes comes as a surprise after they are gone that in our caregiving we have become the recipients of a very precious gift, that of having the privilege of caring for that one who nurtured, loved, taught, and mentored us at an earlier time in our lives. And before long we can become the recipients of the care that we have provided for those who have gone before us.

Questions for Discussion

1. There are over a million cases of elder abuse reported every year, but many are not reported. Why do you think older people are reluctant to tell about abuse from family or caregivers?
2. At a session meeting the pastor was shocked when one of the women elders reported abuse of an older member of the church by her daughter. She said, "I know the daughter was tired and strung out, but I heard her call her mother terrible names and

then even slapped her." Why was the pastor shocked to hear this? What could the session do?

3. An ombudsman was called to a nursing home because a resident complained that one of the certified nursing aides turned on the water of the shower too hot and burned her. The administrator ignored the complaint and said the resident had dementia and had imagined it. If you were the ombudsman, how would you handle that situation?

4. In a church the pastor was quick to report child abuse in a home he visited. A young girl had told him that her stepfather had sexually abused her. He reported the abuse to social service. Yet when an elderly parishioner complained that her children ignored her needs, he attributed her complaint to her confusion. Why was the pastor quick to act in one situation and so hesitant in the other?

5. In a nursing home an eighty-six-year-old member of the congregation told a church visitor, "The other day I had to go to the bathroom and the aide said, 'Go ahead and go. I'm busy now. I'll clean you up later and put diapers on you.'" Was this elder abuse?

6. In this chapter the author states that most elder abuse occurs with older women. Why do you think that is so?

7. You are the caregiver of a mother who is always complaining and laying a guilt trip on you. One day you lost your temper, called your mother names, accused her of ruining your life, and slapped her. Now your mother feels trapped and frightened. How do you solve this problem?

8. What can the church do to support caregivers? Would your church consider the possibility of a support group for adult children caring for aging relatives? What would that group look like? Who would lead it?

9. A large mainline church considered hiring a parish nurse who would not only provide health education for the members but also visit homes and become aware of elder abuse where it existed. Would you see a parish nurse as a valuable member of the church staff?

Notes

1. Quoted in "Abuse and Neglect Is Unacceptable at Any Age," a brochure published by Chief of Elder Rights, Division for Aging Services, 340 N. 11th Street, Suite 114, Las Vegas, NV 89101.
2. Ibid.
3. *Aging Today*, March–April 2002, published by the American Society on Aging, 833 Market Street, Suite 511, San Francisco, CA 94103-1824.
4. Mary Joy Quinn, "Elder Abuse Summit Sets Agenda: Experts Call for National Action," June 9, 2003.
5. Ibid.
6. Anne L. Horton and Judith Williamson, eds., *Abuse and Religion* (Lexington, MA: Lexington Books, 1988), p. 31.
7. *What Everyone Should Know About Elder Abuse*, A Scriptographic Booklet by Channing L. Bete Co., Inc., South Deerfield, MA 01373, p. 1.
8. *Smart Talk*, published by Intracorp, Philadelphia, PA, Spring 2002.
9. Story quoted from *"Aging Me . . . Aging You . . . The Journey of a Lifetime,"* video produced by Media Services, Presbyterian Church (U.S.A.), (800) 524-2612.
10. Andrew Wolfson, "Lawyer Sentenced for Not Repaying Estate," *The Courier-Journal*, Louisville, KY, February 27, 1992.
11. Gina Kolata, *New York Times* News Service, "Elderly Are Often Given Wrong Drugs, Study Says," *The Courier-Journal*, Louisville, KY, July 27, 1994.
12. *The Harvard Health Letter*, October 1995, published by Harvard Publications, P.O. Box 420300, Palm Coast, FL 32141-0300.
13. U.S. Special Committee on Aging, report on Web site by Leslie G. Aronovitz, General Accounting Office, 2003, www.aging.senate.gov.
14. Richard L. Morgan, "Spiritual Help for Caregivers," *AGEnda*, February 2002, published by the Office of Older Adult Ministries, Presbyterian Church (U.S.A.).

Late-Life Depression

Sally L. Campbell

At first glance the reader of this chapter title might think: late-life depression, so what's new? What would you expect? Those who are living in their later years might answer somewhat defensively, "An older person has every right to be depressed!" Perhaps because it is common wisdom that elders in our society will be depressed by the normal aging process, no one makes a big deal about it. Few seem to notice or to intervene in a way that is both caring and effective. If depression is noticed at all, it may be only when it is the most severe form of mental illness. Mental illness in general does not engender a warm and positive response by the public, even the churchgoing public. In our ignorance we may be scared or concerned that it may be "catching" if we get too close. We may also be annoyed by a person who appears fine physically but who seems to have lost interest in what previously had been of interest and may be avoiding interacting with gatherings or individuals formerly enjoyed. We often do not understand this internal process in which a person can feel either helpless or hopeless or both.

Instead of empathizing with or trying to understand the dynamics of aging that sometimes manifests itself as depression, we often seek to explain the depression, which can be dismissive. Juan's spouse just died. Susan's youngest child just married and moved far away. Greg just developed a debilitating chronic disease. Marian never married, so she has no one with whom to grow old. Or perhaps we think more generally, they're just *old* and sad that their lives will soon be over. Why *wouldn't* they be depressed, considering what has happened or what will happen? We hope or assume depressed older persons will get back to their normal way of being if their privacy is respected. We hope, left alone, they can work it out by themselves. Many of us have been taught to "mind our own business" and may be less inclined to intervene when a person seems somewhat more withdrawn or even sadder than usual.

We are not used to considering ourselves our brothers' and sisters' keepers. This avoidance can be seen early on in the development of humankind—in the fourth chapter of the Book of Genesis we find Cain's famous retort to God regarding his responsibility for his brother Abel (Genesis 4:9). It was also behind the lawyer's question to Jesus in Luke's Gospel about who was his neighbor, which led to Jesus' telling the parable we call the story of the Good Samaritan (Luke 10:29). The neighbor is a brother or sister in the community, not necessarily of the same genetic code or even the same tribe. Not expecting to be our sisters' and brothers' keepers is a pervasive attitude in mainstream America. We have accustomed ourselves to think we should pull ourselves up from whatever situation we are in by our own bootstraps. Or, conversely, if it is not possible to pull ourselves up by our own bootstraps (presuming we all have bootstraps to pull), the government or some other group will take care of those who cannot help themselves.

While many older persons will experience periods of sadness, loss, or passing moods, not everyone becomes clinically depressed in his or her later years. Statistics about depression vary. The National Institute of Mental Health (NIMH), a part of the U.S. Department of Health and Human Services, suggests that nearly one in ten Americans over age eighteen are clinically depressed at a given moment (about 18.8 million in 1998). The NIMH says that among older Americans (those over sixty-five), the figures can be as high as one in four, or even one in three. The American Association of Geriatric Psychiatry indicates that between 8 and 12 percent of older adults in the community and up to 37 percent of older adults in a primary care setting (that is, a hospital) may suffer from depressive symptoms. Harold Koenig found that more than 40 percent of older patients in hospitals with medical problems were clinically depressed. N. Breslau and M. R. Haug raise that figure to 56 to 80 percent of nursing home patients who will develop some type of mental illness. Although dementia is one of the most frequent illnesses experienced in nursing homes, psychiatrist Gary

Kennedy notes that depression and depression coupled with dementia are frequently encountered in nursing home residents.

Depression is commonly believed to occur more frequently in women than in men. According to the NIMH, depression is diagnosed almost twice as often in women (12 percent) as it is in men (7 percent). Gender differences may be based more on self-reporting or on women's socially conditioned willingness to seek treatment. We teach little boys not to cry. Is there any societal permission, even encouragement, for younger or older boys to express their emotions and to seek help when they are overwhelmed? It should also be noted that several community studies of depression in older adults did not see a significant gender difference (see especially D. Blazer and C. D. Williams [1980] and J. F. Phifer and S. A. Murrell [1986]).

Untreated, depression can lead to suicide, the intentional killing of oneself. Although older persons made up only 13 percent of the U.S. population in 1997, they accounted for 19 percent of the suicides that year. White males eighty-five and older committed suicide at six times the national U.S. suicide rate (64.9 deaths per 100,000 persons compared with 10.6 per 100,000 nationally). In other words, left untreated, depression can be fatal. Suicide is not usually triggered by one event; however, suicidologists highlight such risk factors in older white males as the loss of loved ones and friends through death, declining health, and diminished sense of purpose and connection after retirement. We may also want to explore the norms in our culture, not only for the expression of sadness, but also for changing roles and for experiencing dependency. Are these behaviors somehow more permissible for women than men? If that is the case, how might we as a society and especially as the church begin to create ways for all in the community to continue feeling their worth in God's eyes? We have the opportunity to look at our usual hands-off responses as individuals, as a society, and especially as members of the beloved community in the church and make a new assessment as to whether it leads to greater well being or loss.

Depression may not appear in an isolated manner. A number of medical conditions are correlated with depression. This is true for heart disease (and especially for those who have undergone bypass surgery), strokes, Parkinson's disease, Alzheimer's disease, and most if not all chronic illnesses (for example, cancer and diabetes). Infectious diseases, such as hepatitis and mononucleosis, often produce depression. In the early 1990s the National Institutes of Health Consensus Development Conference on Diagnosis and Treatment of Depression in Late Life noted the difficulty of diagnosing depression because of its coexistence with many social and physical problems. In addition to cardiovascular and neurological diseases, they pointed to various metabolic disturbances, arthritis, and sensory loss. Florence Safford and George Krell note the secondary depression often associated with endocrine disorders, such as thyroid disease, anemia, uremia, lupus, renal failure, chronic infections (urinary tract infections and tuberculosis), alcoholism, chronic obstructive pulmonary disease (COPD), and influenza. A number of authors note that many patients develop a depression subsequent to the emergence of other diseases as they then face psychosocial concerns and functional disabilities.

In addition, at times depression may be understood as a side effect of medication taken for certain medical conditions. Geriatric psychiatrist Nathan Billig, author of *To Be Old and Sad*, reported that such depression can result from taking blood pressure medications such as antihypertensives, heart medicines such as cardiac antiarrhythmics, anti-inflammatory agents such as steroids, and beta blockers. Other researchers have noted similar effects from some patients' use of sedatives, tranquilizers, hormones, birth control pills, antihistamines, antibiotics, ulcer drugs, anti-Parkinsonian drugs, and diet drugs. In general older persons tend to have more medications prescribed for them than younger folks, so the possibility of depression as an unwanted side effect may be more of an issue for elders than for persons in other stages of life. It behooves all of us as consumers of medical treatment to learn more about the interaction and side effects of the medications we are prescribed. Our elders may have grown up trusting doctors to know best. I have found in my hospital visits that older persons may be reluctant to challenge a doctor's assessment or prescription. Many people can tell me they take X number of pills but not why they take them. We can assist older and younger members of society to ask questions and to expect our physicians and pharmacists to help us understand both what may ail us and how best to find relief, and how to balance the benefits against the burdens of treatments.

As persons age they face new challenges not only physically but also emotionally and spiritually. Most writers in the field note the increase in actual losses that elders face, from retirement from full-time work to physical disability to the deaths of close family and friends. Accompanying these losses may come unwanted changes in socioeconomic status and a fear of outliving their savings. Our society has traditionally not valued the wisdom of elders, choosing to see more their failing health and their inability to participate as actively as they did in the community. Once someone becomes older, younger folks can at times intentionally or unintentionally refuse to "burden" them with duties they might not be able to continue performing. We may wish for "new blood" on committees and teams in the political process and on church sessions and other official boards.

Sometimes we may unconsciously set aside those who hold fast to tradition (really living into the scriptural injunction to "hold fast to what is good"!), who may not always welcome changes, and who can be perceived as ornery or sad that "things are not as they used to be." My paternal grandmother, a very sharp woman living in suburban Boston, told me (when she was in her eighties) that she was angry and sad that her bank had once again changed names after a merger (with corresponding changes in checks and other printed materials). She remarked that she thought banks should "stay the same" because she did not like getting used to something and then having it become something else. She said this on the way to make a deposit at the same bank branch she had always used. She could not focus on what had remained the same but worried about what had changed. Having raised two children in the Depression, she often worried that what she and her husband (long deceased) had saved would somehow be taken from her in the combining of banking institutions. In this day and age, as previously stable financial plans may not prove to be so secure, we may find many older persons terrified that their hard-earned savings may not last through their senior years. It has been predicted for years that as the baby boomers grow older, our Social Security dollars will be maxed out, creating even more anxiety for elders and for the generations behind them as well.

Our disregard of elders can develop into depressive symptoms for persons whose social circle may be shrinking. Concomitant with fewer persons in one's community may be a negative reevaluation of one's worth based on doing less or producing less, resulting in being seen as less valuable to a community, even a community of faith.

Older persons can become existentially depressed based on their perception of themselves as "over the hill" and not wanted by family or others with whom they have had positive, creative, and mutually satisfying relationships in the past. The student chaplains with whom I work often share stories of working with older patients who develop depression. What these chaplains frequently discover as they listen to older patients is a common experience of being dismissed or abandoned by younger family members once their level of disability cannot be handled in the community and they must move into some form of assisted living.

Depression may develop in the younger members of a family as well as they adjust to the growing need of elder members for more care than the younger ones can provide. Some authors have written about the "sandwich generation," middle-aged persons, often women, who are expected to be caregivers for both parents and children. They may find themselves squeezed as they balance work, care of their own homes and lives, and care for persons both older and younger than themselves.

When churches act out resentment of older persons who may need more care, older persons can develop a sour attitude, feeling unappreciated for their years of service and sacrifice and unsure how to stay connected. The unconscious message of the church as an organization may be that "we really value you when you work"—for example, serve on boards and committees, cook, raise money, usher, sing in the choir, teach or direct Sunday school or vacation Bible school. There is a pervasive attitude in our society and church that may emanate from a works-righteousness perspective, subtly or not so subtly conferring worth based on what one does, not on who one is as a child of God. The fact of the matter is that people become depressed for reasons that do not necessarily initially involve the church, and we can consciously or unconsciously participate in enhancing the possibility of persons' developing depression when we treat them as "less than" after a certain age.

One faithful woman of 101 years, who had had both legs amputated due to complications from diabetes and yet still ironed regularly, was heard to remark that she hoped she would get the word from God soon about what she had yet to accomplish. She was sure she was still alive to fulfill some purpose of God's, and she was getting tired but did not want to die without having fulfilled that purpose! She seemed to be questioning the meaning of her life as she became less able, but she also saw challenge in the deciphering of God's will. The church family delighted in her being able to keep the sanctuary's cloth furnishings ironed even as they understood her wish to be free of that duty. I wondered whether her church valued the work she did more than her sharing her increasing tiredness, since apparently no one ventured to ask her if she wanted to delegate that task to someone else. Another possibility might have been for her to be invited to share the ironing of the cloths with someone she might see as her protégé, one to whom she could pass on the traditional ways of caring for the sanctuary cloths.

It is possible in the family of faith to recognize and respond to both the situational depressions that often accompany our experience of the deaths of loved ones or neighbors, disease, or many other forms of loss, as well as to the clinical syndromes related to depression. Whether we are rejoicing or dejected, we are God's children, worthy of care and a place in the kingdom of God.

Identifying Those Who Are "Depressed"

Commonly people use the word *depressed* to describe someone who feels "sad," "blue," "down in the dumps," or "not oneself." Informally we may notice some behavioral changes, such as social withdrawal and perhaps some difficulty sleeping or eating. If these feelings and the corresponding behaviors associated with mild depression do not abate within a reasonable time and if there is no intervening treatment, some persons may progress to a more serious form of depression. In fact, the *Diagnostic and Statistical Manual IV-R* (abbreviated *DSM-IV-R*) of the American Psychiatric Association classifies clinical depression in a number of ways, depending on its symptoms and severity. These kinds of depression range from adjustment disorders to dysthymia to major depression to bipolar disorder.

The mildest form of depression is called an *adjustment disorder with depressed mood.* This disorder is signified by a set of symptoms that are triggered by an identifiable event or stressor and stop when the stressor ceases. A person with this form of depression would normatively display a depressed mood, tearfulness, and/or feelings of hopelessness following one event or stressor within the past three months. These symptoms are more severe than what might be expected as a response to the stressor and significantly affect social and/or occupational functioning. Specifically these symptoms cannot be simply due to bereavement following a death, and once the original stressor(s) cease the symptoms do not last beyond six months.

Examples of situations in which one might develop an adjustment disorder with depressed mood include the onset of an acute or chronic illness or the moving away of a child or close neighbor. The term "adjustment disorder" implies that these changes in mood and behavior are in fact ways that a person attempts to adapt in order to deal with a stressful event and that the symptoms subside once the event is over. Usually persons with this form of mild depression do not seek treatment from a mental health professional but may respond well to overtures of caring from pastors and congregation members. Empathy and outreach to those we hear or know are going through tough circumstances may keep those members from feeling isolated or alone in their distress. We can validate persons' feelings without trying to fix them or demand that they recover within a short time frame.

Closely akin to the adjustment disorder with depressed mood is another form of depression, an *adjustment disorder with mixed anxiety and depressed mood*. As its name implies, persons suffering from this disorder display a wider range of behaviors, including depressed mood, tearfulness, feelings of hopelessness, nervousness, worry, or jitteriness. As with the previous category, this adjustment disorder appears within three months of the triggering event or stressor and disappears within six months after it stops.

Older persons could develop adjustment disorders following a move from independent living to assisted living or after an accident that results in the need for rehabilitation and more assistance than an independent person might like. A person might experience these symptoms around a retirement or job loss or moving from full-time to part-time employment. If someone loses income, there can be a temporary period of depression as he or she adjusts to a different quality of life. This is not only the case with older persons but with younger persons as well who have been downsized out of a job or forced into early retirement. Persons might develop adjustment disorders when they stop driving a car, become separated or divorced, or in response to the move of a favorite sibling or other significant extended family member to a distant place. In each case a definite event has triggered the depression and the person recovers to his or her previous level of functioning within a relatively short period of time.

The American Psychiatric Association categorizes another form of depression as *dysthymic disorder.* This is more persistent than an adjustment disorder and usually does not disappear after the initial event or stressor ceases. It also involves more symptoms than the adjustment disorders. The DSM-IV-R specifies that dysthymia is an appropriate diagnosis when a person has had a depressed mood for most of the day, more often than not, experienced by the person or observed by others, for at least two years. In addition two or more of the following symptoms are also present:

1. poor appetite or overeating
2. insomnia or hypersomnia (sleeping too little or too much)
3. low energy or fatigue
4. low self-esteem
5. poor concentration or difficulty in making decisions
6. feelings of hopelessness

These symptoms do not abate for more than two months during the period being considered diagnostically. The person experiences clinically significant distress or impairment in social, occupational, or other important areas of functioning. In other words, these symptoms noticeably get in the way of normal living.

I consider persons suffering from this form of depression as the "walking wounded" because they continue to function, albeit at a reduced level. They come to worship but do not seem to exhibit the joy of the Lord. They do not seek out or may avoid social occasions. They may disappear after worship, not staying for coffee hour to mingle informally with other worshipers. They will not take on previously enjoyed roles in the church. They seem to be conserving their energies for life's basics. They may complain that life is "difficult" or that they just do not feel themselves. They may experience going through the motions of normal life, but they are not volunteering for new projects or may not have much patience with others who are either very happy or down in the dumps themselves. Others will recognize someone who seems emotionally and spiritually to be dragging themselves through the motions of their former life. Part of the difficulty in diagnosing dysthymia is that many older persons experience more tiredness and difficulty in sleeping and/or eating than before, so they may not recognize the combination of symptoms as signaling depression. Note how many of these signals are not related to an emotion like sadness. The emotion must be inferred from the behaviors.

If a church member complains of one of the symptoms of dysthymia, one response a caring person might use is to wonder with that individual whether he or she has ruled out a physical problem by having a physical examination by a physician. It is not always a mental health–related issue when a person exhibits some of these signs. Many of depression's symptoms are also signs of medical conditions, diseases, or disorders. It is wise to think of persons holistically and to treat body, mind, and spirit. As with persons suffering from an adjustment disorder (or any other condition), it is not usually helpful to tell those with dysthymia to "snap out of it." They may wish to do so but cannot. Do not assume that they are deriving any pleasure from feeling the way they do. There is little to no "secondary gain" from depression. Few people volunteer to help persons with depression as they might someone with a physical disability or disease. This is due in part to the invisibility of emotional distress. We may also misread depression as orneriness or shyness.

Persons with dysthymia need consistent loving presence from church members, inquiries about how things are going, and offers to listen when the person is ready to talk. Pathologizing, or making persons with milder forms of depression feel abnormal, may cause them to talk less about what they are feeling and become even more isolated and alone with their disease. On the other hand, it is a good thing to express concern. It can be helpful to say, "I haven't seen you in a while and I was concerned about you. How are you doing?" Do not be put off if the person brushes off the concern expressed by saying a quick "Fine." Our society seems to reward persons for appearing fine even when they are not. Do not be afraid to risk a follow-up comment, "Well, you may be fine, but you seem a little down to me" and see what the person does with that assessment. When you persist gently, you are not playing therapist; rather, you are sharing what you see and giving the other person the gift of an observation without a judgment. Then the person with whom you are talking might nod in appreciation of your observation without continuing to talk with you, or may tell you more of what is going on. Active listening and conveying of positive regard for another person are key strategies for professional counselors, but they are also good ways to enact our duty to care for one another as human beings.

The most serious of the depressive disorders is denoted in the DSM-IV-R as a *major depressive episode*. The key indicators are the presence of at least five of the following nine symptoms (the first and second must be included in the five), which are present over the same two-week period and represent a marked change from the person's previous functioning:

1. depressed mood most of the time, most days (either by self-report or other observation)
2. very diminished interest or pleasure in all or most activities most of the time, most days (again, by self-report or other observation)
3. weight loss or gain although not dieting (more than 5 percent of body weight) or decrease or increase in appetite most days
4. sleeping too much or too little most days
5. restlessness or slowing down (noticeable to others, not just by self- report)
6. fatigue or loss of energy most days
7. feelings of worthlessness or excessive or inappropriate guilt most of the time (not merely guilt about being sick)
8. decreased ability to think or concentrate, or indecisiveness, most days (again, either by self-report or other observation)
9. recurrent thoughts of death (not just fear of dying), recurrent suicidal ideation without a specific plan, or a suicide attempt or a specific plan for completing suicide

In addition to their presence, these symptoms cause clinically significant distress or impairment in social, occupational, or other important areas of functioning. They are not signs of direct physiological effects of drug abuse or other medication or a general medical condition. These symptoms are not those due primarily to bereavement; that is, the symptoms last longer than two months after the loss and include significant impairment in functioning (being preoccupied with worthlessness, suicidal ideation, psychotic symptoms, or slowing down).

While it is possible to see a connection between the symptoms of an adjustment disorder with depressed mood and dysthymia and major depression, note the severity of the symptoms in the major depressive episode and the presence of significant and recurring thoughts of worthlessness and suicide. This is well beyond the realm of a bad day or week, beyond the occasional down mood that accompanies a sad occurrence or lifestyle change. A depressed person cannot cope with the everyday tasks of living. Yet sometimes people with this disorder suffer in silence, fearing what people will think, wondering and worrying if they are "crazy."

Depressed people sometimes come to church to reach out in a passive way, hoping beyond hope for rescue from their own thoughts, feelings, and behaviors, which seem so self-defeating. They may not be able to pray or take advantage of the community of care and accountability within the church. They are literally walking in the valley of the shadow of death. When left untreated, major depression can lead to suicide. Would that we could share our concerns more freely with our neighbors in this kind of need and so avert the self-inflicted death that often leaves families and communities of faith reeling with guilt, sadness, and anger.

Bipolar disorder, formally named manic depression, is seen in persons who cycle back and forth between depression and mania. While relatively rare (the surgeon general's report on mental health suggests it afflicts less than 1 percent of the population), bipolar disorder can be variously diagnosed, depending on the recurrence of depressive periods and mania. A manic episode, as the DSM-IV-R defines it, appears to be a period of an abnormally elevated, expansive, or irritable mood persisting at least one week. More than being in good spirits, persons suffering from manic episodes display at least three of the following symptoms:

1. has inflated self-esteem
2. has decreased need for sleep (only needs about three hours per night)
3. is more talkative or seems pressured to keep talking
4. experiences flight of ideas or racing thoughts
5. exhibits distractibility
6. shows an increase in either focused activity or agitation
7. has excessive involvement in pleasurable activities at high risk for having painful consequences (such as spending sprees, sexual indiscretions, or foolish financial gambles)

Bipolar disorder involves a person's experiencing alternately depressive and manic episodes, sometimes with more of one than the other. Persons seeking to relate to an individual with bipolar disorder may be confused by the major changes they see. We may not be as alarmed to see someone emotionally "up" as "down," yet each is potentially dangerous. Observation of change in normal functioning may help persons in congregations with long-term knowledge of the individual to diagnose this condition. While persons who experience a manic episode may consider themselves able to leap tall buildings at a single bound, when experiencing a depressive episode they may be more likely to consider themselves incapable of stepping over a stick on the sidewalk.

Treatment Issues

Most recent secular resources recommend for depression psychotherapy, medications, and electro convulsive therapy (also called ECT or shock therapy), and perhaps socialization. Not many materials speak of a faith community's involvement with depressed older persons as a potential resource. Perhaps that is because we do not tend to get involved. There are many social, emotional, and spiritual ills that get short shrift in the church as we focus (or perseverate) on hotter topics. I suggest that there are several reasons for older persons not getting the treatment that is available. There are ways we of the beloved community might be more effective keepers of one another.

Top Ten Reasons Older People of Faith May Not Seek Help for Depression

1. "Depression is just a normal part of aging—everyone is feeling it."
2. "This is God's will that I suffer through 'the valley of the shadow of death.'"
3. "I am being punished for having done something wrong—if I repent, it will disappear."
4. "'This, too, shall pass'–just be patient—tomorrow something else will hurt!"
5. It is embarrassing to have a mental rather than physical problem.
6. "It costs too much" (this may be true for older folks on a fixed income).
7. "I am not sure of where to get help—and there are so many crazy folks who treat mental illness."
8. A medical doctor does not pick up on the signals and refer people to others. (Part of denial—"See, if I were really depressed surely the doctor would have said something.")
9. "If I just have faith or pray or read the right Scripture, the depression will lift" (like the weather).

10. "I don't want to be seen as a complainer (and maybe no one will care if I tell them I feel awful)."

On a more positive note, Harold Koenig cites several studies that correlate religious beliefs and practices with positive coping with depressive symptoms.[1] There appears to be renewed interest in the medical community for research in "spirituality," that is, observing, describing, and perhaps also recommending connection with a person's spiritual roots, with a community of shared faith, ritual, and caring as a resource for coping with many of life's ills, especially in later years. Perhaps in years to come practitioners of holistic healing will more routinely prescribe attendance at worship, private prayer, and involvement in the social and outreach life of local faith communities as preventive measures for dealing with depression and other ills. Will the church be ready to receive persons who may find it hard to hear and act on the good news of the gospel because of clinical depression? Will we be hospitable welcomers of those who doubt God's (and people's) care? Will we be glad when depressed folks darken our doors, or resent yet another government program ending with the benediction to mental health consumers to "find a faith community and be well"?

An effective response from the Christian community will depend to some extent on our level of reliable information about medical and alternative forms of treatment for depression. We need to educate ourselves about mental illness in general and depression in particular. There are an increasing number of resources available for professionals and the lay public. Multidisciplinary conferences are another good source of information about the issues of identifying and getting the most vulnerable folks into effective treatment that is holistic, not merely medication-related. Members of church committees that advise pastors might inquire about the nature of continuing education events in which the pastors (and churches) invest time and money. Do any include an updating of information about mental health and ways the church can facilitate good care one-on-one and on the wider levels—community, regional, and national? I believe there is baseline knowledge that all pastors need, not only specialized ministers who focus on pastoral counseling. Many persons, especially older adults, will be more likely to approach their own pastor than to seek out a pastoral counselor or secular mental health professional.

There is excellent material in both book and pamphlet form about help from the medical community and self-help groups concerning the efficacy of medication for depression. Perhaps a parish nurse, pastor, and members of a congregational health ministry committee might look for resources to add to a congregation's library or pamphlet display area. Members of a congregation might consider reaching out to local physicians as well since older members may feel more comfortable initially thinking of what ails them as a physical problem.

There is mixed commentary in the media and professional journals about the effectiveness of psychotherapy (especially by those who subscribe to the biological theories of depression). This can make older folks who may be leery anyway about seeking treatment even less likely to seek help. It would be wise to advise people who are ready to explore whether therapy might be an effective option for them to inquire about the therapist's specialty. Depression, like grief, is not just a garden-variety mental health issue with which everyone with a counselor's degree can deal equally well. Encourage members of your congregation to interview a couple of therapists to check the "fit" between the professional and the patient. It may be helpful to ask about the professional's experience with older depressed persons as well as his or her credentials. Geriatrics is increasingly being studied and taught and practiced in our community by psychiatrists, psychologists, clinical social workers, nurses, and pastoral counselors, so some professionals will be more versed and experienced than others in dealing with the special issues involved in treating depression in older persons.

Within the psychotherapeutic community promising work is being done through the cognitive behavioral approach as opposed to the more traditional psychodynamic approach. Cognitive behavioral therapists help persons identify and challenge negative messages they give themselves that result in depressive symptoms. Much of professional mental health literature emphasizes utilizing a combination of approaches including psychopharmacological (drug therapy) as well as supportive psychotherapy. Geriatric psychiatrists are increasingly voicing concern about the overmedication of older patients. It is crucial that any physician prescribing antidepressant medication should be aware of all the medications a person is taking in order to minimize the potential for injurious drug interactions.

I would counsel pastors and laypersons not to neglect any means that may assist a depressed person, including talk therapy, drug therapy, prayer, and the other means of grace accessible through involvement in a congregation that is sensitive to holistic health and healing. Sometimes persons who are farther along in their own recovery process might be terrific older or younger sisters or brothers in faith, spiritual and emotional mentors. Of course this presupposes that a recovering person is ready to be open about his or her own health/illness continuum and can bear the burden of another's struggle with depression. A pastor must exercise great care to respect privacy while also taking the initiative to recommend or suggest connections that might encourage a person (young or old) to seek help, to believe help is available, and to follow through until the symptoms disappear and wellness is maintained.

Some pastors have sought out consultants so that they have a forum for discussing those in their care about whom they have grave concerns and may strategize concerning more effective responses. Even the helpers need help to keep identifying and responding to those in our congregations who can deny, resist, and otherwise frustrate those who would be hospitable companions when life's way is burdensome and heavy-laden. Pastors and other caregivers may need assistance in setting limits when a parishioner asks more than a pastor can give or practice and support when the person is consistently thwarting the pastor's efforts to tell the truth and help the parishioner reach out for the assistance that is available. Sometimes the helper wants to help more than the parishioner wants to be helped. Sometimes the pastor's own depressive tendencies are touched by what he or she sees in the parishioner, and the pastor may need support to sort through whose issue it is. To be the beloved community is to be wise and compassionate with our own unfinished selves as well as recognize that we cannot be all things to all people. Often the pastor is in an excellent position to observe a parishioner over time and to tell the truth in love, to express care for the person, and to offer pastoral support. This can be what Seward Hiltner calls effective "pre-counseling," setting the stage for a referral later for more specialized help. The pastor's task is to become knowledgeable about the signs and symptoms of depression and about referral resources, as well as to continue to care while a person is receiving treatment beyond the church.

Recommendations for Dealing with Depression in Older Persons

Recognize the signs

1. Have materials about depression in the pamphlet holders in your church.
2. Invite a mental health professional or pastoral counselor or chaplain to address an adult class in your congregation (or presbytery or other judicatory gathering).
3. Plug into denominational and national materials on destigmatizing mental illness.
4. Have some materials on depression and other mental illnesses in your church library; check with your presbytery or other judicatory's resource centers for curricular materials and references.

Relate with care

1. Include prayers for persons with depression in worship as you do with those having physical illnesses.
2. If you have healing services, welcome those with all kinds of illnesses.
3. Include references to biblical characters and others from literature (classic and newer) who suffer from depression or other mental illness in sermons, adult education forums, and so forth.
4. Confront with love those who mock or joke about a disability.
5. Encourage people of all ages to join in community, regional, and national events to raise awareness and funds for care, research, and education about mental illness.
6. Think systemically—what resources can be accessed in your community by whom? Consider the economics of mental health and how a community cares for persons of all colors and socioeconomic classes; raise questions in political and other arenas so that quality affordable health care is accessible to all.

Respect differences

1. Remember that not all who suffer from depression will display the same symptoms/signs and not all will respond to the same treatments. (Do not suggest that because Mabel or Henry responded well to ECT everyone with depression should receive shock therapy.)

2. Women may be more open about their feelings; men may be more circumspect; encourage everyone to share what is on their hearts and minds as they can. (Do not assume that if you do not hear about someone's experience of depression, he or she is not suffering with it.)

3. Seek to understand cultural norms about mental illness in the community in which you minister and in the families that are part of your congregation.

Reframe

1. By making the invisible illnesses visible through prayers and references in sermons and by including educational opportunities on mental health in general and depression in particular you will help to demythologize and reduce the stigma many still feel about suffering with a mental illness.

2. In conversations and routine pastoral care visits, help those who struggle with depression and their families and friends to understand that depressed persons are not crazy, lazy, or purposely intending to drive others crazy—advocate for getting professional help as an adjunct to the care a congregation can offer.

Refer

1. Know your community resources—when you are new in a community, look in the phone book under "Mental health services" and call each one and ask about what the professional's specialty is and how one would become a patient. Ask about waiting time before a first appointment, the fee scale, and acceptance of insurance plans.

2. At ecumenical clergy gatherings, inquire about resources other leaders have found helpful.

3. Be able to give some specifics about what treatment is like. Older persons, as well as younger ones, may have stereotyped views of those who might "shrink" their heads.

4. Investigate local chapters of self-help support groups for those suffering with depression.

5. Consider accompanying a person to a first appointment for support.

Follow-up

1. Ask how things are going—go with your gut feeling when "Fine" does not ring true.
2. Keep a close eye on those who are depressed (especially anyone who has expressed suicidal ideation, intention, or plans).
3. Continue to invite persons with depression into the regular fellowship of the church community.

We ought not placate, pacify, or pontificate, and we definitely ought not ignore depressed persons. Instead, we need to notice one another, to bear one another's burdens, to not make assumptions, and to emphasize God's care for all God's creatures under all circumstances (especially when our souls and countenances are downcast). We all need to encourage one another in our individual walk in faith and to realize that we will all feel empty, sad, at a loss, and frustrated from time to time, but we need not feel abandoned in the Christian community. If we truly act out "keeping" our brothers and sisters in respectful, caring ways, we will demonstrate the love of God that embraces us in all our conditions and at all times in our lives.

Questions for Discussion

1. An elderly member of the church lives in a retirement community, but hardly ever leaves her room. She spends most of the day in bed, watching TV, and even has meals brought to her room. Is she just a loner, or is she suffering from depression?
2. How can you differentiate between passing moods and clinical depression?
3. Discuss whether some older people are overmedicated for depression. What alternatives are there?
4. The author says depression occurs more often in women than men. Can you give reasons why this is true?
5. As visitors of older people in the congregation, how can you detect symptoms of depression?
6. As a pastor, how can you know when a person needs professional help for depression?
7. If you have suffered from depression and found ways to handle it, would you be willing to share this with church members?
8. Baby boomers, a more affluent and educated generation than previous ones, will begin retiring in 2011. Do you think the boomers will struggle with depression? Why? Why not?

Resources on Depression of the Elderly

Books

Clark, David C., ed. *Clergy Response to Suicidal Persons and Their Family Members.* Chicago Theological Seminary. Chicago: Exploration Press, 1993.

Cooper-Goldenberg, Juliana. *A Spirituality for Late Life,* Older Adult Issues Series. Louisville: Geneva Press, 1999.

Dean, Amy E. *Growing Older, Growing Better; Daily Meditations for Celebrating Aging.* Carlsbad, CA: Hay House, 1997.

De Leo, Diego and Rene F. W. Dykstra. *Depression and Suicide in Late Life.* Toronto, Canada: Hogrefe and Huber Publishers, 1990.

Diagnostic Criteria from DSM-IV. Washington, DC: American Psychiatric Association, 1994.

Doka, Kenneth J., ed. *Living with Grief; Loss in Later Life.* Washington, DC: Hospice Foundation of America, 2002.

Dunlap, Susan J. *Counseling Depressed Women.* Louisville: Westminster John Knox Press, 1997.

Dymski, J. Daniel. *A Caregiver's Companion: Ministering to Older Adults.* Notre Dame, IN: Ave Maria Press, 1997.

Eckford, Leslie and Amanda Lambert. *Beating the Senior Blues.* Oakland, CA: New Harbinger Publications, 2002.

Gilbert, Binford W. *The Pastoral Care of Depression.* Binghamton, NY: Haworth Press, 1998.

Gregg-Schroder, Susan. *In the Shadow of God's Wings; Grace in the Midst of Depression.* Nashville: Upper Room Books, 1997. Also has a study guide.

Hills, Helen. Aging Well; *Exploring the Land of Our Later Years.* Athol, MA: Haley's Publishing, 1998.

Hulme, William and Lucy. *Wrestling with Depression; A Spiritual Guide to Reclaiming Life.* Minneapolis: Fortress Press, 1995.

Ilardo, Joseph A. *As Parents Age; A Psychological and Practical Guide.* Acton, MA: VanderWyk and Burnham, 1998.

Kennedy, Gary J. *Geriatric Mental Health Care; A Treatment Guide for Health Professionals.* New York: Guilford Press, 2000.

Kimble, Melvin, Susan McFadden, James Ellor, and James Seeber, eds. Aging, *Spirituality and Religion: A Handbook.* Minneapolis: Fortress Press, 1995.

Koenig, Harold G. and Andrew J. Weaver. *Counseling Troubled Older Adults: A Handbook for Pastors and Religious Caregivers.* Nashville: Abingdon Press, 1997.

Koenig, Harold G. and Andrew J. Weaver. *Pastoral Care of Older Adults.* Minneapolis: Fortress Press, 1998.

Miletich, John J. *Depression in the Elderly; A Multimedia Sourcebook.* Westport, CT: Greenwood Press, 1997.

Mosher-Ashley, Pearl M. and Phyllis W. Barrett. *A Life Worth Living; Practical Strategies for Reducing Depression in Older Adults.* Baltimore: Health Professions Press, 1997.

Pipher, Mary. *Another Country; Navigating the Emotional Terrain of Our Elders.* New York: Riverhead Books, 1999.

Raines, Robert. *A Time to Live: Seven Tasks of Creative Aging.* New York: Dutton, 1997.

Randall, Robert L. and James B. Nelson. *Walking Through the Valley: Understanding and Emerging from Clergy Depression.* Nashville: Abingdon Press, 1998.

Safford, Florence and George I. Krell. *Gerontology for Health Professionals; A Practice Guide.* Washington, DC: NASW Press, 1992.

Sheikh, Javaid, ed. *Treating the Elderly.* San Francisco: Jossey-Bass Publishers, 1996.

Stone, Howard J. *Depression and Hope: New Insights for Pastoral Care.* Minneapolis: Fortress Press, 1998.

Vaillant, George E. *Aging Well; Surprising Guideposts to a Happier Life from the Landmark Harvard Study of Adult Development.* Boston: Little, Brown, and Co., 2002.

Pamphlets and Fact Sheets

Caregiving: Communicating with Health Professionals, American Association of Retired Persons, 1995–2001.

Depression. National Institute of Mental Health, 2000.

Depression: A Serious but Treatable Illness. National Institute on Aging, U.S. Department of Health and Human Services, Public Health Service, National Institute of Health, 1996.

Depression and Alzheimer's Disease, Information from Your Family Doctor series, American Academy of Family Physicians, 2000.

Depression and Older Adults: What It Is and How to Get Help, Information from Your Family Doctor series, American Academy of Family Physicians, 2000.

Depression Can Break Your Heart. National Institute of Mental Health, 2001.

Depression: How Medicine Can Help, Information from Your Family Doctor series. American Academy of Family Physicians, 2000.

Depression Research at the Institute of Mental Health. NIMH, 2001.

Depression: What It Is and How to Get Help, Information from Your Family Doctor series, American Academy of Family Physicians, 2000.

Geriatrics and Mental Health—The Facts. American Association for Geriatric Psychiatry, 2001.

If You're Over 65 and Feeling Depressed: Treatment Brings New Hope. National Institute of Mental Health, 1990 (revised 1995).

Older Adults and Mental Health (fact sheet). U.S .Administration on Aging, U.S. Department of Health and Human Services, 2001.

Older Adults: Depression and Suicide Facts. National Institute of Mental Health, 2001.

Articles

Blazer, D. and C. D. Williams. "Epidemiology of dysphoria and depression in an elderly community population," *American Journal of Psychiatry*, v. 137 (1980), pp. 439–444.

Blixen, Carol E. and Christopher Kippes. "Depression, social support, and quality of life in older adults with osteoarthritis," *Journal of Nursing Scholarship*, v. 31, n. 3 (Third Quarter, 1999), pp. 221–226.

Bothell, William Lee, Joel Fischer, and Cullen Hayashida. "Social support and depression among low income elderly" in *Making Aging in Place Work*, ed. Leon Pastalan. Binghamton, NY: Haworth Press, 1999.

Gallo, Joseph J. and Peter V. Rabins. "Depression without sadness: alternative presentations of depression in late life," *American Family Physician*, vol. 60, n. 3 (September 1, 1999), pp. 820–826.

Hagerty, Bonnie M. and Reg A. Williams. "The effects of sense of belonging, social support, conflict, and loneliness on depression," *Nursing Research*, vol. 48, n. 4 (July/August 1999), pp. 215–19.

Hughes, Colin P. "Community psychiatric nursing and the depressed elderly: a case for using cognitive therapy," *Journal of Advanced Nursing*, vol. 16 (1991), pp. 565–72.

Jurlowicz, Lenore H. "Social factors and depression in late life," *Archives of Psychiatric Nursing*, vol. 7, n. 1 (February 1993), pp. 30–36.

Kennedy, Gary J. "The geriatric syndrome of late-life depression," *Psychiatric Services*, vol. 46, n. 1 (January 1995), pp. 43–48.

Lander, Mark, Keith Wilson, and Harvey Max Chocinov. "Depression and the dying older patient," *Clinics in Geriatric Medicine*, vol. 16, n. 2 (May 2000), pp. 335–355.

Lazaro, Luisa, Teodor Marcos, and Manuel Valdes. "Affective disorders, social support, and hospital status in geriatric patients in a general hospital," *General Hospital Psychiatry*, vol. 17 (1995), pp. 299–304.

"Looking Out for Depression, ElderAction: Action Ideas for Older Persons and Their Families." U.S. Administration on Aging, 2000. http://www.caregivers.com/Category_Pages/document_display.asp?id =1968.

Phifer, J. F. and S. A. Murrell. "Etiological factors in the onset of depressive symptoms in older adults," *Journal of Abnormal Psychology*, vol. 45 (1986), pp. 282–91.

Reynolds, Charles F. and David J. Kupfer. "Depression and aging: a look to the future," *Psychiatric Services*, vol. 50, n. 9 (September 1999), pp. 1167–1172.

Robinson, Karnen Meier. "Predictors of depression among wife caregivers," *Nursing Research*, vol. 38, n. 6 (November/December 1989), pp. 359–363.

Steiner, David and Bernice Marcopulos. "Depression in the elderly; characteristics and clinical management," *Nursing Clinics of North America*, vol. 26, n. 3 (September 1991), pp. 585–600.

Stone, Howard W. "Depression," in *Clinical Handbook of Pastoral Counseling*, vol. 2, eds. Robert J. Wicks and Richard D. Parsons. Mahwah, NJ: Paulist Press, 1993.

Wade, Barbara. "Depression in older people: a study," *Nursing Standard*, vol. 40, n. 8 (June 29, 1994), pp. 29–35.

Note

1. Harold Koenig, "Religion and Health in Later Life" in *Aging, Spirituality and Religion: A Handbook.* eds. Melvin Kimble, Susan McFadden, James Ellor, and James Seeber (Minneapolis: Fortress Press, 1995), pp. 9–29.

Coping with Alzheimer's Disease

Steven Sapp

A case can be made that Christianity attained its present position as the world's largest religion because it provides an answer to the fundamental human problem of death. It is ironic, then, that contemporary American Christians—like most of their fellow citizens—have so much trouble accepting their mortality. This difficulty has a direct effect on the way most congregations respond to aging because acknowledging aging directly enough to devise institutional responses requires admitting that human beings age and die. Programs to help feed the homeless or to provide comfort to persons with AIDS—though problematic for other reasons—are still relatively "safe" for most members of congregations because they can rationalize that they will never find themselves in such unhappy circumstances. Aging, however, is rather different. In the youth-worshiping culture of contemporary America most people do not want to be reminded of the fate that awaits us all, even if those who are people of faith have reason to believe in an *ultimately* favorable outcome.

What is true of the members of congregations in general applies to their leaders as well. Clergy do not seem to be any more comfortable accepting their mortality than are those they serve, and this may be one reason that truly effective and meaningful ministries for the aging are not more widespread than they are. A longtime geriatric social worker who was regional director for a company that builds and manages facilities for people with Alzheimer's disease once told me—echoing a lament I have heard from others—that he continued to experience frustration because of the difficulty of encouraging clergy to visit facilities like his. He was familiar with many of the factors that seemed operative: lack of time, ignorance of the need, and denial. He definitely believed that there needs to be more collaboration between churches and these facilities.

And if Christian clergy and congregations have trouble dealing with aging in general because of its association with mortality, how much more is this so in regard to Alzheimer's disease and other dementias. These illnesses not only remind us of our limited life span—as of course do others such as cancer and cardiovascular disease—but dementia also robs us of the very characteristics that our society says give us worth, such as our rationality and independence. The inevitable result is that most dreaded fate in America—"becoming a burden." No wonder our churches do such a poor job of meaningful ministry to those affected by Alzheimer's disease if in doing so both clergy and congregations would have to face up the fact that a similar fate is a very realistic possibility for them.

But what exactly is this malady that strikes such fear into our hearts? Let us consider briefly what it is that makes this chapter necessary, and then we can proceed to look at some of the issues Alzheimer's disease raises for Christians, concluding with some possible responses.

Is Alzheimer's Disease Really a Problem?

First of all, it may be necessary to justify my claim that clergy and congregations need to pay more attention to Alzheimer's disease.[1] Currently around four million people in the United States suffer from Alzheimer's disease. If we assume that each of these persons has only four close family members, twenty million people feel the impact of the disease directly. Adding friends and coworkers to this number explains why a survey in the early 1990s found that thirty-seven million Americans said they knew someone with Alzheimer's.

But the situation is even worse than these numbers suggest because of the well- known "graying of America." In 1900 only 4 percent of the people in this country were sixty-five and older (three million); today almost 13 percent are (nearly forty million). By the middle of this century this number will be closer to 25 percent (about seventy million). And as the whole population ages, so does the older segment of it. People eighty-five and older currently make up about 10 percent of those sixty-five and older, but that proportion may reach 30 percent by the middle of this century, or close to twenty million people.

The relevance of these numbers for us is that Alzheimer's disease afflicts primarily older people, and the incidence increases as people get older. At age seventy-five, for example, the chance of developing Alzheimer's may be as high as one in five, and it approaches one in two by eighty-five. Because those over eighty-five are the fastest-growing segment of our population, experts predict that by the end of this decade six million people in the United States will have Alzheimer's, and perhaps fourteen million by the middle of the century.

Apart from the "normal" response of wanting to care for those in need that such numbers should prompt in Christians, another compelling reason exists for churches to become knowledgeable about Alzheimer's and more involved in responding to it. The percentage of older members in many congregations is even higher than in the population as a whole. In the Presbyterian Church (U.S.A.), for example, 67 percent of the members are over the age of forty-five, 57 percent are over fifty, and 35 percent are sixty-five or older. Half of all the people in this country are older than thirty-six and half younger; in the PC(USA) that median age is fifty-four. Most mainline denominations report at least 20 to 25 percent of their members sixty-five and older. So it is especially important that clergy and laypeople prepare now to confront the challenges that Alzheimer's disease will increasingly present to the nation and to the church.

These numbers lead me to a brief but important tangent: I am becoming increasingly impatient with the attitude of churches that "older adults" are somebody "over there" to whom "we" must minister and for whom "we" must figure out programs. The elderly are *not* a needy subgroup within the church—they *are* the church to a great extent and will only become increasingly more so, as we just saw in the statistics. Indeed, Mel Kimble, a longtime leader in the field of religious gerontology, estimates that on average clergypersons spend about half of their time working with older parishioners and their families.

So we need to stop thinking about "older adult ministry" or "ministry with the aging" as *missionary* work to those "old folks over there." The late Barbara Pittard Payne, another true pioneer in the field, aptly expressed my point when she said, "Don't feed me and pray with me on Thursday unless you're going to include me all the other days." Continuing to talk about ministering to "those old folks over there" in light of contemporary demographic realities simply does not make sense when "those people over there" are who we are as the church.

What Is Alzheimer's Disease?

A fundamental fact must be understood clearly: Alzheimer's disease is not *normal* aging and thus *not* an inevitable result of growing older. Rather, it is an irreversible degenerative disease of the brain characterized by specific identifiable symptoms, though the course of the illness varies widely; the time from diagnosis to death ranges from two to twenty or more years, with an average of about eight. Alzheimer's is the most prevalent form of dementia, a condition defined as serious enough loss or impairment of mental capacity to affect normal functioning. Many types of dementia exist, 20 to 30 percent of them resulting from *treatable* conditions (for example, depression, dehydration, infection, or prescription medication problems), and these are partially or often completely reversible.

Only a complete examination by a physician experienced in treating dementia can determine what is causing the symptoms. This process consists of a thorough medical history, a complete physical examination to rule out other causes, and a psychological ("mental status") screening. This is time-consuming, tiring, and expensive, and caregivers often need help to get through it, especially if their loved one has progressed to the point of being difficult. If the pastor is too busy to spend the time needed, one or more members of the congregation can accompany the caregiver through the process to lend moral and practical support.

Despite recent progress in research, the cause of Alzheimer's remains unknown.[2] The most promising path to this knowledge currently lies in the realm of genetics, but other factors like environmental influences and body chemistry are likely to be implicated. No cure exists for the illness, though four drugs are currently approved for its treatment and many more are under study. The ones available now, however, at best can slow the rate of decline and improve the quality of life for a relatively short time.

Many other possible treatments have received varying amounts of publicity and some may even offer promise. Among these are vitamin E, estrogen replacement therapy, various anti-inflammatory agents, lipid-lowering agents (statins), gamma- and beta-secretase inhibitors, and gingko biloba. None of these has been shown to be truly effective in either preventing or treating Alzheimer's, however, and all claims to that effect should be taken with considerable caution; furthermore, all have potentially dangerous side effects. One service that knowledgeable clergy can provide caregivers in their congregations is to urge them to learn all they can about a possible treatment from reputable sources before committing any of their resources to it.

What Are the Symptoms of Alzheimer's Disease?

Because of the variability of the illness, it is impossible to say that "this is *exactly* what to expect" as it progresses. Still, the symptoms of Alzheimer's can be described accurately as long it is remembered that their appearance and severity will vary. Given that the brain is the organ that is failing, it should come as no surprise that the uniqueness that God gives each of us continues to manifest itself.

Memory loss is of course the best-known sign of Alzheimer's, affecting short-term memory first but gradually progressing to the point that the person cannot recognize or name even a spouse or adult child. Related to this is an inability to learn even the simplest new facts and tasks no matter what ingenious techniques the caregiver devises. Problems with language also appear, with regard both to expressing oneself and to understanding what others are saying. Difficulties with performing simple actions like eating, dressing, and toileting become common, and eventually incontinence and lack of coordination leading to falls cause problems for both persons with Alzheimer's and their caregivers.

Not surprisingly, personality changes and mood swings take place throughout the course of the illness, often causing the caregiver to feel that he or she is living with a total stranger. The person with dementia becomes disoriented in relation to time and place, perhaps thinking the present is a time far in the past or the current home is one from childhood. Impaired judgment also appears and increases, causing behavior that can range from the bizarre to the outright dangerous, especially with regard to driving. Hallucinations and delusions are not uncommon, leading to suspicion and paranoia directed toward even a lifelong spouse or loving adult child.

With most terminal illnesses physical decline is marked, and though caregivers may have to provide almost total care, the recipient of that care is relatively immobile. With Alzheimer's the problems occasioned by the loss of cognitive function are not accompanied by an initial loss of mobility and strength, considerably complicating the caregiving task. Among the most troubling symptoms for caregivers are agitation, restlessness, and wandering, often accompanied by disrupted sleep cycles, which can lead to physical exhaustion of the caregiver. Given these symptoms, there is little wonder that studies have found depression rates among those caring for a person with dementia to be over 50 percent. But the impact of the illness on families stretches far beyond even something as serious as depression.

What Does Alzheimer's Disease Do to Families?

Almost three-fourths of people with Alzheimer's disease live at home, and about the same proportion of their care in the home is provided by family and friends. Both those with the disease and their caregivers consistently affirm that this is the way they want it. But no serious illness—least of all one that is progressively debilitating and invariably terminal—leaves unscathed those who interact closely with the afflicted person. Alzheimer's disease is especially pernicious in this regard for several reasons.

First, one of the most frustrating things for many caregivers is that for some period of time (often quite lengthy) persons with Alzheimer's remain physically robust and very active, even if they have progressively less purposive control over their behavior and are less and less able to interact with others in meaningful ways. Often the individual with Alzheimer's knows that he or she should "do something" but simply cannot remember or discern what it is. One part of the person's cognitive machinery is working, but others are not, and often the person remains quite capable of performing some functions but totally unable to carry out some others. Thus it is complicated both emotionally and ethically to decide if—and to what extent—a caregiver should "take over" the person's life. Furthermore, during the early stages of the disease, and at least at times in later stages, the person is conscious that "I am losing my mind" but is powerless to do anything about it, which can lead to anger and frustration, especially if those around the person fail to recognize the cognitive capacity that remains.

Second, related to this mix of abilities is another difficulty: The changes brought about by the disease take place in different people at an extremely variable rate, making it virtually impossible to determine at any given moment exactly what the person's mental capacity is or even what particular behavioral manifestations will appear. Although the overall direction of the illness is invariably down, a person may plateau for periods of time or even show temporary (but short-term) improvement, further confusing the situation, not least by evoking false hope in caregivers that the improvement will continue.

Third, these problems are compounded still more by the loss of contact with reality (or perhaps existence in a different reality) that characterizes the disease. Because the person often appears otherwise normal, caregivers are constantly tempted to try to "bring the person back" into the caregiver's reality, provoking further confusion and sometimes even anger and hostility. Today the preferred approach is to "live into" the demented person's reality as much as possible (if no personal danger to either party is involved in doing so) and allow the person to enjoy whatever he or she is experiencing.

Beyond these general comments about the impact of Alzheimer's disease on family caregivers, a number of other specific issues arise that caring clergy and congregations need to be aware of if they are to devise appropriate ways to support those who—in the words of the title of one of the first and still best guidebooks[3] on the topic— face endless "thirty-six-hour days" of caregiving. Space permits only the briefest of summaries of the most important of these issues here.

Role Changes and Family Conflicts

As Alzheimer's disease progresses, the ill person can no longer fulfill responsibilities normally carried out, and the caregiver—most commonly the spouse—has to assume more and more of formerly shared tasks. This reorientation in patterns of living developed over decades is extremely hard on everybody involved. Even more difficulties may arise if an adult child is the primary caregiver and the "child" must gradually become more and more the "parent," particularly with regard to matters like dressing, toileting, and bathing (which is even more difficult when the parent is the opposite sex).

Christian spouses frequently wrestle with the meaning of their wedding vows to love and honor the partner "for better, for worse, in sickness and in health," and adult children may struggle with the meaning of the Fifth Commandment's admonition to "honor your father and your mother" (Exodus 20:12) in this situation. Clearly clergy should be able to help caregivers work through these issues appropriately, even to the point of concluding that if a particular situation is truly impossible for everybody, loving and honoring a demented spouse or parent may sadly mean moving that person to a facility that can provide the quality care that has become simply beyond the family's capability.

Sibling conflicts can also create problems when decisions about parents' care arise, especially if one adult child is the primary caregiver and the others periodically offer "suggestions," often without full awareness of what the caregiver faces day in and day out. Clergy who stay aware of caregiving situations among their members can offer valuable assistance by offering to moderate family conferences if such tensions arise. Trained and experienced in interpersonal relationships and group process and objective in their judgment, they may help family members identify underlying issues that they fail to see because of their emotional involvement and long-practiced ways of relating to one another. This process can assist them in finding points of conflict and avenues of resolution that may be impossible for them to discover themselves.

Grief

If one word summarizes the impact of Alzheimer's disease on families, it is loss, which inevitably occasions grief. In this case the condition causing the grief can go on for years, during which the loved one gradually slips away, though for some time remaining physically robust and outwardly appearing "normal." In addition, caring for a person with Alzheimer's forces caregiving spouses (and children and grandchildren) to come face-to-face with their own aging, another kind of loss for many people in this country. Acknowledging one's mortality as the first step toward spiritual fulfillment is a basic principle of Christianity, however, and the sensitive clergyperson can help a family caregiver struggling with this particular kind of grief to understand this.

Whatever the course of an individual's journey with Alzheimer's, the outcome is the same. And whatever opportunity the slow progression affords family members for "anticipatory grief," for most the physical death is painful. Compounding normal grief, however, is the physical, mental, emotional, and often financial exhaustion caregivers feel, and especially problems occasioned by the common wish along the way that the person's suffering finally end (along with the caregiver's burden). A caring minister and congregation can help lift some of this burden and offer appropriate ways to deal with the result of Alzheimer's disease in the lives of family caregivers, often made worse by these virtually universal feelings.

Guilt

Guilt is something the Christian faith is well equipped to address, and when it comes to Alzheimer's, offering caregivers help in this area is a desperately needed service. I never fail to be amazed when I hear family members who are expending themselves in almost unbelievable ways in caring for a loved one say that they are not doing enough, or that they must have played some role in causing the person to have Alzheimer's, or that sometimes they wish for the person's death.

Of course in some cases the guilt may have a basis, such as when the heavy weight of caregiving leads to verbal or even physical abuse of the ill person. Elder abuse in general is increasing in the United States, and clergy and congregational visitors have an important role to play in assuring the safety of those at risk. In the first place, compassionate support of caregivers can help prevent the exhaustion and frustration that can spark abuse. Beyond this, those who are regularly visiting in the home can be alert for signs of problems that may need to be addressed through social services or in extreme cases judicial avenues.

A major source of guilt that wise counsel may prevent (or more likely only *lessen*) is the agonizing decision to move the ill person to institutional care. Alert clergy and congregational visitors can detect the need for such action and can begin to broach the issue with the caregiver, who will almost always be resistant. If the caregiver has made the unwise promise never to institutionalize the loved one, the guilt at having to do so may delay the decision until much later than it should have been made.

Clergy are especially suited to help caregivers understand that though they perhaps cannot avoid guilt feelings in their situation, their love, compassion, and self-sacrifice more than compensate for any shortcomings in the care they provide, real or imagined. Certainly many resources exist in our faith tradition that can be brought to bear on this matter, and the support of a loving faith community can help caregivers retain a positive self-evaluation in the face of a situation that often makes them question themselves.

This cannot be overstressed: *Caregivers must take care of themselves without feeling guilty for doing so.* It is critical that caregivers learn to balance the needs of the person they are caring for and their own. Many devout people think their faith calls them to sacrifice themselves for loved ones, perhaps even to "lay down their lives" for them. It is hard to disparage such altruism, which after all is at the core of the Christian faith. Caregivers need to be reminded constantly, however, that Alzheimer's disease makes patients of the entire family and that genuine concern for the ill person means that the caregivers must stay healthy if they are to go on providing care.

Again, clergy especially can be of great service to caregivers by "giving them permission" to take care of themselves and by assuring them they should not feel guilty for getting away occasionally (or preferably regularly). They are simply following the example of Jesus himself, who frequently withdrew "to a lonely place" for revitalization when the demands of his responsibilities threatened to overwhelm him. Familiarity with resources in the community, such as good day care or other respite programs, can be invaluable, and every congregation can develop a program that sends members to the homes of families coping with dementia so that caregivers can leave their loved ones with trusted and caring friends for short periods.

The vast majority of family caregivers *want* to keep their loved ones at home as long as possible if not until death or the "final illness." Clearly this is too heavy a burden for one person. What if, however, churches took the lead in developing an approach analogous to hospice? I am not referring to the "terminal illness" aspect but rather to the concept of a "team" approach that utilizes a number of different people with different kinds of skills and abilities, a characteristic of most congregations. Hospice has shown this approach to be less expensive and more compassionate than hospitalization for end-of-life care; certainly it stands to reason that it would be cheaper than any kind of institutionalization for persons with Alzheimer's disease as well. But even more important, it would have the person-centered benefit of allowing the ill persons to stay in the most familiar environment possible and their caregivers to satisfy their wishes to keep them there. The late Tom Kitwood, a trailblazer in the humane treatment of people with dementia, noted that quality care for persons with dementia is always the work of a team of folks together performing work that they are good at and that they enjoy. This kind of care requires intentionality.[4] It would be wonderful if Christian congregations showed the way in replacing the chance factor with an intentional movement in this direction.

Anger

I have already mentioned another almost inevitable result of Alzheimer's caregiving: anger. The nature of the illness increasingly precludes the expressions of gratitude we normally expect when we do something for another person, and often the person with dementia blames various problems on the caregiver or even accuses that person of mistreatment. Given what the caregiver goes through to assure the person's well-being, such behavior cannot help but evoke hurt and anger. In addition, because the person with dementia may appear so normal outwardly, it is difficult sometimes to accept that the individual cannot really be held responsible, and then when that realization forces its way back into consciousness, guilt over being angry arises. Clergy who maintain regular contact with caregivers can find ways to offer gentle reminders that the illness is causing the cognitively impaired person's actions and that they are not really "personal."

Often anger is directed, not at the ill person, but at others, including family members who do not help, physicians who have no cure, friends who abandon the family in their time of greatest need, and God, who may be seen as letting a very bad thing happen to good people. Again, feelings of guilt may then arise for being angry with God. Clergy clearly have an important role to play here through sensitive counseling and perhaps referral to resources that many Christians may find helpful, such as psalms that express anger and disappointment and anger at God for permitting misfortune or tragedy.

Embarrassment

Although hardly as serious a concern as guilt and anger, many family caregivers feel intense embarrassment because people with dementia behave in ways that range from bizarre to offensive. Because they often do not *look* sick, there is a tendency to think they should "know better," which of course they do not. When the elderly mother who has always been prim and proper starts cursing the visiting pastor or making sexual advances, the caregiving daughter cannot help but cringe and try to explain and apologize. Sadly, a common response is simply to try to avoid situations in which such embarrassment might occur, thus isolating the person, to the detriment of both that individual and the caregiver.

Visitors who are knowledgeable about dementia can reassure caregivers that they understand and are not offended by such behavior. Congregations that foster an atmosphere in which caregivers are comfortable bringing their loved ones despite their problems and in which they find love and support will be rendering a tremendous service by providing the opportunity for them to be among people who genuinely care and at least try to understand.

In fact, I strongly encourage continuing to include persons with Alzheimer's in religious observances, even when it seems that they no longer comprehend what is happening and may not always behave "appropriately." Many reports exist that familiar rituals, prayers, Bible verses memorized decades earlier, and especially hymns evoke strong positive responses from people who otherwise seem completely inaccessible, and empirical research has begun to support this anecdotal evidence. If this is so for late-stage Alzheimer's, the comfort and reassurance people in early stages can receive from such sources is surely much greater. Entire worship services can be structured specifically for the cognitively impaired and their families.[5] When the individual can no longer attend corporate worship of any kind, the "old, old story" can still be told and old familiar hymns can be played and sung by caring fellow church members.

Isolation

Alzheimer's caregivers often comment that their friends are uncomfortable interacting with someone who is cognitively impaired, and because the disease allows no hope for recovery or even improvement, many people choose to avoid the caregiver as well because they do not know what to say. The isolation and abandonment caregivers feel are also increased because they find it so hard to leave their loved ones, a situation that gets worse as the disease progresses.

In addition to assuring that the pastor and other visitors from the congregation continue to call on families stricken with Alzheimer's, a very helpful way to combat isolation is to encourage caregivers to attend a support group. In fact, congregations should explore sponsoring such groups because churches are ideal places for them to meet. In support groups caregivers learn specific and practical ways to deal with their loved ones, receive information about the disease and resources available to them, and gain emotional support from others having the same experiences.

It is important for clergy and congregations to be aware also that early diagnosis of Alzheimer's disease is becoming increasingly common, meaning that more people know they have the disease while they can still understand what is happening to them. With the variable course of the disease many people are only mildly impaired for a relatively long time, and support groups are appearing for persons with Alzheimer's. These groups can be very helpful in encouraging their participants to continue to live life as fully as possible. Congregations can contribute to this goal if they realize that some people in the very early stages of Alzheimer's can continue to do volunteer work or perform familiar tasks such as ushering.

An essential resource for everyone who is concerned about dementia and wants to help those wrestling with it is the Alzheimer's Association, the nationally recognized leader in addressing such illnesses. Most large communities have a local chapter that can provide information about the disease and help with support groups. For the number and location of the nearest Alzheimer's Association chapter, call the national office in Chicago at (800) 272-3900, log on to www.alz.org, or write to the Alzheimer's Association, 919 North Michigan Avenue, Suite 1100, Chicago, IL 60611-1676.

Fear

Although fear is an element in many of the issues already discussed, it deserves special consideration. Diseases like Alzheimer's evoke myriad fears: fear of the loved one's death; fear of one's own death first, leaving no one to care for the ill person; fear of financial disaster; fear of inability to continue to care for the person at home, thus requiring institutionalization; fear of loss of friends; and many other fears. These fears need to be taken seriously and provisions made to address the situations that prompt them.

Beyond this response, however, clergy and congregational visitors can remind caregivers of the role faith can play as a resource in dealing with fear. In the Old Testament familiar psalms like 23, 27, and 46, as well as others less familiar, can provide great comfort by showing the timeless nature of the fears and other feelings that caregivers experience. Furthermore, they can remind those who face the seemingly endless and hopeless burden of caregiving that many people have found in their faith the strength to overcome great hardship (even when that faith is tested and seems to be inadequate). For Christians the New Testament contains numerous familiar expressions of the comforting love and presence of Jesus Christ, such as John 14:1, 27 and Philippians 4:11–13, especially verse 13.

Ministers who make the effort to identify such texts can read them together with caregivers (and those they are caring for) and help them find their applicability for the situation in which they find themselves.

Clergy and congregational visitors should encourage caregivers to make use of one of the greatest resources they have to cope with the terrible stress of caring for a person with dementia: prayer. If reminded of Tennyson's affirmation, "More things are wrought by prayer than this world dreams of," caregivers at the end of their rope and feeling totally alone and isolated can turn to prayer to find the source of that "perfect love [that] casts out fear" (1 John 4:18). Reinhold Niebuhr's "Serenity Prayer" is particularly relevant for those who care for people with dementia:

> God grant me the serenity
> To accept the things I cannot change,
> The courage to change the things I can,
> And the wisdom to know the difference.

Helplessness and Loss of Hope

Serenity, sadly, is not a state of mind that most caregivers would ever apply to themselves. Indeed, among the worst effects of dementia are the sense of helplessness and the loss of hope that almost all caregivers feel at one time or another, and with good reason. Caring for a person with dementia has been described as "the funeral that never ends," with no chance of the positive outcome—recovery— that we can hope for with many illnesses. If, as is so often the case in our culture, hope is understood to mean "getting better," Alzheimer's is a hope*less* situation. I regularly hear people say—and they are mostly serious—"If I'm ever diagnosed with Alzheimer's, I'm going to kill myself before I get too far gone to do it," and caregivers certainly can understand that feeling.

The great Prussian philosopher Immanuel Kant wrote: "All the interests of my reason, speculative as well as practical, combine in the following three questions: (1) What can I know? (2) What ought I do? (3) What may I hope?"[6] The importance of knowledge and morality (though the latter is perhaps honored more in the breach than in the observance) is widely acknowledged in our society's constellation of values, but a thinker as profound as Kant realized that hope must also be seen as an equal member of that essential triumvirate on which the meaning of human life rests.[7] And Alzheimer's disease is an especially efficient destroyer of hope.

Some excellent advice to offer to those who are caring for a person with Alzheimer's disease and are struggling to cling to any shred of hope is that given by poet-statesman Vaclav Havel when he said: "Hope is not about believing you can change things. Hope is about believing you make a difference." No one can change the ultimate outcome of the situation in which these caregivers find themselves, but they can be helped to find comfort and satisfaction in the fact that they are making a great difference in the lives of their loved ones.

Beyond this, the basic message of the Christian faith can be a source of genuine hope in the face of despair, recognizing as it does the full reality of the pain and suffering caregivers experience (remember Jesus on the cross, suffering so terribly that he cried out that God had forsaken him, and yet beyond the suffering lay the new life of resurrection). As someone once said, "Hope has to do with the presence of God, not the absence of struggle," an affirmation that calls to mind the words of Martin Luther King, Jr., "We must accept finite disappointment, but we must never lose infinite hope."

Indeed, from the Christian perspective, it seems that struggle and suffering are necessary for hope. Remember Paul's statement in Romans 5:3–5 that we "boast in our sufferings, knowing that suffering produces endurance, and endurance produces character, and character produces hope, and hope does not disappoint us." How could Paul see suffering as the basis for hope? Simply because "God proves his love for us in that while we still were sinners Christ died for us" (v. 8) and was raised by God, "the first fruits of those who have died" (1 Corinthians 15:20). In short, *the resurrection of Christ is the source of the Chris-tian hope,* and this is precisely the message that clergy and congregational visitors can bring to families facing the apparent hopelessness of Alzheimer's disease.

As Paul makes clear, however, before the resurrection was the *cross.* So Christian hope is never an unrealistic refusal to accept the negativities of life but a realization that even those negativities, even a whole world "groaning in labor pains" (Romans 8:22), even something as vicious and damnable as Alzheimer's disease, cannot prevail against the power of God. As Victor Frankl has taught us, this matter of hope and meaning can be summed up in the equation D=S-M—despair equals suffering without meaning. If we can find some meaning, some purpose in suffering and struggle, then we can avoid despair. Certainly the church has the resources to be a major source of meaning for those struggling with dementia, and it should fulfill its responsibility.

I conclude with a word to clergy who may find themselves interacting with families touched by Alzheimer's disease. I culled the following sentences from my class notes from Pastoral Psychology 170, "Pastoral Conversation," taught by Richard A. Goodling at Duke University Divinity School in the fall of 1969. No commentary seems necessary (though given that Dr. Goodling *spoke* these words, I suppose the emphases must be mine):

> Being a minister is more than just delivering the message. It is meeting the recipient, becoming responsible for him or her through love. The effect of the message depends to a large extent on the messenger who brings it. The minister's function is to make real the love of God in his or her own attitudes. . . . One of the essential characteristics of the pastoral conversation is that it is a *hopeful* conversation, backed by the pastor's faith in God. The Christian faith calls forth expectancy, that of being saved *from* as well as *for* or *to*. Pastoral conversation is a means of implementing that expectancy.

The Role of the Church

Now we know something about Alzheimer's disease and what it does to families. I have offered some suggestions about how clergy and congregations can begin to address some of the specific issues that caring for a person with dementia raises for the caregiver. Before I present an example of how Christian theological reflection can be relevant to the issue, I want to explore the church's role in this important area a little further.

First, the church is uniquely situated to help families with Alzheimer's for several reasons. Jesus made clear his expectation that his disciples must care for those in need. Echoing a fundamental teaching of Abrahamic religion perhaps best articulated before him by the Hebrew prophets, Jesus did not make such assistance optional (see Matthew 25). The early church followed its Master's example and command, as illustrated by Paul's admonition in Galatians 6:2: "Bear one another's burdens, and in this way you will fulfill the law of Christ."

There is no reason to think that Christians today do not carry the same obligation, and it is simply a fact that people with Alzheimer's (and many other older people who do not have dementia) reach the point at which they cannot fend for themselves, where they become the "needy" persons that our religious tradition has always affirmed demand the selfless attention of those who stand in that tradition. That does not make them any the less important—if anything, it is exactly the opposite: our obligation toward them *increases.*

Second, because of this fundamental theological/ethical commitment, churches were providing what we today know as "social services" long before governments came to accept doing so as their responsibility. Indeed, religious congregations have long been a source of assistance and services of many kinds for their older members and their families, and often for other elders in the community who may not be formally affiliated with the particular congregation. Support for those affected by Alzheimer's disease is in keeping with this practice, and in this era of downsizing of public programs this tradition needs to be continued. Furthermore, in many congregations, perhaps especially smaller ones in less urbanized settings, the same people have known one another for many years, leading to a natural tendency to offer support and assistance when needed. So, strong precedent exists for developing programs to assist Alzheimer's families.

Third, some families are reluctant to access even the public resources that are available, especially if they have always seen themselves as independent and "able to make it on our own." This reluctance may be compounded by the fact that our society has not yet overcome a longstanding prejudice against "mental illness" and a "blame the victim" attitude that is not so prevalent with more clearly physical ailments such as cancer or stroke (despite the fact that those who suffer from those diseases may actually have done more to contribute to them than do people with Alzheimer's). The difficulty in acknowledging that a family member has an illness that causes such strange behavior with no obvious physical symptoms for a relatively long period can lead many caregivers to try to do everything themselves. But the nature of the clergy-parishioner relationship grants access and initiative to pastors (and other representatives of the congregation) that is simply unavailable to public programs, however commendable.

Fourth, but by no means less significant, because of the nature of Alzheimer's disease and the unrelenting burden of caring for someone suffering from it, caregivers almost always reach the point that spiritual support is essential if they too are not to become victims of the disease. Obviously the church is where they should feel comfortable turning for such sustenance, and programs should be in place to reach out to caregivers in the event they do not take the initiative.

Fifth, congregations bring together people who possess a wide variety of expertise, experience, and connections. Thus they naturally enjoy the resources for the kind of creativity needed in this area, the fresh, "outside the box" perspectives that might not be found among those trained in a specific discipline, even in gerontology. In addition, Christians generally see things in a way that does not despair at seemingly insurmountable odds but rather persists in pushing for action that improves the human condition (though admittedly what constitutes "improvement" is not always universally agreed upon, even among church people). This perspective tends to help members of congregations affirm meaning and purpose in the face of what often seems to be chaos, which is no small plus as one grows older and especially as one faces dementia. Indeed, Christians live out of a sense of *hope*, an attitude that can be called upon to encourage a little more creativity and courage when it comes to creative programming, even if the odds appear stacked against success.

Finally, although religious groups are not exempt from financial realities, they tend not to look at the "bottom line" first and last to determine what they should do, thereby promoting a more community-oriented outlook in contrast to the individualism and self-interest rampant in contemporary America. This approach again opens the way for forging some truly creative programs that more bottom line-oriented organizations would lack the courage to try.

Sadly, among the reasons most often cited by leaders of religious institutions for not providing services for the elderly that promise great potential benefit to the community—such as respite programs for Alzheimer's caregivers—is the two-pronged deterrent of a burdensome state regulatory process and the fear of liability, with the attendant expense of securing adequate insurance protection. I would certainly never advocate allowing a congregation to set up any kind of program it wants without oversight (especially given the alarming stories about elder abuse), and it has become an apparently God-given right for Americans to sue over even the slightest wrong—real or perceived. Still, some kinds of regulatory accommodations or compromises might allow congregations to provide at least some basic programs for the elderly without much of a threat to First Amendment interpretations that fear state involvement with religion. Such programs could be a real service not only to a church's own members and to others in the community but also to states whose already strained public resources are going to become only more heavily burdened in the coming decades. Tom Kitwood again offers wise words of counsel: "However tight the restrictions imposed by law, and however severe the financial constraints, there is always some freedom for movement, some possibility for doing new things."[8] Certainly Christian churches should be eager to assist in God's work of "making all things new" to whatever extent they can.

The "Hypercognitive Culture"

With the clear mandate to help those in need and with the resources at its disposal, what is deterring the church from being in the forefront of developing creative and innovative ways to help families struggling under the burden of Alzheimer's disease? Earlier I said American Christians, clergy and lay alike, have a great deal of trouble accepting their mortality in general and acknowledging and responding to dementias like Alzheimer's in particular. The reasons for this difficulty are many, but when it comes to Alzheimer's disease, our predominant cultural values contribute greatly. In a felicitous phrase coined by ethicist Stephen Post in his excellent book *The Moral Challenge of Alzheimer Disease*,[9] we have become a "hypercognitive culture," one "that is the child of rationalism and capitalism, so clarity of mind and economic productivity determine the value of a human life." The result is that when people's mental capacities fade, when their reason and memory no longer function "properly," they begin to lose full moral standing in our society and thus become devalued.

Although we do not do a very good job of accepting people with any kind of disability in a society such as ours, dementia generates a particularly malignant response from most people, probably because it evokes some of the worst anxieties Americans can face. Here in one package—even more than in normal aging, though many observers believe it happens there as well—we see the loss of virtually everything our society says gives us value: youth and all the physical attributes we associate with it, cognitive function and rational control of our actions, economic productivity, and of course the most terrifying threat of all, the loss of our autonomy and *independence*, the ability to "do it our way." However, unlike many other anxiety-producing conditions such as being homeless or HIV-positive, we cannot really get away with saying, "It will never happen to me," because we know the odds are excellent that if we live long enough we *will* suffer from dementia or be close to someone who does, and we will certainly get old.

As much as I admire the work of Carl Eisdorfer, a pioneer in this field who was one of the founders of the national Alzheimer's Association and is currently my colleague as chair of psychiatry at the University of Miami, I think he and his coauthor Donna Cohen chose a very unfortunate title for their generally excellent book on Alzheimer's disease: *The Loss of Self*.[10]

Why do I say that? Because in a hypercognitive culture such as ours, in which we have come to live pretty much *for* self, if we suffer the "loss of self" most people now associate with Alzheimer's—and many with simply getting old—what else is there worth living for? As Frank Sinatra put it, "For what is a man, what has he got? If not him*self*, then he has naught." Sinatra's attitude is increasingly likely to be held by others toward old people, and especially *toward* those with dementia.

If we buy into the predominant attitudes of our society—compounded by trying to find a defense against the anxieties people with dementia evoke in us—we make judgments about the worth of such individuals and our responsibilities to them. We are then likely to consider them less than fully human, not really *persons* because they fail to meet our criteria of personhood. This allows us to exclude and isolate them from society. We might say it becomes a matter of "out of [their] mind, out of [our] sight"!

To coin a word, we can say that such people are *dismembered*, removed from being seen as part of the organic entity—the *body*—that constitutes any social grouping. Sadly, this is as true of the church—the earthly body of Christ—and other faith communities as it is of the broader society.

In many ways the predominant model of Alzheimer's disease has served our society's values well, making it much easier to deal with people with dementia in a perfunctory, superficial way. After all, if we are not really dealing with a *person*—at least one who is a rational, subjective being with awareness of self and others—why take the time and energy to go through all those motions we associate with appropriate, caring interaction with persons? It certainly is easier to deal with the problems *we* perceive if we convince ourselves that they are unaware of them.

But Post reminds us that "human beings are much more than sharp minds, powerful rememberers, and economic successes."[11] When Christians make such an assertion, of course, it is based on a deeply held belief that is in direct contrast to the dominant values of our hypercognitive culture. Our religious beliefs lead us to affirm instead the inherent value of *all* human beings as created in God's own image, made "little less than angels," regardless of the level of their cognitive function or economic productivity. And that says something very different about how we respond to them and interact with them.

The problem is—in Kitwood's words—"the strategic task is one of cultural transformation, at a time when many of the circumstances are not propitious."[12] I cite just one example of how Christian beliefs can serve as a foundation for the cultural transformation Kitwood says is necessary if we are to resist our hypercognitive culture's tendency to treat people with dementia as less than fully human beings created in God's own image. I present this point in the context of a particularly vexing problem most caregivers face and suggest how the Christian "countercultural" view can offer a solution to that problem.

A dominant characteristic and source of pride for contemporary Americans is our strong sense of independence, practically an obsession for many people today. With regard to the concerns of this chapter, this trait manifests itself most noticeably in many caregivers' inability to accept help. Whatever its source, such fierce independence causes problems in acknowledging the inability to care for the person with dementia com-pletely on one's own. Even when people offer assistance, they may be turned away because the caregiver cannot admit the need for any kind of help, even spiritual support.

It is understandable that those who have been meeting all of the ill person's needs feel that they are the best ones to do whatever has to be done, which may often be true. A fierce attitude of "I can do it by myself," however, deters offers of help that may still be made and can even hinder the provision of the best care possible by failing to utilize resources that are available in the family, religious institution, or community.

Total responsibility for the care of a person with Alzheimer's disease can wreak havoc on the physical and emotional well-being of anyone. Caregivers must be encouraged to take advantage of offers of assistance and even to ask for help when needed. Debbie Anderson, director of Senior Health Service at Overlake Hospital in Bellevue, Washington, offers a helpful approach when she points out that true independence is not living without help but rather knowing when to ask for help so that you can truly do what you want to do. Sensitive clergy and congregational visitors can lead caregivers to understand that it is really a *sign of strength* if they are able to ask for help instead of an indication of weakness as many see it.

One of my favorite comments from an Alzheimer's caregiver is relevant here (and in situations beyond this, including many in which clergy often find themselves): "Even Superman is Clark Kent most of the time!" Instead of trying to do it all themselves, caregivers can make a list of people who say, "Let me know if I can help." Then when they need help, they can ask for it.

But what does the Christian faith specifically have to contribute to this discussion that can counter the predominant attitude in our culture that leads caregivers to try to maintain their independence despite the near impossibility of the task they face? Just this: the Christian gospel boils down to one thing in the final analysis—it is *God's* act alone that is sufficient to restore the relationship between God and human beings, not anything we can do *on our own*, by ourselves, independently. This central affirmation of the apostle Paul—echoed by Augustine, the formative thinker for Roman Catholic theology, and emphasized by the Protestant Reformers as the heart of their message—forces us to acknowledge our absolute dependence on the unmerited and freely offered grace of God, and we just do not like to do that. We are not satisfied with being "in the *image* of God"; we want to be *like* God, independent, *self*-sufficient. Therefore we have real problems facing up to the possibility of growing old and especially of dementia because it forces us to admit that we are *not* self-sufficient and able to "go it alone."

In a very real sense, then, the inevitable results of aging and of Alzheimer's disease that strike such fear into the hearts of contemporary Americans can serve as a *model* for what Christianity says it means merely to be a human being: at its very heart, the Christian faith affirms that human beings *are* dependent, that we do not live on our own and only for ourselves at *any* point in our lives. The problem humans always have to struggle with is precisely the difficulty of accepting the totally free grace of God (which is nothing more than acknowledging utter dependence upon God). Perhaps if we could do a better job throughout our lives of accepting that we are totally dependent upon the creating, redeeming, and sustaining God, it will be easier to accept the prospect of the dependence upon other human beings that aging often and dementia always necessitates, whether as the person with the illness or as the caregiver. If the church can communicate this message to caregivers—as it should to all its members—they may be able to accept offers of help and not be so determined to try to get along only on their own.

At any rate, this perspective should again give pause to Christians who might fall into the cultural trap of devaluing and therefore dis-membering people who become dependent through the loss of cognitive capacity: if in fact we are *all* really totally dependent, the difference between the dependence of the person with dementia and of those evaluating such a person is a matter of degree, not substance. There seems to be a clear message here for those of us who are, in Daniel Callahan's telling phrase, "currently able-bodied" (or perhaps "able-minded").

I have briefly and all too superficially sketched the beginnings of one part of a response to the prevailing values of our hypercognitive culture that lead to the devaluation of people with Alzheimer's disease and the consequent failure to provide their caregivers with the assistance and support they so desperately need. But where might reaffirming these basic beliefs lead believers and the congregations? In *The Moral Challenge of Alzheimer Disease* Post raises what he calls "the critical ethical question" with regard to this illness: "How can we weave people with dementia into the web of caring connectedness that promises to spare them the cruelty and abuse into which they have been and are easily thrown?"[13] Contemporary American values tend to dismember people with cognitive deficits, to remove such persons from the public eye, and then to rationalize doing so by arguing that, after all, such beings are not really "persons"—or at least they do not really meet the criteria for being *human*—at all. If Christians keep before them the fundamental truths of their faith they will refuse to allow people with dementia in their congregations (and their caregivers) to suffer this dis-membering, this removal from the body (whether the body politic or the body of Christ), this being cast aside as no longer fully human and worthy of our complete moral attention.

Of course the reluctance of pastors and congregations to get involved in Alzheimer's care—or at least their extreme discomfort with people who are suffering from cognitive deficits and therefore their tendency to exclude them implicitly if not explicitly—is not particularly surprising, for all the reasons presented earlier. The truth is that here as in too many other places, faith communities have bought into society's dominant values, perhaps not so malignantly as to deny *any* value to people with dementia but certainly enough to convey to them (and their caregivers) that they are somehow less than fully welcome. Obviously this is wrong and—difficult though it may be to overcome—also unnecessary if proper training is provided for clergy and lay leaders.

The religious community—through its clergy and congregations—must refuse to yield to contemporary assessments of the cognitively impaired as less than fully human and instead *remember* such persons, *incorporating* them as fully into the body of believers as their condition allows. By doing so we not only maintain their hope for as long as they are aware of it (and their caregivers certainly remain aware!); we also sustain *our own* hope that if we are ever in similar circumstances the community will not abandon us but will strive to keep us as fully connected as possible.

A similarity exists between this and a central concept of Robert Putnam's provocative *Bowling Alone: The Collapse and Revival of American Community*. His notion of "generalized reciprocity," on which he says a functioning democracy is based, is: "I'll do this for you now, without expecting anything immediately in return and perhaps without even knowing you, confident that down the road you or someone else will return the favor."[14] This idea certainly falls somewhat short of the true Christian ideal of selfless, neighbor-regarding love (*agape*), but functionally it seems much the same and perhaps is the most we can realistically hope for in our society at large. Within the church, however, we ought to be able to do even better.

Alzheimer's disease has been described as a "biopsychosocial" illness: besides the terrible cost of the disease to a person's body and mind, there is no question that it exacts a horrible toll with regard to the ill person's (and caregivers') place in society as well, isolating and excluding them. And it seems unarguable that, as Margaret Mohrmann puts it, "the damage done to a person's self-identification as a member of a community can be healed only by the ministrations of that community."[15]

Again, then, is it any wonder that the traditional model of dementia care—feeding off the understandable fears and anxieties mentioned earlier—has tended to isolate persons with Alzheimer's disease, to cut them off from meaningful human interaction? This in turn has led many to hopelessness, despair, and a more rapid decline than has likely been necessary. But if the community of faith refuses to continue to take this approach, if it insists on remembering such people (and their caregivers), it can take a huge step toward in-spiriting them instead of disspiriting them. By congregations' insistence on not allowing even something like Alzheimer's to remove a person from the community, they witness to the truth that nothing can separate us from the love of God, incarnated and made manifest in the body of Christ, not even an illness that robs us of that aspect of our being that many in our society say is precisely what gives us our value as persons.

We also proclaim an equally important theological truth, one our culture has sadly lost sight of. Mohrmann again makes the point well: none of the negativities of life—however devastating—is "absolute in this world." Their elimination is not required for us to be able to live a fully human existence. She concludes: "What is required for a truly human life is not the absence of pain but the presence of others, the maintenance of living bonds with other human beings. . . . As part of their healing, those who suffer require from us assurance that our relationships with them endure."[16]

The term I have used, *remembering*, is obviously intended to be a catchy double-entendre, but it conveys significant substance as well. When we make a conscious effort to keep people with Alzheimer's disease "in the community," when we remember or reincorporate them into the body of believers, we are actually *recalling* many things of importance to us as that community of faith. We recall, for instance, what our own faith requires of us with regard to those less fortunate and in need; what the body of Christ is all about (cf. 1 Corinthians 12); who those who no longer remember once were and the contributions they made; indeed, who we ourselves are (or at least ought to want to be) and how we would (or will) want to be treated if (or when) we are no longer quite "ourselves." And through this act of remembering them (which is also an act of *reminding* ourselves)— in this proclamation and assurance that nothing can separate the

Christian from Christ's body—lies the essential mooring point that those suffering from Alzheimer's disease, either directly or as caregivers, must hold onto: hope.

A Concluding Suggestion

Although it may appear at first somewhat afield from the topic of this chapter, I cannot conclude without saying something about the preparation of pastors in most of the seminaries in this country. Recall the figures cited earlier about the age composition of the PC(USA), with more than half the members over the age of fifty and one out of three sixty-five or older. This is a trend that is found in all the mainline Christian denominations and most Jewish congregations as well, indicating that American congregations are aging even faster than the general population. And studies show that clergy are often the first people many of their congregants turn to, not only for "spiritual" needs but for many other needs as well, including various mental health concerns. In light of these two factors, it is obvious that clergy need to have not only passing acquaintance with gerontology but in fact specialized training in working with older people.

Yet how many seminaries offer any kind of meaningful "geriatric" training program? How many make any effort to combat the deep-seated (but rather anachronistic) notion that youth ministry and coming up with new ways to get young families into the church are the *only* ways to assure the long-term health (or even survival) of Christ's earthly body? I am not so naive as to assume that people's attitudes can be radically changed by what happens during their seminary training. Kitwood has observed: "Attitudes are the key. It is relatively easy to help a person to gain in knowledge and skill, but attitudes are difficult to change. Ageism, rigidity, and that arrogance which bespeaks a lack of openness to new learning are particular drawbacks."[17] Nonetheless, as long as theological/pastoral education fails to recognize the importance of this particular ministry, I fear it will only continue to be neglected by new pastors and their congregations, to the detriment of all.

Questions for Discussion

1. Mel Kimble is quoted as saying that about half of the time of the average clergyperson is spent working with older adults and their families. If this is true, why is this ministry not seen as a top

priority of the church and given the full support of the congregation, the pastor, the session, and the budget?

2. What are the symptoms of Alzheimer's disease? What effect does it have on family life?

3. What can the church do to alleviate some of the burden of a family that is dealing with a family member with Alzheimer's disease?

4. Why would the author encourage the inclusion of persons with Alzheimer's disease in religious observances, even when it seems that they no longer comprehend what is happening and may not always behave "appropriately"?

5. Vaclav Havel is quoted as saying, "Hope is not believing you can change things. Hope is about believing you can make a difference." What difference would believing this quote make in the life of an Alzheimer's patient and family?

6. How can a faith community be supportive to the caregiver who faces the absence of the person he or she knew, but continues to have that person's bodily presence? What has faith to say when consciousness and communication is absent?

7. The author raises the question: What is deterring the church from being in the forefront of developing creative and innovative ways to help families struggling under the burden of Alzheimer's disease? Answer this for your own congregation.

8. The author states that we as Christians are not satisfied with being "in the image of God." It seems we want to be like God, independent, self-sufficient. At the same time, the author says, "At its very heart, the Christian faith affirms that human beings are totally dependent upon the creating, redeeming God." How can these two positions be reconciled?

9. In pastoral care of people with dementia, how can the church be encouraged not to see such persons as less than fully human and instead remember them, incorporating them as fully into the body of believers as their condition allows?

10. A dementia unit at a nursing home asks you, the pastor, and elders to conduct a worship service for the residents. Realizing their mental situation, design such a worship service that relates to their needs.

11. How can seminaries be encouraged to offer "geriatric" training programs in addition to the focus on youth ministries?

Notes

1. The medical name for this illness is slowly changing to "Alzheimer disease," as occurred with the transition from Down's syndrome to Down syndrome. I have decided to retain the more common form here.

2. For a good overview accessible to non-medical readers, see the articles in the January 31, 2000, and July 17, 2000, issues of *Time*. A wealth of information is also available from the Web sites of the Alzheimer's Association (www.alz.org), the Alzheimer's Disease Education and Referral Cente, part of the National Institute on Aging of the National Institutes of Health (www.alzheimers.org), and the Administration on Aging's Alzheimer's Disease Resource Room (www.aoa.gov/alz/index.asp).

3. Nancy Mace and Peter Rabins, *The 36-Hour Day: A Family Guide to Caring for Persons with Alzheimer's Disease, Related Dementing Illnesses, and Memory Loss in Later Life*, 3rd edition (New York: Warner Books, 2001).

4. Tom Kitwood, *Dementia Reconsidered: The Person Comes First* (Philadelphia: Open University Press, 1997), p. 110.

5. A helpful guide for those who wish to continue to offer worship experiences for cognitively impaired people is Elizabeth Pohlman and Gloria Bloom, eds., *Worship Services for People with Alzheimer's Disease: A Handbook*, available from the Alzheimer's Disease Assistance Center, 2212 Burdett Avenue, Troy, NY 12180.

6. *Critique of Pure Reason*, trans. Norman Kemp Smith (New York: St. Martin's Press, 1965), p. 635.

7. One cannot help but think of the apostle Paul's similar affirmation, though he used different concepts for the other two elements: "And now faith, hope, and love abide, these three" (1 Corinthians 13:13a).

8. Tom Kitwood, *Dementia Reconsidered*, p.142.

9. Stephen Post, *The Moral Challenge of Alzheimer Disease* (Baltimore: Johns Hopkins Press, 1995), p. 3.

10. Carl Eisdorfer and Donna Cohen, *The Loss of Self: A Family Resource for the Care of Alzheimer's Disease and Related Disorders*, revised and updated (New York: W. W. Norton, 2002).

11. Stephen Post, *The Moral Challenge*, p. 3.

12. Tom Kitwood, *Dementia Reconsidered*, p. 133.

13. Stephen Post, *The Moral Challenge*, p. 61.

14. Robert Putnam, *Bowling Alone: The Collapse and Revival of American Community* (New York: Simon & Schuster, 2000), p. 134.

15. Margaret Mohrmann, *Medicine as Ministry: Reflections on Suffering, Ethics, and Hope* (Cleveland: Pilgrim Press, 1995), p. 85.

16. Ibid.

17. Kitwood, *Dementia Reconsidered*, p. 112.

A Call to Love in Life's Dark Places

Andrea Reiter

Asserting the Call

The premise of this chapter is that faithful older adults have a significant vocation to fulfill in their later years. At the intersection of their faith life and their lived experience, seniors are among some of God's best-equipped people to respond to the challenging invitation of extending Christ's healing love. The world's "dark" places desperately need them.

Seniors are optimally positioned for such a call, and not simply because of the large numbers of older adults expected to dominate the scene in the "graying" of America and of the church.[1] Because of spiritual opportunities inherent in older adult life, seniors can be especially suited to the spiritual care of others.

Older adults bring the validity of having undergone and survived a vast array of challenges. As they continue to live they also continue to model for everyone—other seniors, younger adults, and even children—alternative ways and deeper values by which to cope with life's challenges and its fullness. Seniors have had a longer opportunity in which to develop compassion. Having "been there," they offer a great capacity to understand the struggles of others, even in rapidly changing times. The authors of *A Gospel for the Mature Years* affirm that as persons age, their spiritual maturity "is tested and refined" through the frequent experience of loss, in the form of illness and disability, death of loved ones, and changes in social position.[2] Older adults have indeed been seasoned in the boot camp of life.

Availability: The Time to Be There

With an increase in unstructured time from the shifting of child-rearing and career responsibilities[3] older adults are gifted with the possibilities of both availability and patience—crucial credentials for representing God's caring presence to others.

Also, later life has long been recognized by psychologists and philosophers as a time hallmarked for deeper personal growth. For the Christian this season of later-life "transcendence" (the desire to go beyond one's self in life)[4] is a time that allows for more openness to the activity of the Holy Spirit and for the emergence of deeper sensitivity to vocational calls into service.

John Koenig referred to this trend among even frail elderly people when he noted that even when Christians face loss of various kinds, including disability, what remains real above all else is transformation, a transformation that results from continual self-resensitizing to God's goodness. This is the source of ministry by older persons. The Spirit's "empowering self-disclosure" finds a home in the life of anyone who is open to it.[5]

His words rang true in my fond remembrance of a "caring and bearing" Christian support group, that was once sponsored by my congregation at a local assisted-living facility. There were generally a half-dozen participants who attended that group, both male and female. For the most part they ranged in age from their mid to late eighties. Physically, slowly, but ever so faithfully, they would patiently drag themselves to the weekly sessions by cane or by walker as we met together for two months. They represented a varied mix of different Christian traditions.

Some of our members were quite highly educated and financially secure individuals, but "Emma" was not. Barely having completed grade school, Emma nevertheless displayed a sense of call that deeply enriched us all. Blinded by macular degeneration and sustaining injuries from an increasing number of falls, Emma rarely missed a meeting. After several weeks she shared her personal perspectives about the one additional job she felt God had for her to do before her "time was up"; it involved both prayer and badgering! Having outlived two husbands who both had passed away from lung cancer, Emma believed it was her special mission to get young people to quit smoking.

How intentional she was about that call! She could identify with her residual sight and hearing each and every one of the staff members who frequented her apartment in the course of their daily duties. She knew their names, and she knew about their families. She discussed with them their hopes and dreams—and their habits. She was pleasant and cooperative, but frank. When she inquired about their smoking, she did it with a smile and with a warning that she intended to pray for their habit to stop. Emma was genuinely concerned about their welfare, despite the fact that they were the paid caregivers in her life. By this point she could name at least two staff women who had become "healed of their smoking." It caused her great joy, and she was always careful to give the credit for these life transformations to God.

Besides contributing to the health of the staff Emma contributed to the spiritual health of our group. Each of us learned to love and respect her sense of call as it impacted our own thoughts and values. The group often asked her to open or to close the sessions with prayer, and we cherished the simple, clear cadences of concern and gratitude, that she always expressed when we would be in prayer for one another.

Being Grounded in Reality

Over the past century improved health care and economic conditions have greatly extended human longevity and are expected to continue to do so in developed countries. But an increase in longevity is also often accompanied by an increase in the number of years a person may live with chronic conditions of pain or diminishment. As this becomes so, elder Christians like Emma may find themselves in the position of encountering their own late-life aging in ways that provide an important faith witness to others. Christian hope may be directed toward that which is unseen and rooted in the promises of the Resurrection, but faith is lived out—not in the future, but in the now—for all to see.

Aging and mortality may be facts of life, but the attitudes and responses with which older adults face them provide a powerful witness, one way or another, to Christian beliefs about the sovereignty of God in our lives and about the role of faith as a life-giving reality. Not that we encounter our aging without a common sense of ambivalence. T. Herbert Driscoll, author and retired rector, has expressed this commonly felt double-mindedness toward our own mortality in terms of his own poignant experience:

> I shall age in the company of many spirits, welcome and unwelcome. Now halfway through my sixth decade, I

sometimes detect the cloying presence of a spirit of self-pity, sometimes a spirit of fear, frequently a spirit of anxiety. All can at this stage be repulsed by activity, involvement, creativity, but I am under no illusion that these diversions will forever be available as allies against the invasion of those dark shadows of my being. Which spirit will be the richest and closest companion of my senior years? I do not yet know. I know what my hope is: that I may encounter one who offers new creation in exchange for my diminishing powers, bright visions for my failing sight, and intimations of resurrection for my expectations of death.[6]

A Call to Wisdom between Generations

The need to be grounded in the reality of our own aging is not confined to the later years. There is a clear and gnawing hunger in our youth-oriented society for a permanence of meaning that lasts a lifetime. Perhaps it is older adults alone who can serve as the generational vanguards on this battlefront of meaning. It is through their genuine grappling and courage in the face of their own aging that we are mentored in the art of living abundantly.[7]

Hence we can understand the immediate popularity of such books as *Tuesdays with Morrie*. This book provides us with a living example of the capacity to develop wisdom and courage even in the face of adversity and death. We clearly can have an amazing impact upon others.

Morrie Schwartz, the hero of this story, was a college professor teaching sociology during the real-life student days of the book's author, Mitch Albom. When the two reconnect, the older man is in the last months of his life, struggling with Lou Gehrig's disease. But it is the younger man who is the one spiritually dying. Caught up in the exhaustively demanding lifestyle of his success-oriented career, readers experience "their rekindled relationship" as "one final 'class' in how to truly live."[8] They see how it is possible to laugh in the face of decline and death.

Understanding Call

A vocation, according to the dictionary can be paraphrased as:

1. The work at which one is regularly employed.
2. A summons, or a strong inclination, to a particular course of action, especially a religious one.
3. The special function of an individual or group.[9]

Whether we receive payment for it or not, vocation also comes to us as "the gift which God has given us in our selfhood."[10] It always requires an examination of those dreams and values that we cherish. Its locus can be found in these words of Frederick Buechner, who pinpoints our calling: "at the juncture where your heart's deepest gladness meets the world's deepest hunger."[11]

There is no shortage of places in which older adults can help the darkness that shadows our world. But what is the locus of our deepest gladness as older adults?

- Are we drawn to the circle of life in the support, the loving, and sometimes the caregiving time that we extend to our own children and grandchildren?
- Are we inclined toward offering a helping hand to vulnerable adults in our own families, or groups, or communities?
- Have we thought about encouraging or mentoring troubled youth?
- What are the special hobbies or abilities and personal career skills that we could share?
- Is respect for and renewal of God's created order near and dear to our hearts?
- Do we feel the desire to learn new things and grow in new ways that were never open to us before? Do we believe in being equipped for modeling or mentoring something new?
- What can we do to leave the world a better place, help to lessen its inequities, violence, and social injustice?

Since the word *vocation* itself is related to the Latin word *vocare* (to be called), Christians listen for the voice of God in the urgings of their heart and in their immersion in the life and needs of their community. The pursuit of God's will for our lives in the reshaping of our later years helps to clarify our continuing purpose and direction for the future.

While older adults of faith may no longer be occupied in paid positions, they can identify from all the stages of their past life the earlier shapes of vocational call. Perhaps they can discern from years of paid employment or years of being caregivers of children that those earlier jobs and tasks were ways of accomplishing a service for God. Perhaps those *relationships* associated with work or family or school were the outlets through which they lived out their Christian sense of call.

But as seniors do we ever think about the implications of being called as a group? Longevity has been biblically described as an abundance of days. If so, and if life is a gift dispensed moment by moment and year after year, how much richness have we known across our lives? What are we being called to do with that richness in our senior years? What are some of the new ways of being, some of the untried roles that are possible through our membership in this "Lots of Days Club"? Is it possible that we are even being called to serve in some of life's dark places?

While not everyone is gifted for ministry with those who are very vulnerable, we need to exercise caution about the reservations we may feel at the prospect of serving those in distress. At any age the temptation exists to make diminishing assumptions about ourselves. We are so ready to translate these ideas into explanations for opting out. When Moses protested his lack of confidence and speaking ability, God did not automatically excuse him from the call that was his. Disability does not seem to be a legitimate barrier to service in the "dark places" of life.

The answer for Moses came in God's alternative options—a team leadership approach by Moses and Aaron. In numbers there can usually be found the needed strength and diversity of gifts to meet a challenging call.

In our own current era there is a more contemporary story paralleling this point. In San Francisco a group of senior men were called upon to perform a specialized ministry for those suffering the darkness known as Alzheimer's disease.[12] It was felt that the ministry of these senior men could make a tremendous impact on the welfare of frail elderly male residents who resided in the special Alzheimer's unit of a local nursing home. The prospective "caregivers" in this situation were other retired men—members of a local church—whose contact, it was hoped, would reduce the loneliness and depression so often associated with isolation. This program would never have come to be, however, had these church members not overcome two common stereotypes:

1. Men are not relational and would never want to just visit and talk, one-on-one, *especially* with long-term care residents suffering from dementia.
2. The discomfort of relating to extremely frail older people would be too threatening to allow for any long-term commitment.

While it was true that the volunteers expressed both anxiety and discomfort at the initial program proposal, a short-term trial run was initiated. The early training and after-support came from a trained social worker who encouraged the group and helped it gain confidence. Furthermore, in the sharing of their experiences together the volunteers found the strength to continue risking this new way of serving. As the program became better established, the group of visitors met together weekly for breakfast on the day of their nursing home visitation. They talked about their experiences and how they were growing in the face of this new challenge. A call into "darkness" does not have to be so dire and drear that the challenge cannot be met collectively with the help of others.

The sense of call that developed for these men not only became clear and doable, but catching! Later program expansions began to include younger businessmen who arranged to conduct their visits with residents over the course of their business lunch hours.

Being Equipped for the Call

When guidance counselors direct younger people into their early vocational choices, a combination of testing and evaluation procedures are used to find out if the young person's interests match their abilities. In later life our own skills and abilities certainly can still be part of the undertakings that we follow. But the decision to respond to a call from God brings with it another dimension. There is a degree of "unmanageable risk" that seems to come with a spiritual call.

Responding to God's vocational call may not be as simple as selecting a career path on our own. Part of the problem lies in the fact that spiritual equipping may only happen *during* the course of our responding to a call rather than before our plunge into the effort.

If we dare as older adults to step out in the humility of our insecurities, we are in very good company. There are ready examples of those who have done this very thing across the ages. From the Old to the New Testament, as Eugenia Benignus has pointed out, "When God wanted to bring about a significant change in the world, old people were called to the fore . . . Abraham and Sarah . . . Moses, Aaron and Miriam . . . Elizabeth and Zechariah . . . Simeon and Anna."[13]

A host of older men and women were called out for special service. Most of them were suffering some sort of difficulty, either because of their societies, their families, or their health. But the one thing that they seemed to have in common was their openness to God and the possibility of something new happening. They may not have had currency that read "In God We Trust." They may have lacked pension plans for the stability of their futures, but by allowing their lives to be used, they impacted centuries and continents far beyond the reach of their imaginations.

In a more recent example, former President Jimmy Carter and his wife, Rosalyn, returned from Washington, D.C., to their home in Plains, Georgia, following Jimmy's unpredicted presidential defeat in 1980. The family left office to return to the family business of peanut farming—only to discover that the farm had been devastated by the incompetence of others during their absence.

Nevertheless, the Carters founded the Carter Peace Center despite their personal financial crisis, their sense of shock and despair, and their lack of outside funding. They came into a new sense of call by taking the initial steps toward realizing what had been an obscure dream in their lives all along—working together to answer a call in the midst of the global darkness of conflict and poverty.[14]

Their work through the center continues to grow. In terms of a direct and personal impact upon the international darkness of conflict and poverty, more goodwill and understanding has been achieved by their simple sense of call and faithfulness to God's vision than perhaps ever could have been accomplished during the years that they spent in Washington, where they once lived lives of high political profile.

Regardless of our station in life or our age, our vocations come to us with the reassurance that we are not alone in the quest for direction and meaning. The same voice that calls us through the ages also saves us from meaninglessness and equips us with courage:

> [You] who have been borne by me from your birth,
>   carried from the womb;
> even to your old age I am he,
>   even when you turn gray I will carry you.
> I have made, and I will bear,
>   I will carry and will save (Isaiah 46:3–4).

Living Out the Call—It's All about Relationships

Living out the vocational call to become a sustaining presence for others presumes the centrality of prayer in our personal and corporate prayer life. Since there are so many excellent resources available on the subject, we will not be specifically developing that theme here except to say that living out a call to love presumes certain facts about relationship:

1. Prayer is our relationship with God. We need it for our own sustenance.
2. Love is the expression of that relationship with others, especially when they are in "dark places."
3. In our call to the darkness of life, whether that darkness is in others' lives or our own, we need the support of other people.

Supportive relationships function creatively in the form of care teams, creative relationships of mutuality and practical loving. Care teams represent one of at least three different ways in which older adults can live out their call to love in caring relationships. These include relationships formed around sharing journeys, around providing a listening presence, and around providing active support.

Accepting the Call—Decision and Courage

In a specialized way older adults are called to serve as special ambassadors of God's love and presence. But this first requires that they accept service as a necessary and important mission. Responding to God's call involves the key word *decision*, a word suggesting the intent to act.

A call is not a casual weather report, informing us about the outdoors around us. Rather, it is an invitation to action. It may be "felt," but it can never come to fruition without the consent that only we can give it by action. The very least that we can do is to begin a fuller exploration of what the call to love in life's dark places may mean for us.

Continued courage is the next requirement. Pursuing one's call is going to require some level of persistence. Stepping out into the dark places of life is not exactly an invitation to a party. It requires courage even to begin thinking about the prospects, and it requires perseverance to overcome the inevitable obstacles that will arise—beginning with our own ambivalence and doubts.

Courage and persistence, the two most needed qualities for living out this call, also happen to be two of the gifts that are most possible for seniors. They are gifts acquired both from the lessons of our own lives and from the actions of the Holy Spirit. In many ways when we enter our later years we are like the Old Testament figure of Jacob, who contended long and hard with a heavenly stranger.[15] Jacob, who wrestled with him all night long, must have been fairly confused at the beginning of the story. While camping alone en route to confront his brother he was blindsided in the dark and awakened from a fitful sleep. He had no clue about the person with whom he was contending that night. He just knew that he was being assaulted. At some point in the long struggle during his persistent flailing Jacob seems to have made a decision. Contending, cantankerous, cunning and persistent Jacob!

Was it near daybreak that he began to feel the vague truth that God was somehow touching his life in this struggle? He shouts into the fray: "I will not let you go, [sputter, sputter] unless you bless me." What hutzpah! However, women and men in later life have always had to have some of the same pluck that Jacob did, for in the words of Bette Davis, "Old age is no place for sissies." Like Jacob, senior Christians may have emerged victorious from their struggles with some kind of a battle scar. (Jacob's was a limp.) But to be unaware of the strengths that have developed from our own wrestlings and to see only the limp is to be crippled in the worst sense of that word.

We always are walking on toward promises that are still ahead. We need to leave the scenes of our struggles and move on, but we also need to do so with the realization that we have triumphed through much. By the time the first hairs on our head have grayed, life may have repeatedly pinned us down, and we may have repeatedly had to wrestle our way back up. We have contended and survived, and sometimes even been victorious in terrible battles between loss and renewal, disruption and redirection, transition and rootedness, disease and healing, despondency and hope, survival and sufficiency, doubt and assurance, fear and faith. It is in the very fabric of our lives, within our stories, that our victories are enmeshed. If we never make the effort to recapture and claim our stories, especially those of faith, we lose sight of the journey that we have been on, and we ignore or forget the many circumstances of life in which God has personally been journeying with and strengthening us.[16]

One of the major ingredients in the shaping of our call rests in our attitudes about who we are. To examine our life journey offers us the powerful potential of recognizing that which God is helping us to become and to understand that we are not alone. Before we can be called to represent God's love to others in their journey we must first understand how our own trip has gone.

A Deterrent to Call:
Ageism—the Chill that Keeps on Giving

Ageism was ushered into Western society as a cultural prejudice with the nineteenth century. The Industrial Revolution brought with it unprecedented national economic development, but not without a serious cost in terms of human welfare. Societal and family structures began to change as progress, technology and production became more central to our lives than family and relationships. As the traditional role of elders in the family and community diminished, long-lived practices such as the oral tradition of storytelling and the personal sharing of "elder wisdom" began to disappear.[17]

Although much work has been done over the last twenty-five to thirty years by governmental, social and religious bodies to recognize and to reverse the effects of ageism, its vestiges still remain with us systemically in American life. Ageism covertly influences our thinking and our behavior. It hangs around our sentiments like an untended cobweb, whispering thoughts of despair into the corners of our mind. It ushers many of us in later life along a hallway to depression: "I have nothing worthwhile left to offer" or "My life is useless." For those in younger life, ageism holds only the promise of lifelong anxiety: "I *never* want to get old!"

Ageism is a powerful silencer of our stories and a potent extinguisher of the dreams to which God calls us at every age. Although the church was founded upon a gospel that is fundamentally countercultural,[18] it still remains influenced by the culture in which it is immersed. So much so that when congregations submit to the nuances of ageism, they hardly recognize it. Yet it tacitly affects the faith and spiritual energy of every generation in the religious community. Harold Koenig has written that congregational ageism is the general view that the older generation is expected to content itself with attending church services and social functions, volunteering at church bazaars, or doing mindless tasks. Ageism causes congregations "to neglect the spiritual and emotional needs with which persons past middle age must grapple."[19]

The perspective of concern for the spiritual welfare of older people focuses on the church's relationship with its independent, active older members. But there is an even greater indictment of congregations that marginalize their frail elderly members: "Abandonment in a time of need ought not be excused. . . . A neglect of any member weakens the witness of a congregation. A congregation's identity is distorted, and its mission compromised when confessions of love and care are hollow statements."[20]

Congregations that do attempt to counter ageism are faith communities that understand that older adult ministry is more than volunteerism for its own sake, that it is more than busy work or social activities intended primarily to promote a balance of health, welfare, or self-esteem. As Juliana Cooper-Goldenberg has said, the church is not merely a social service agency. It is a spiritual service agency.[21] If it is to be about the business of bringing God's kingdom more fully into the world's darkness the church also needs to resist the tide of cultural influence inside and outside of its walls and to reaffirm in visible and concrete ways that God's call is ageless.

We have come a long way from the days when aging in a congregation meant waiting patiently for one's eternal reward. We are doing more and more to move beyond the stereotype of older adult ministry as something done only *for* and *to* the aging. Generally, however, the proclamation of calling for senior Christians still needs to be developed as a major focus of faith within the congregation. It is when this happens routinely as a part of congregational life that the church of Jesus Christ will cease "compounding society's sin"[22] and be better prepared to surf the age wave that is predicted to crest over the next fifty years.

Implementing the Call: The Need for Journey Sharing

Examining our life story is a faith adventure that deepens our own spiritual life. But by their very nature stories are corporate entities, intended for telling. Our own faith story can contribute to the building up of the body of Christ and has the capacity of both engendering trust in God in others and increasing God's praise.

Learning to do some form of journey sharing is important to the call that we have been considering for older adults, because there will be times when the sharing of our own story is exactly what is needed. Yet journey sharing may itself be one of the most difficult obstacles to overcome. For some older adults it is a daunting exercise that flies in the face of how they were raised.

In his first best-selling work, *The Greatest Generation*, Tom Brokaw wrote about the contributions of the women and men whose youth and prime had been lived during the great conflict of World War II. Why did he feel specifically compelled to write this book? It was because of what he learned working with this particular population during his journalistic career. After years of interaction Brokaw observed that very few of this age group were inclined to talk either about themselves or about the often-heroic wartime contributions and sacrifices they made. Often they displayed the attitude that they simply "did what they had to do" in the best way that they could, and then just tried to move on with their lives in the aftermath.[23]

Serving as their personal interpreter to the public, Brokaw published their life vignettes and shared their stories for them. The book's instant trajectory to the best-seller list reflects his keen perception about the mood of the country—that there was a hunger for vision, especially among the young. For Brokaw the food of inspiration and dignity was present in these untold stories. Telling the stories was necessary, not for the personal acclaim of the people involved, but to build up the national community. If that was true before September 11, 2001, it has certainly become more evident in the darkness that burst upon the world scene afterward.

Dark Places: Post–September 11

That dark winter came in 2001, not with the usual northern blasts of ice and snow, but with flailing storms of global terrorism. The world was in a dark place, seemingly fixated on hatred and destruction. We braced ourselves against the chilling blasts of relentless media images, where suffering, grief, and chaos blitzed across our screens.

Young and old alike were fully immersed in the moment, each one prompted to examine "the season" of his or her life, and to make revisions. Young survivors of the infernal explosions spoke about wanting to make their redeemed lives count for something, and collective bereavement impelled families of all ages to connect with one another whether they lived near or far apart. It was a crisis of immeasurable proportions.

The Chinese word for "crisis" uses two symbols to depict disaster, one for *danger* and the other for *opportunity*. Although everyone was being called upon in this tragedy to extend love into life's darkest places, older adults were among those who had a newly acknowledged opportunity. Barely a few months after the "war on terrorism" began, a poignant e-mail arrived whose focus was like a clarion call. Its emphasis was upon healing, and it simply read:

> Are current or past events weighing heavily on your heart? Sharing stories could help heal both old hurts and new. Taking time this weekend to listen to the stories of elderly friends or relatives who have lived through similarly trying times can help inform, inspire, nurture, or heal both parties. Stories from the past not only help put events into perspective, but they also help communicate meaning and reinforce feelings of connectedness between generations.[24]

What this mental health bulletin addressed in psychological terms was fundamentally a spiritual issue—the truth that sharing meaning through our stories is vital to the welfare of others. Without claiming the stories of our lives we can neither grasp nor develop our sense of call. In fact, the refusal to share our journey with others can sometimes be detrimental to them. In his book *Let Your Life Speak* Parker Palmer describes the emptiness he felt as a young man struggling with the first dark signs of depression. He criticizes the seniors in his life for clinging to the cultural facades of success when what he needed more than anything from them at the time was their genuineness:

> The experience of darkness has been essential to my coming into selfhood. . . . Many young people today journey in the dark, as the young always have, and we elders do them a disservice when we withhold the shadowy parts of our lives. When I was young, there were very few elders willing to talk about the darkness; most of them pretended that success was all they had ever known. As the darkness began to descend on me in my early twenties, I thought that I had developed a unique and terminal case of failure.[25]

Seniors offer us the unparalleled opportunity of seeing firsthand how the stresses and strains of life are not just obstacles to be coped with, but pathways towards healing, wholeness, and personal transformation. One of the questions most frequently asked by the frail elderly is a basically spiritual one: "Why am I still here?" It is a question that can be either a psalm-like lament, laced with despair, confusion, or bitterness, or a daily open inquiry. Both can be forms of prayer.[26]

Why indeed are any of us here, at any age, on any particular day? What is it to which we are being invited on *this* day? It is at the very crossroads of our life experience and our faith that we ultimately find the meaning of abundant life—a junction that points us to service. Elder Christian disciples can manifest through their lives qualities of commitment, candor, strength, wisdom, courage, and selflessness. They can enrich us with the gifts of persistence, hope, centeredness, joy, humility, wisdom, vitality, and prayer, perhaps even better than they could in their younger years. These disciples represent and make real to others the presence, love, and grace of God, especially to those whose life course is taking them through darkness, difficulty, or meaninglessness.

As in the parable of the talents (Matthew 25:14–30), in which resources were distributed to the servants before the master's business trip, our own gifts of experience and wisdom are resources given for investment—not as possessions to be buried under the ground of our lives, where they remain dormant and wasted, never enabling anyone to grow in the light of grace.

Good things can grow out of our "dark places," becoming the avenues by which we travel with one another on our journeys. When we walk with each other God's presence is brought between us as surely as Christ's presence came and walked between two disillusioned disciples who were fleeing Jerusalem after the darkness of the crucifixion. God caught up with them on the road to Emmaus with the fresh breezes of a renewed vision: "Were not our hearts burning within us while he was talking to us on the road, while he was opening the scriptures to us?" (Luke 24:13–35). They were able to go back to the place they were running from with new vigor and joy.

There are probably numerous ways of implementing this call to love in life's dark places. But in addition to the sharing of stories at least two other avenues are listening with love and acting in compassion.

The Call to Love: A Listening Presence

> For everything there is a season . . . a time to keep silence and a time to speak . . . (Ecclesiastes 3).

One of the greatest gifts that one person can give to another in distress is time to truly listen. The dark times of a personal crisis might also require many forms of practical assistance, but healing the wounds that are felt deeply within requires something more. In order for the personal darkness of a life situation to be lifted, people need to be heard at the deeper levels of their feelings. They need the assurance that they have been heard.

Jesus' words are for us a model of effective Christian caring: "Where two or [more] are gathered in my name, there am I in the midst . . ." (Matthew 18:20). We best reflect and represent Christ when we remember that it is the other person's relationship with God that will be the source of all that they will ultimately need. Not our advice, our suggestions, a rehearsing of our own ailments, or the inappropriate use of quoting Scripture. Mature Christian senior adults have a great capacity to communicate, both verbally and nonverbally, that we belong to God. And if they are in need of improved skills for effective listening, they have at their disposal both a God-given capacity for lifelong learning and a wide range of congregationally based programs and printed resources on active listening.[27] It can be done.

One example of a listening ministry model is a program designed for seniors to help support one another. In Rochester, Minnesota, older adults are trained to become peer counselors, offering support "to other elders who are experiencing difficulties, which helps to combat situations of loneliness and isolation, and a host of other common issues. The program is spiritually based by helping people to explore God's role in their lives, or by discussing their search for or return to a religious community." In weekly home visits the peer counselors "help people identify the symptoms of depression, make changes in relationships, accept their physical limitations and value who they are."[28]

The call to love in life's dark places does not require an advanced degree in the helping professions, but it does require the desire to care effectively and the capacity of learning better ways of loving, reaching out, and relating.

The Call to Love by Concrete Service—Dual Aspects of Aging and Ministry: Caregiving and Care Receiving

Caregiving and care receiving are two sides of the same coin of the "care-sharing" equation. It presumes that we are all rooted in God's loving concern for us, and that we are each made in God's image and likeness. There is no denying that the tensions and difficulties of living with either role are challenging and stressful. It seems that everyone in a care-sharing situation is struggling to maintain a sense of identity, meaning, and balance in the face of challenging demands.

> Family caregiving studies indicate that the burdens of the family caregiving experience have negative consequences on the physical and mental health of caregivers. Caregivers commonly suffer stress, depression, anxiety, and fatigue. Research has also linked chronic stress of caregiving to breakdowns in the cardiovascular and immune system over time. It addition to the physical strain, the accelerating costs of health care often leave the financial resources of caregivers depleted before they can access any type of state or federal assistance.[29]

"Good" caregiving requires the hallmarks of respect, dependability, and compassion. "Good" care receiving requires humor, cooperation, and respect for the caregiver(s). Together they form a circle of care that is in its own way a small covenant community.

However, this is a community in need of the broader support and connection of others. Thus there have been growing dialogues concerning:

1. Using the ministry services of parish nurse programs to link individuals and families with helpful resources and caring support
2. The establishment of inter-program links between hospital chaplains and local pastors or church care teams to better serve the physical and spiritual needs of parishioners undergoing hospitalization and rehabilitation protocols[30]
3. Promoting the development of congregation- or community-based care teams by which the lives of both care receivers and caregivers are enhanced, and the workload is effectively shared

Care Team Approaches

The family management model of a care team

Companion and Caregiving Solutions is the story of one family in which adult siblings successfully worked together as a unique kind of family care team. To them it was unacceptable that their declining and ailing mother should live her remaining years in a nursing home if that possibility could be averted. It was their particular way of honoring their mother. Although it was financially necessary for all the adult children in that family to remain employed, they nevertheless wished to help their parent remain in her own home as long as possible. They were unable themselves, however, to provide her with the ongoing supervision and care that she required. Neither could they financially afford to purchase home health care services for an extended period of time.

The story of their successful creativity aired on ABC-KATV on the "Senior Spirit Report" in June 1998. Shortly afterward they published a booklet describing the strategies and evaluations they used in meeting the caregiving needs of their parent.[31] They became a family care team by identifying a trustworthy live-in caregiver with whom they could negotiate and barter services. They approached the entire process and the tasks involved creatively, but with a lot of careful thought. In the process of collaboration the family was shaped into a Care Team of Family Management, and they were able to meet the needs of their mother in a way that was acceptable to her and that offered balance and mutual support to all family members involved.

Community care teams

By virtue of scattered efforts around the country, the early development of care teams emerged as a community response to improving the quality of life for those living and dying with HIV/AIDS.[32] Soon people observed that this concept was applicable to other situations of chronic and terminal suffering. By 1994 this helpful model was being applied to the needs of in-home care of frail seniors in Houston, Texas, in a program called Second Family Care Teams.[33]

The development of congregational care teams has its roots in these early movements that grew from the compassionate responses of community efforts. Today it is increasingly being replicated and promoted within the mission and ministry strategies of several denominations because of its simple yet effective design.

Congregational care teams

When illness, frailty, or disability strikes we are threatened with more than the obvious pain and inconvenience that become part of daily life. We also feel the deep emotional and spiritual suffering of isolation. It is often a situation in which the loss of community can be as devastating to both caregivers and care receivers as is the actual loss of abilities. Community seems to be a vital healing ingredient in problems relating to the sharing of care.

Recognizing the essential role of the congregation as the ground of community, many denominations have begun encouraging the development of congregational care teams as an effective modality for caring ministry. It is not designed to replace the pastoral care extended by clergy, elders, or deacons, but to be a flexible model by which to augment those ministries. Care teams enable the pressing practical needs of members to be addressed in a nurturing and consistent way that reduces both stress and isolation for the caregivers and care receivers in a family.

The Presbyterian Health, Education, and Welfare Association (PHEWA) of the Presbyterian Church (U.S.A.) sponsors education and training for the development of this model in Presbyterian congregations. In any individual church the team consists of "a group of volunteers working together to offer practical, emotional, and spiritual support to those in need . . . from a developmental or physical disability, a prolonged physical or mental illness, limitations brought on by the aging process, or other life-challenging situations."[34]

Persons who receive care team training become trainers and in turn teach members of their own congregational volunteer group. Caregiving volunteers offer only those services that they themselves feel led to rendering. To avoid burnout the volunteers' participation is limited to a reasonable time frame, typically a period of service up to one year. Care teams also often have a volunteer coordinator whose function it is to promote clear communication between the team and the team's care recipient(s) or "care partner(s)." Special attention is given to the autonomy of the care partners and their families, who are regarded as integral parts of the team's life and mission. Periodic meetings help the team function effectively and responsively. A volunteer resource person tries to identify and connect everyone with helpful resources that may be available from the larger community. The duplication of services is also avoided. Best of all is the perspective that every person on the care-sharing team, both the care partners (recipients) and the caregivers, are in the dual roles of giving their own gifts and receiving the gifts of others.

The role that older adults can play in the implementation of a church's care team is enormous, given their life experience, availability, and call to service. With the coming of the age wave so often described in population projections, older adults will inevitably and increasingly participate in the roles of both caregiving and care receiving, and even now they can be integral in the development of these kinds of ministry efforts.

But whether seniors find themselves led to service in practical outreach efforts such as these or ministries of listening and sharing, it is patently true that it is in our later days that we most clearly "come to experience [our] true vocation."[35] May we hear in that an invitation to come and serve with love in life's dark places.

Questions for Discussion

1. Who are the active elders (older adults) today? Consider your congregation and those you might consider "senior adults." What roles have they played in the life of your church and how has it changed in the last five, ten, or twenty years?

2. Think scripturally about the power of intergenerational faith transmission. Read about Samuel and Eli (1 Samuel 3) or Paul and Timothy; pray and meditate on the relationship between Elizabeth and Mary.

3. Identify and interview congregants whose lives after retirement have demonstrated a new and redirected sense of call. To what do they attribute their ability to move forward with grace and to trust in uncharted waters?

4. While our culture presses on in fast-paced sound bytes and a driven sense of productivity, older persons experience a sense of slowing in their physical or mental processes. Explore what older adults may be able to teach us about acceptance and "pace versus peace." Offer an intergenerational class on Christian spiritual practice(s).

5. How can homebound congregants remain a vital part of the church by also sharing their gifts? Discuss which aspects of church can be made more connectional. Worship? Prayer? Christian education?

6. Loss and bereavement are a universal experience of the aging. Consider ways in which members can be a rich resource in the church for others who have lost children, siblings, spouses, parents.

7. Ask widows in the congregation to faithfully telephone the newly widowed and ask them to join a social group in the church.

8. All Saints Day can be a healing bridge into the holiday season to follow. Suggest that families who wish to remember a loved one bring a candle and light them from the altar candles. The lit candles serve as a memorial to the great cloud of witnesses of the church.

9. Add a category to the weekly prayer list, "Pray for grandchildren." This includes biological grandchildren of all ages and "special children" for whom we have concern in the church, in global missions, and in the news.

Notes

1. Miriam Dunson, ed., *Older Adult Ministry: A Guide for the Session and Congregation* (Louisville: Office of Older Adult Ministry, Congregational Ministries Division, Presbyterian Church [U.S.A.], 2000), pp. 12–13.

2. Harold G. Koenig and Tracy and Betty Lamar, *A Gospel for the Mature Years: Finding Fulfillment by Knowing and Using Your Gifts* (New York: The Haworth Pastoral Press, 1997), p. 25.

3. Charles J. Fahey, "Ethics and the Third Age" in *Affirmative Aging: A Creative Approach to Longer Life* (Harrisburg, PA: Morehouse Publishing, 1994), p. 17.

4. Zalman Schachter-Shalomi and Ronald Miller, *From Age-ing to Sage-ing: A Profound New Vision of Growing Older* (New York: Warner Books, 1995), pp. 135–158.

5. John Koenig, *The Older Persons' Worth: A Theological Perspective*, Symposium at Union Theological Seminary (New York: Presbyterian Senior Services, 1980).

6. T. Herbert Driscoll, "Aging: A Spiritual Journey" in *Affirmative Aging*, p. 2.

7. Report on the Task Force on Older Adult Ministry, Older Adult Ministry: Growing in the Abundant Life (Louisville: Office of the General Assembly, Presbyterian Church [U.S.A.], 1992), p. 13.

8. Mitch Albom, *Tuesdays with Morrie: An Old Man, a Young Man, and Life's Greatest Lesson* (New York: Doubleday, 1997).

9. *Merriam Webster's Collegiate Dictionary*, 10th edition (Springfield, MA: Merriam Webster Publishing Company, 1998).

10. Parker J. Palmer, *Let Your Life Speak* (San Francisco: Jossey-Bass, 2000), p. 10.

11. Frederick Buechner, *Wishful Thinking: A Theological ABC* (New York: Harper & Row, 1973), p. 95.

12. Pat Schroeder, "Connections Between Men: Meeting the Spiritual Needs of Elders With Dementia," *Aging & Spirituality Quarterly*, The American Society on Aging's Forum on Religion, *Spirituality and Aging*, vol. X, no. 3, p. 3.

13. Emma Lou Benignus, "Challenge to Ministry: Opportunities for Older Persons" in *Affirmative Aging*, p. 27.
14. Jimmy Carter, *Living Faith* (New York: Times Books, 1996).
15. Emma Lou Benignus, op. cit., p. 36.
16. Richard L. Morgan, *Remembering Your Story* (Nashville: Upper Room Books, 1996).
17. Zalman Schachter-Shalom et al., From *Age-ing to Sage-ing*, p. 63.
18. Juliana Cooper-Goldberg, *A Spirituality for Late Life* (Louisville: Geneva Press, 1999), p. 14.
19. Harold G. Koenig et al., *A Gospel for the Mature Years*, p. 5.
20. Earl Shelp and Ronald Sunderland, *ibid*. p. 55.
21. Juliana Cooper-Goldenberg, *A Spirituality for Late Life*, xi.
22. Emma Lou Benignus, loc. cit., p. 25.
23. Tom Brokaw, *The Greatest Generation* (New York: Random House, 1998).
24. Real Age Tip of the Day, realage.com.
25. Palmer, *Let Your Life Speak*, pp. 18–19.
26. Miriam Dunson, *A Very Present Help in Trouble: Psalm Studies for Older Adults* (Louisville: Geneva Press, 1999).
27. Stephen Ministries, 8016 Dale, St. Louis, MO 63117-1449.
28. *Aging & Spirituality, Newsletter of the Forum on Religion, Spirituality and Aging*, vol. 14, no. 1, Spring 2002.
29. "The Changing Context of Caregiving," *Church & Society*, March/April 2002, p. 13.
30. Ronald H. Sutherland, "Care Teams and Pastoral Professionals: Response to the Health Care Changes of this Decade," *The Journal of Pastoral Care & Counseling*, vol. 56, no. 2 (Summer 2002), p. 157.
31. Cheryl Suzanne Browne, *Companion and Caregiving Solutions* (Prestige Press, 1992).
32. Pat Gleich, Bob Gillespie, and James Tippett, "From Epidemic to Caring Endeavor: A History of the Care Team Movement," *Church & Society*, March/April 2002, p. 18.
33. Ronald Sutherland, "Care Teams and Pastoral Professionals," p. 158.
34. *The Care Team Exploration Guide* (Louisville: Office of Health Ministries, Presbyterian Church [U.S.A.], 2000), p. 5.
35. John Koenig, quoted in *Affirmative Aging*, p. 28.